THE BOOK OF Virgin Golf Records

THE BOOK OF

Virgin **Golf Records**

ROB PEGLEY

Virgin

First published in Great Britain in 1998 by Virgin Books
an imprint of Virgin Publishing Ltd.
Thames Wharf Studios, Rainville Road, London W6 9HT

A catalogue record for this book is available from the British Library.

ISBN 1-85227-771-8

Printed in Belgium by Proost N.V.

Design and repro by Prima Creative Services
Additional illustrations by Oliver Frey

Introduction

An antiquated, ritualistic and misogynous group of men who continue with a meaningless and futile pursuit of small improvements without significant results. No, not the House of Lords, but a stereotypical view of the golf world.

Until recently, that is. Young players like Justin Rose and a certain Eldrick Woods, known to his friends as Tiger, have suddenly made it cool to like golf again. Everybody is in on the action. Shearer and Sheringham take on Owen and Scholes between World Cup matches. And Chris Evans is on Channel 4 with David Leadbetter telling him to keep his head down. Yes, everybody wants to be Tiger Woods.

But then, like me, you always knew what a great sport golf was. However, like me you were probably put off by the stuffy nature of many other golfing tomes. Where was the one volume which had all the facts at your fingertips, together with explanations of all the historical references and terms you never quite grasped? And which included the weird and wonderful anecdotes with which to impress your friends on the course?

Now that book is in your hands. Simply read and memorise the next 155 pages and watch your popularity soar. Assuming you play once a week, at a conservative estimate there should be enough here to drop into conversation for the next 53 years, by which time, who knows, Tiger Woods mania may have subsided. Perhaps, by then, you might have made a hole-in-one. (At which point you can inform playing partners that 'it is estimated that a golfer has to hit an average of 12,000 tee shots before making one'.) Or, you may have been struck by lightning, upon which occasion you will, hopefully, pick yourself up, dust yourself down, and tell the rest of your threesome that the same thing happened to Lee Trevino in 1975. Or, if you develop the 'Yips', you can at least tell people that Tommy Armour coined the phrase for this nervous putting condition.

From Aaron (Tommy, US Masters Champion in 1973) to Zoeller (Fuzzy, second on the US Tour in 1983) there are a hundred and one ways to make you a complete bore at the nineteenth hole, or while away those evenings in between practice putts on the lounge carpet.

Everything you need is here, from best rounds to course lengths, from former champions to bizarre deaths. Players are listed with their detailed career statistics, such as earnings and wins. Courses have complete histories and major events, together with playing details. Championships are included with winners and scores. Terms, equipment, rules and nations all come under consideration and everything has an exciting story to back it up.

There's something for everyone. If you have a basic understanding then it can be improved. For those who wish to study there are complete statistics. And there is even the weird and wonderful for those who think they know it all.

But if that's still not enough, then tell us what you want to see. The next volume is already under way. If you think we've missed something out then write to:

Virgin Publishing, Thames Wharf Studios, Rainville Road, London W6 9HT.

In the meantime, do you know who designed Royal Birkdale? Well you will know by page 111.

Rob Pegley
July 1998

TOMMY AARON

Born: Gainesville, GA, USA – 22/02/1937
First US Tour: 1961
US Tour Wins: 2
Major Wins: 1 (US Masters 1973)
Ryder Cup appearances: 2
First Senior Tour: 1987
Senior Tour Wins: 1
Senior Tour Earnings: $2.2 million

TOMMY AARON first came to prominence as part of the Walker Cup team that visited Britain in 1959. The team also included Deane Beman and Jack Nicklaus. The American team, made up mostly of college boys, beat an experienced British team 9–3.

● MORE SUCCESSFUL on home soil than abroad as a tournament player, Aaron was never really in contention for a British Open – indeed, on his way to shooting 91 at a windswept Lytham in the third round of the 1963 Open, he pulled out a white handkerchief and shouted, 'Where do I go to surrender?'

● RUNNER UP TO Gary Player in the US PGA at Oakland Hills in 1972, Aaron recorded his only major win the following year, winning the US Masters at Augusta. Peter Oosterhuis led by three shots going into the final 18 holes but eventually finished third, two shots behind Aaron. The two competed again that year when Aaron played in his second and final Ryder Cup competition in Scotland.

● THE MASTERS had provided Aaron's other most famous moment five years previously. In the 1968 tournament he filled in the card of playing partner Roberto de Vicenzo incorrectly, writing 4 instead of 3 at the 17th on the last day. Although de Vicenzo had actually scored a three, the carded score had to be taken and de Vicenzo lost to Bob Goalby by one shot, missing the opportunity of a play-off. Aaron was mortified, but probably not as upset as his partner.

ACCIDENTS

THE WORST INJURY to be sustained by a professional in a major tournament was when Richard Boxall drove off the ninth tee at Birkdale in the 1991 Open third round. With Boxall three strokes off the lead, a loud crack was heard as he played his drive and he collapsed in agony with a stress fracture of his leg.

● BOBBY CRUIKSHANK suffered a self-inflicted injury when in contention for the US Open in 1934. Having played a bad shot, he threw his club in the air and it fell on his head, temporarily concussing him. Dazed,

Lee Trevino was lucky to escape with only a minor injury after being struck by lightning during a tournament.

he drifted out of contention.

● THERE HAVE BEEN fatal accidents as well on the golf course. One Richard McCulough, playing at Ponoka Community GC, Alberta, Canada, in May 1973, banged his club against a golf cart in a fit of pique during a round. The shaft of his club broke and flew up, cutting his carotid artery and killing him.

● ANOTHER DEATH on a course occurred when John Mosley had an argument with a green fee guard at Delaware Park, Buffalo, in 1972. The guard shot him dead and was sentenced to seven and a half years in jail for manslaughter. John Mosley's wife, perhaps the first real golf widow, received $100,000 compensation.

● TONY LEMA is the only world-class pro to have been killed in the name of golf. He died in 1966 in a light aircraft crash on the way from the US PGA to an exhibition match in Chicago. Ironically, the plane crashed on the seventh green of a course in Illinois.

● LEE TREVINO was once struck by lightning during a tournament and was lucky to escape with injury only.

Did You Know?

Perhaps the luckiest golfing escape of all was that of Harry Vardon. He was due to attend the 1912 US Open but illness prevented him from sailing on the Titanic.

ADMINISTRATION

THERE ARE TWO major powers responsible for the administration of golf – the USGA in America and the Royal & Ancient in Great Britain.

● DESPITE BEING a private club with the idiosyncrasies that entails, the R&A is actually the governing body for the entire golf world except the US and Mexico. It is responsible for the Rules of Golf and those governing amateur status, organization of the Open and other championships in Great Britain, and the selection of teams to represent Great Britain and Ireland.

● THE ROYAL & ANCIENT was formed on 14 May 1754, when it drafted 13 rules for playing the game.

● THE USGA is only just over 100 years old, a mere puppy compared to the R&A. It was formed in 1894 by Charlie MacDonald, who was frustrated by the seeming inability of the Americans to organize a major championship properly.

● THE AMERICAN approach to the game is slightly different to that of the British, with America preferring matchplay to the British love of strokeplay, and allowing the picking up, marking and cleaning of balls.

● A 1951 RULES CONFERENCE helped realign the two factions and now a joint committee regularly reviews the rules to ensure changing conditions and technological advances are treated equally on both sides of the Atlantic.

Administration Contacts

Royal & Ancient Golf Club
St Andrews
Fife
Scotland KY16 9JD

United States Golf Association
Far Hills
New Jersey 07931

AGE

TIGER WOODS is the most prodigious talent of the late 20th century and in winning the Masters at the age of 21 surpassed both Ballesteros and Nicklaus, each of whom won the US Masters at the age of 23.

● EVEN WOODS, though, didn't match the feat of Tom Morris Jnr, who in 1868 won the British Open at the age of 17 and had won it four times by the time he was Woods' age. His father, Tom Morris Snr, became the oldest champion of the British, Open at 46, a record which has always seemed unlikely to be broken. However Hale Irwin won the US Open in 1990 at the age of 45, and as Faldo, Ballesteros et al approach a ripe age it will be interesting to see if any records will actually fall.

● AT 21, WOODS is already too old to break any other records held by young players – but he may yet set new records for the number of trophies racked up.

THE GENERATION GAME

Youngest Champions

— British Open —
Tom Morris Jnr, 1868
(17 years 5 months)
Seve Ballesteros, 1979
(22 years 3 months)
— US Open —
John McDermott, 1911
(19 years 10 months)
— US Masters —
Tiger Woods, 1997 (21 years 3 months)
— US PGA —
Gene Sarazen, 1922 (20 years 5 months)
— European Tour —
Dale Hayes, 1971 Spanish Open
(18 years 9 months)
— US PGA Tour —
John McDermott, 1911 US Open
(19 years 10 Months)

Oldest Champions

— British Open —
Tom Morris Snr, 1867 (46 years, 99 days),
Roberto de Vicenzo, 1967
(44 years 93 days)
— US Open —
Hale Irwin, 1990 (45 years 0 months)
— US Masters —
Jack Nicklaus, 1986 (46 years, 2 months)
— US PGA —
Julius Boros, 1968 (48 years 4 months)
— European Tour —
Neil Coles, 1982 Sanyo Open
(48 years 0 months)
— US PGA Tour —
Sam Snead, 1965 Gt Greensboro Open
(52 years 10 months)

ALBATROSS

AN ALBATROSS is three strokes under par for a hole, in other words a two at a par five, or a hole in one at a par four. It is also known as a double eagle.

● GENE SARAZEN hit perhaps the most famous of these on his way to the US Masters title in 1935. His second shot, a four-wood, carried some 210m (230yd) before rolling into the 15th hole at Augusta. It eventually helped take him to a play-off victory, and was perhaps the greatest shot of all time.

● BILL GRAHAM once hit a double eagle two at the massive 550m (602yd) par-five 16th hole at the Whiting Field course in Florida. A drive followed by a three-wood, was enough for the 196cm (6ft 5in) 27-year-old, who had a 40 kmh (25mph) hour tail wind to aid him.

AMY ALCOTT

Born: Kansas City, MO, USA – 22/02/1956	
First LPGA Tour: 1975	
Highest Ranking: 3rd (1979, 1980)	
Tour Wins: 29	
Major Wins: 5 (US Open 1980, Dinah Shore 1983, 1988, 1991, Du Maurier Classic 1979)	
Tour Earnings: $3 million	

AMY ALCOTT JOINED the US Tour straight from high school at the age of 19. A brilliant putter, the only thing she missed, she said, was not a tough four-footer, but 'my mother's homemade soup'.

Amy Alcott has won major tournaments in all three of the decades in which she has competed, from the Du Maurier in 1979 to the Dinah Shore in 1991.

● A CONSISTENT PLAYER over her 20 years on tour, in her first 15 years she was never worse than 18th, and was five times in the top five. She has recorded 29 wins to date and accumulated four wins in a year three times, in 1979, 1980 and 1984.

● HER BEST YEAR was 1980, when she was voted Golf Magazine Golfer of the Year and won the US open by nine strokes in 38°C (100°F) heat at Nashville. Her 280 total was four better than the previous best, and the final 36-hole total of 140 equalled Mickey Wright's in 1959.

● SHE ALSO WON the Du Maurier Classic in 1979, its first year as a major, but it is the Dinah Shore which has brought her most success. She was the only player to have won the Shore three times until Betsy King equalled her feat in 1997.

Helen Alfredsson may have blonde hair, a long drive and a fiery nature, but there comparisons with John Daly end.

HELEN ALFREDSSON

Born: Gothenburg, Sweden – 09/04/1965
First LPGA Tour: 1992
Highest Ranking: 5 (1993, 1997)
Tour Wins: 2
Major Wins: 1 (Dinah Shore, 1993)
Solheim Cup Appearances: 4

THE SIX TIMES Swedish Champion is a fiery athlete, and a stunning blonde who has many fans around the world – plenty of whom have started shrines on the internet to her. Not just a pretty face and a brilliant golfer, she also has a degree in International Business from the United States International University.

● ALFREDSSON FIRST came to prominence with British fans after winning the 1990 British Open at Woburn in a play-off. She then helped win the 1992 Solheim Cup for Europe and experienced her first year on the LPGA Tour.

● IN HER FIRST YEAR she won Rookie of the Year and the following year finished in the top five, coming second in the US Open and winning the Dinah Shore. In 1994 she tied for her ninth place in the US Women's Open held at the Indianwood Golf club, but she hit a 63 in the opening round which is the lowest recorded in the US Women's Open by two shots.

● THE YEAR OF 1996 was a poor one for a player who can reach great heights and she finished outside the top 20 for the first time ever. However, 1997 saw her return to form and she was second in the European Amex Tour behind Alison Nicholas.

Peter Alliss has been the voice of British golf for over 25 years.

Robert Allenby with the 1994 Heineken Australian Open trophy.

PETER ALLISS

Born: Berlin, Germany – 28/02/1931
Turned Pro: 1946
Career Spanned: 1950s to 1969
Highest European Ranking: 1st (1964 & 1966)
Tournament Victories: 20
Major Wins: 0
Ryder Cup Appearances: 8

THE SON OF Percy Alliss – a great player in his own right – Peter had an excellent career as a player, although it is as the voice of BBC golf that he is best known.

● A BRILLIANT commentator with a laid-back style, Alliss was first invited to contribute to BBC coverage after a producer heard him entertaining fellow pros on a plane trip between tournaments.

● AS WELL AS presenting golf coverage, Alliss is also a writer and raconteur on the sport, and once had his own TV programme, Around with Alliss, which combined his two favourite pursuits – golf and talking.

● IT IS OFTEN forgotten how successful a player Allis was. He turned pro at the age of 15 and before retiring from competition in 1969 recorded 20 wins, including three successive wins in Europe in 1958 – the Italian, Spanish and Portuguese Opens.

● ALLISS PLAYED in every Ryder Cup team bar one from 1953 to 1969. The only time he missed was 1955, when he and fellow youngster Bernard Hunt were left out. In the

ROBERT ALLENBY

Born: Melbourne, Australia – 12/07/1971
First European Tour: 1992
Highest Ranking: 3rd (1996)
European Tour Wins: 4
Major Wins: 0

ALLENBY WAS thought to be Greg Norman's successor after a good season in his native Australia, a high finish (joint 12th) in the 1995 Open and a win in the 1994 Honda Open in Europe.

● A CAR CRASH in Spain cut his 1996 season short, though, and he had to take one shot in the Volvo Masters at Valderrama with a fractured sternum to qualify for a £75,000 bonus. Having painfully completed the shot, he gave the money to cancer charities.

● AN IMPRESSIVE three times win in Europe in 1996 gained him third place in the Order of Merit that year. However, despite a creditable tenth in the 1997 Open, Allenby tumbled in the European Order of Merit to 60th in 1997.

previous Ryder Cup, in 1953, the two rookies had made mistakes that lost the cup when victory had been almost assured.
● PETER AND Percy Alliss were the only father and son to have played in the Cup until Ignacio Garrido played in 1997, following his father Antonio, who played in the 1979 matches.
● ALLISS HAS PLAYED ten times for England in the World Cup and his record of three wins in the PGA Championship (1957, 1962, 1965) is only bettered by Nick Faldo.
● IN THE 1960 Open Alliss broke the St Andrews Old Course record with a 66 in qualifying proper, but failed to make the cut once the tournament started.
● ALLISS HAS latterly been involved with course design, he and David Thomas being responsible for the design of the Belfry course used for the Ryder Cup.

AMATEURS

THERE ARE MILLIONS of amateur golfers all over the world, and unless you've accepted payment for playing you are included among them. The exact definition is thus: an amateur golfer is one who plays the game as a non-remunerative or non-profitmaking sport. Even the giving of golf lessons can infringe this.

● AMATEUR STATUS has changed radically over the century as riches to be had on the Pro Tour have increased. Prior to World War II leading amateurs used to win major championships, John Ball, Harold Hilton and Francis Ouimet all achieving success in the British and US Opens. The most notable amateur, however, was Bobby Jones, who won an incredible four US Opens and three British Opens. In 1960 Jack Nicklaus, then amateur, finished runner-up to Arnold Palmer in the US Open.
● AMATEUR GOLF still thrives, however, and until players qualify for a tour it can provide a rich breeding ground. The Walker Cup and Curtis Cup are held to let the best male and female amateurs from America and Great Britain and Ireland compete, in much the same way as the Ryder Cup and Solheim Cup. The British and US Amateur Championships have also recorded some notable winners.
● TIGER WOODS was the US Amateur Champion in 1994, 1995 and 1996, while other past winners include Justin Leonard (1992), Phil Mickelson (1990), Lanny Wadkins (1970, with Tom Kite runner-up), Craig Stadler (1973), Jerry Pate (1974) and Hal Sutton (1980). Jack Nicklaus won in 1959 and 1965, and Arnold Palmer in 1954.

Hal Sutton – an amateur who made it.

The Major Amateur Competitions

British Amateur Championship
First Staged: 1885, Hoylake
Most Titles: John Ball (8),
Michael Bonallack (5)

US Amateur Championship
First Staged: 1895, Newport, Rhode Island
Most Titles: Bobby Jones (5),
Jerome Travers (4)

Walker Cup
First Staged: 1922, National GL, New York
US – 31 wins, GB & Ireland – 4 wins,
one match halved

Curtis Cup
First Staged: 1932, Wentworth
US – 20 wins, GB & Ireland 6 wins,
three matches halved

AMERICA

AMERICA HAS dominated golf in the 20th century, ever since Francis Ouimet won the US Open in 1913.
● FIRST REFERENCES to golf in the USA appear in the late 18th century, and in 1888 a St Andrews club was formed by John Reid on a cow pasture at Yonkers in New York. Shinnecock Hills at Long Island soon followed and in 1894 the USGA formed in New York.
● THE FIRST US Open was held in 1895 and early competitions were won by the British, but golf was becoming popular in the USA and by the turn of the century 1000 clubs were in existence.
● JOHNNY MCDERMOTT was the first native-born US Open winner in 1911 and 1912. Ouimet followed and then the great Walter Hagen began his dominance in 1914. In 1916 the US PGA was established, and today three of the four major golfing tournaments are held in the USA.
● IN ADDITION to the individual tournaments, after World War I the Ryder cup, Walker Cup and Curtis Cup were also dominated by the Americans. Bobby Jones, Walter Hagen, Watson, Nicklaus, Trevino – the list has been endless and on the US Tour the Australian Greg Norman is the only man since the South African Gary Player to break US dominance on home soil.

Major American Competitions

US Open
First Staged: 1895, Newport, Rhode Island
Most Wins: Willie Anderson, Bobby Jones,
   Ben Hogan and Jack Nicklaus (4),
   Hale Irwin (3).
USPGA Championship
First Staged: 1916, Siwanoy CC,
   Bronxville, New York
Most Wins: Walter Hagen,
   Jack Nicklaus (5), Gene Sarazen,
   Sam Snead (3)
US Masters
First Staged: 1934
Most Wins: Jack Nicklaus (6),
   Arnold Palmer (4)

Ten Famous US Players

Ray Floyd
Walter Hagen
Ben Hogan
Bobby Jones
Jack Nicklaus
Arnold Palmer
Gene Sarazen
Lee Trevino
Tom Watson
Tiger Woods

The Top Ten US Courses

Augusta National, Georgia
Baltusrol, Springfield, New Jersey
Medinah, Illinois
Merion, Ardmore, Philadelphia
Pebble Beach, Monterey, California
Pine Valley, New Jersey
Pinehurst, North Carolina
Oakmont, Pennsylvania
Shinnecock Hills, Southampton,
   New York
Winged Foot, Mamaroneck

JAMIE ANDERSON

Born: St Andrews, Scotland – 1842
Career Spanned: 1850s–1880s
Major Wins: 3 – British Open (1877, 1878,
   1879)

ANDERSON IS ONE of only three men
to have won three consecutive British
Opens. The others are Young Tom Morris
and Peter Thomson.
● THE SON OF David Anderson (Old Daw),
a St Andrews caddie, Jamie Anderson
played golf from the age of ten and was the
best iron player of his time. At the 1878
Championship at Prestwick he recorded the
first hole-in-one in British Open history.
● PLAYING LONG before the golfing
riches of today, Anderson died in 1912 in a
poorhouse in Perth.

WILLIE ANDERSON

Born: North Berwick, Scotland – 1878
Career Spanned: 1897–1910
Major Wins: 4 (US Open 1901, 1903,
   1904, 1905)

WILLIE ANDERSON was a Scot who died
at the age of 32 after winning the US
Open four times. His premature death may
have been caused by alcoholism.
● ANDERSON'S HAT-TRICK of US Opens
from 1903 to 1905 has never been equalled.
He also achieved a second, a third, two
fourths and three fifths in the US Open, as
well as four wins in the Western Open, then
the second tournament behind the US
Open.
● HE HAD EVEN led the US Open in 1897
as a 17-year-old immigrant until Joe Lloyd
eagled the final hole. He was the first
professional at Baltusrol in New Jersey, and
he was well-liked for his modesty and
unflappable temperament.

● AT AN EXHIBITION game in Pittsburgh,
Anderson seemed noticeably tired after the
last few holes. Afterwards, sprawled in a
golf shop chair, he said that he wouldn't
play another round that year. He returned
to his home in Philadelphia and died two
days later.

PRINCE ANDREW – THE DUKE OF YORK

A KEEN PLAYER and patron of St Andrews,
Prince Andrew presented
the 1992 Curtis Cup at
Hoylake and was an
enthusiastic cheerleader at
the Ryder Cup in
Valderrama. He was more
than just a royal observer
and was indeed out on the
course at 4.00am watching
the groundsmen prepare the
course for the day.

ISAO AOKI

Born: Chiba, Japan – 31/08/1942
First Tour: 1981
US Tour Wins: 1
Major Wins: 0
First Senior Tour: 1992
Senior Tour Wins: 6
Senior Tour Earnings: $3.7 million

UNDOUBTEDLY his country's finest golfer,
Aoki is a great putter with a very
confident style, really rattling the ball in.
He has been the leading money-winner
in Japan five times.
● BECAUSE THE Japanese Tour is so
lucrative, few Japanese players venture
abroad. Aoki is an exception, and as a
result, he is one of the very few Japanese

*Aoki at the 1994 Dubai Desert Classic, one of
the few tournaments for which he makes a trip
out of Japan.*

Chipping in

'No, I thought they were cheering for me.'
(Nicklaus, when asked if the cheering at the
1980 US Open had put him off).

Stuart Appleby is the latest golfer to challenge Greg Norman's Australian supremacy.

who have come close to winning a major. He has achieved more than 50 victories worldwide and is the only Japanese player to have won on the Japanese, Australian, US and European tours.

● OCCASIONALLY INSPIRED, he broke the scoring record in the 1980 US Open but still finished behind Jack Nicklaus, while his 63 in the third round of the British Open at Muirfield equals the lowest-ever shot for a round.

● ALTHOUGH HE has never won a major, Aoki won the 1978 World Matchplay at Wentworth, and the 1983 European Open. He has also won the Open of Japan twice, the Hawaiian Open in 1983, and the Japanese PGA Championship five times. He now competes on the US Senior Tour and in one season won over $500,000.

STUART APPLEBY

Born: Cohuna Australia – 01/05/1971
First US Tour: 1994
Highest Ranking: 18 (1997)
US Tour Wins: 1
Major Wins: 0
Tour Earnings: $2 million

WITH THE SLUMP in form of compatriot Robert Allenby, Appleby is the latest to be dubbed the next Greg Norman. His rise in the World rankings was the biggest increase in 1997, and 1998 looks set to be a great year for the young man from Cohuna.

GEORGE ARCHER

Born: San Francisco, CA, USA – 01/10/1939
First US Tour: 1964
Highest Ranking: 5 (1968, 1971, 1972)
US Tour Wins: 12
Major Wins: 1 (US Masters 1969)
First Senior Tour: 1989
Senior Tour Wins: 17
Senior Tour Earnings: $5.2 million

ARCHER IS ONE of the greatest putters of all time, yet remains a modest and unassuming man. Very tall at 197cm (6ft 5$\frac{1}{2}$in), he crouches and goes down the shaft for greater control. In the 1980 Heritage Classic he set a tour record of 94 putts for four rounds.

● ARCHER WON US Masters in 1969 when Charles Coody bogeyed the last three holes to finish two shots behind. It is his only major victory.

● HE HAS BEEN more successful on the Senior Tour, and from 1990 to 1994 averaged $750,000 per year, twice getting near the million mark.

Chipping in

'Baseball players quit playing and take up golf, football players quit and take up golf, what are we supposed to take up when we quit?'

Putting genius: George Archer.

TOMMY ARMOUR

Born: Edinburgh, Scotland – 24/09/1895
Career Spanned: c.1924–c.1939
Major Wins: 3 (British Open 1931, US Open 1927, US PGA 1930)

ONCE DESCRIBED as having 'a mouth like a steel trap, a nose like a ski-jump, hands like the fins of a shark, and eyes which indicate he would enjoy seeing you get a compound fracture of the leg', Armour was an imposing sight. In World War I he lost the sight of an eye during combat after his tank was hit by enemy fire. He climbed out and

strangled a German soldier with his bare hands.

● ARMOUR WON all three of the majors available to him in the 1920s and early 1930s, beating Harry Cooper in a play-off for US Open and Gene Sarazen in the final of the US PGA.

● A NOTORIOUSLY slow player, Armour once said, 'Whoever said golf was supposed to be played fast?' He had 25 hole-in-ones during his career, all of which he dismissed as luck.

● ARMOUR RETIRED to teach and write golfing instruction books and today his name is associated with a range of golfing products.

Chipping in

'Golf is an awkward set of bodily contortions designed to produce a graceful result.'

Did You Know?

When Neil Armstrong landed on the moon in 1969 he got out a club and started playing, perhaps demonstrating the love of golf in the States. It was difficult for him to find a fairway, but there were plenty of bunkers around.

AUGUSTA NATIONAL

Where: Georgia, USA

Par: 72

Yardage: 6,925

Opened: 1933

Designer: Dr Alister Mackenzie and Bobby Jones

Major Events Staged: US Masters 1934–42 and 1946 to present

AUGUSTA IS the only course to hold a major Championship every year and as such is instantly recognizable. The back nine can almost be memorized, especially the crucial stretch, Amen Corner, which rounds at 11, 12 and 13.

● THE CLUB was founded by Bobby Jones after he retired from golf in 1930 at the age of 28. His friend, the banker Clifford Roberts, helped organize the club, and Bobby Jones worked with Dr Mackenzie on the course design, Mackenzie's work at Cypress Point having impressed him.

● JONES WANTED a course that would test the very best players but would still be a pleasure for all golfers to play. He achieved this with wide fairways, few bunkers and no rough. Instead the defences are the greens – huge and severely contoured.

● MANY FAMOUS moments have been witnessed at Augusta, including Gene Sarazen's double eagle at the 15th in 1935 – possibly the most famous stroke of all time –

and Sandy Lyle's great bunker shot at 18th in 1988. From 128m (140yd) in a bunker, he hit to 3m (10ft) from the flag and got the birdie he needed for a Masters win.

Tommy Armour: Best seen from a distance.

This par-three 12th hole is part of Amen Corner at Augusta, so-called because players pray as they approach it.

A

AUSTRALIA

MORE THAN 1 in 30 people belong to a club in Australia and there are 1,400 courses. After the UK and USA, Australia has traditionally been the third biggest force in golfing history.
● GREG NORMAN has increased that popularity and importance over the last two decades. Alex Reid formed the Tasmanian Midlands in 1829, one of the earliest recorded clubs.

Ten Famous Australian Players

Rodger Davis	Graham Marsh
Steve Elkington	Kel Nagle
Ian Baker-Finch	Greg Norman
Wayne Grady	Peter Senior
David Graham	Peter Thomson

Top Five Australian Courses

The Australian	Royal Melbourne
Kingston Heath	Royal Sydney
Metropolitan	

Contacts

Australian Golf Union
Golf Australia House
155 Cecil Street
South Melbourne
Victoria 3205

THE AUSTRALIAN OPEN

First played: 1904
Most Wins: Gary Player (7),
    Jack Nicklaus (6)
Lowest 72-hole Score: 264
    (Gary Player, 1965)

THE DEPRESSION of the late 1980s hit prize money severely in the Australian Open, but by 1994/5 it had recovered to over £3 million and it remains the most important competition in the southern hemisphere. Past winners include Bobby Locke, Jack Nicklaus, Arnold Palmer, Gary Player, Gene Sarazen and Tom Watson.

Australian Open Last 25 Winners

Year	Venue	Winner	Score
1972	Kooyonga	Peter Thomson	281
1973	Royal Queensland	JC Snead	280
1974	Lake Karrinyup	Gary Player	277
1975	The Australian	Jack Nicklaus	279
1976	The Australian	Jack Nicklaus	286
1977	The Australian	David Graham	284
1978	The Australian	Jack Nicklaus	284
1979	Metropolitan	Jack Newton	288
1980	The Lakes	Greg Norman	284
1981	Victoria	Bill Roger	282
1982	The Australian	Bob Shearer	287
1983	Kingston Heath	Peter Fowler	285
1984	Royal Melbourne	Tom Watson	281
1985	Royal Melbourne	Greg Norman	212*
1986	Metropolitan	Rodger Davis	278
1987	Royal Melbourne	Greg Norman	273
1988	Royal Sydney	Mark Calcavecchia	269
1989	Kingston Heath	Peter Senior	271
1990	The Australian	John Morse	283
1991	Royal Melbourne	Wayne Riley	285
1992	The Lakes	Steve Elkington	280
1993	Metropolitan	Brad Faxon	275
1994	Royal Sydney	Robert Allenby	280
1995	Kingston Heath	Greg Norman	278
1996	The Australian	Greg Norman	280
1997	Metropolitan	Lee Westwood	274

*reduced to 54 holes

PAUL AZINGER

Born: Hoylake, MA, USA – 06/01/1960
First US Tour: 1982
Highest Ranking: 2 (1987, 1993)
US Tour Wins: 11
Major Wins: 1 (US PGA 1993)
Ryder Cup Appearances: 3

AZINGER WAS a great player who developed cancer at the age of 33 just as he was likely to become a huge star. PGA Player of the year in 1987, he lost the British Open to Nick Faldo by one shot after dropping shots at the last two holes.
● THEN, IN 1993, his game peaked with ten top three finishes – the best since Tom Watson in 1980 – and a win in the US PGA. But a troublesome shoulder was diagnosed as lymphoma and his career, perhaps even his life, seemed to be over. Fortunately he recovered and late in 1994 returned to better form.
● HIS BOOK 'Zinger', about his struggle with cancer, has been a great success.

BAGS

The first golf bags appeared in the 1880s. Until then, caddies had carried clubs under their arms. Even club captains, like William Innes (above right, circa 1830s) of Black Heath, had to struggle with an armload. Traditionally bags have been leather, but latterly PVC and nylon have all been used.

Having made a full recovery from illness, Paul Azinger is slowly returning to top form.

B

● FOR THE PROFESSIONAL, expensive leather bags provided by sponsors remain the norm, but for the average player a lightweight waterproof bag is essential – particularly so now that trolley bans are imminent.

IAN BAKER-FINCH

Born: Nambour, Australia – 24/10/1960
Turned Pro: 1979
First US Tour: 1988
US Tour Wins: 1
European Tour Wins: 2
Major Wins: 1 (British Open 1991)

IAN BAKER-FINCH's fall from grace has been a long one. After a brilliant final-day win in the 1991 Open at Royal Birkdale he was troubled by back and shoulder injuries, among other problems, and won only the 1993 Australian PGA over the next four years. In 1994 and 1995 he qualified for the final two rounds only once in eight majors and went 16 months without winning a cent. This ended with a paltry $1,250 for 33rd place in Sydney in 1996.

● AFTER FIVE BIRDIES in the first seven holes of the 1991 Open Baker-Finch looked good. When he played the first nine in 29 he looked great, and at one point, taking 61 strokes for 18 consecutive holes, he was outstanding. He eventually won by two shots.

● IN 1984 he had been in with a chance of Open success. A 68 and 66 gave him a three-stroke lead, a third-round 71 then left him equal leader, but after a bad first hole on the final round his confidence fell apart and he finished with a 79, eight shots behind the St Andrew's winner, Ballesteros.

● BAKER-FINCH won events in Europe, the US and Japan before he started missing cuts galore. He has also won events in his homeland, as well as the New Zealand

Ian Baker-Finch's daughter thinks the British Open trophy's good enough to eat.

Open. He has competed in the States since 1988 and by end of 1991 had won 15 events worldwide and come second in twice that number.

● ON WINNING THE 1988 Bridgestone/Aso Open in Japan, Baker-Finch received a cow as a prize. He sold it back to the organizers for $5,000.

B

A.J. BALFOUR

THEN LEADER of the Tory party and later prime minister, Balfour agreed to become PGA president. Just like Eisenhower in the USA, he was a big ally of golf and did everything in his powers to raise the profile of the game. As a result he was nicknamed the Father of English Golf.

● HIS LOVE of the game was such that when he was Chief Secretary for Ireland he played the occasional round at Phoenix Park, protected by two plain-clothed guards. Five years earlier two government officials had been murdered there.

Chipping in

'I am quite certain that there has never been a greater addition to the lighter side of civilization than that supplied by the game of golf.'

JOHN BALL

Born: Hoylake, England – 24/12/1861
Career Spanned: 1880s to 1921
Major Wins: 1 (British Open 1890)
Major Amateur Wins: 8 (British Amateur Championship 1888, 1890, 1892, 1894, 1899, 1907, 1910, 1912)

JOHN BALL was the great British Amateur Champion. His eight wins are still a record, and he was also twice a beaten finalist. Only Bobby Jones was a better amateur on the world stage.

● BALL WAS ALMOST disqualified from amateur status at a young age, though. As a boy of 14 or 15, he tied Bob Martin for fourth place in the 1878 Open at Prestwick, for which he won 10 shillings (50p). Not sure what to do with the money, his chaperon, John Morris, told him to put it in his pocket. Later a committee ruled he was too young for this to have been a professional act and from then on it was agreed that only if you won money over the age of 16 could you be considered a professional.

● BALL'S PEAK was in the 1890s when he competed with professionals, and in 1890 he was the first Englishman to win British Open – and also the first amateur. He won the British Amateur Championship the same year.

● JOHN BALL'S strength was his iron shots to the flag. Until he came along players had been content just to aim for the green, but Ball always went at the pin. He wasn't a great putter, but his swing and accuracy made up for it.

● BALL ONCE had a wager that in dense fog he couldn't complete 18 holes at Hoylake in under 90 without losing a ball. It was a day when you couldn't see a flagstick from the tee. He painted his ball black, completed the round in $2^{1}/_4$ hours and scored an 81.

Seve Ballesteros is determined to get his playing career back on the rails.

B

SEVE BALLESTEROS

Born: Pedrena, Spain – 9/4/1957

First European Tour: 1974

Highest Ranking: 1 (1976, 1977, 1978, 1986, 1988, 1991)

European Tour Wins: 54

Major Wins: 5 (British Open 1979, 1984, 1988, US Masters 1980, 1983)

Ryder Cup Appearances: 8

IN A RECENT poll in 'Golf Monthly' magazine Ballesteros was voted the fifth best player of all time and also the professional with the best short game, with over a third of the votes. His poise and rhythm have made him one of the best-known modern golfers and he is certainly the most charismatic player ever seen on the European tour.

● A REAL NATURAL, Ballesteros has perhaps not won as many majors as he should have done, with much of his success coming early in his 20s. This is mainly because his driving is wayward. But it is his recovery from water, woodland or deep rough for which he is famous. 'Seve's got shots the rest of us don't even know,' Ben Crenshaw once said.

● IN 1976 the 19-year-old Ballesteros tied for the 1st-round lead of the Open at Royal Birkdale with a 69 and told the press he 'might take 80 if the wind gets up tomorrow'. A star was born. The next day another 69 in fact meant a two-shot lead, and he still led on day three, but eventually finished second to Miller. His win that year in the Dutch Open was his first European victory.

● THREE YEARS later at Lytham he won his first Open. On the final round his ball hit a host of BBC vehicles but still recorded a birdie. His playing partner Hale Irwin 'could not believe somebody with such bad driving could win the Open'. He was the youngest champ since 1872, despite missing the last six fairways.

● NEXT YEAR he won the US Masters. A 66, a 69 and a 68 gave him a seven-stroke lead on the final day and he eventually won after erratic play eroded a 10-shot lead (at one point it was down to two). Again he was the youngest champion and also the first European to win. He won the Masters again in 1983, this time by four strokes.

● THE YEAR OF 1984 brought a second Open title at St Andrews. This time steady play and pars rather than birdies were rewarded, and he came home by two shots from Langer and Watson. His 1988 British Open, in which he beat Nick Faldo and Nick Price with a final-round 65, was described as 'the best of my life'. It was also his last major to date.

● SEVE WAS Ryder Cup captain at Valderrama and marshalled the team brilliantly, if being a little overbearing at times. The day after his side's win, he maintained that he did not want to be captain for the 1999 Ryder Cup at Boston. He would perhaps like to do the job again in the future, but quite rightly wants to concentrate on his own game after his poor form of late.

● SEVE (Sebbie to the Spaniards), comes from a small village of farmers and fisherman on the northern coast of Spain. His uncle Ramon Sota was considered to be Spain's best golfer, prominent in the 1950s and 60s, and his three older brothers are golf professionals. He had a club in his hand as soon as he could walk, and turned professional before he was 17.

● HE IS A GREAT Ryder Cup player, determined and ambitious; only Faldo has won more points in Ryder Cup competition. He also has five World Matchplay titles and his score of 54 European wins is a record, as is his being six times leader of the European Merit table.

Chipping in

'I'd like to see the fairways more narrow. Then everybody would have to play from the rough, not just me.'

BALLS

The dimpled golf ball is now one of sport's most recognizable images, but wooden balls were the first to be seen on a golf course. They were followed by balls made by stuffing feathers into a leather casing before a solid gutta-percha ball was developed in 1859.

● MADE FROM the juice of the Malayan percha tree, this ball was cheaper and could be remoulded when damaged, unlike the feathery type, which could explode when wet. It became instantly popular.

● THEN CAME the Haskell ball, patented in 1898. This was a three-piece ball, based on the resilience of rubber bands wound under tension. It was soon to command the market.

● THE HASKELL ball was called a 'pill of quicksilver' by the great US amateur Chick Evans. Playing with a ball of rubber bands inside a cover of gutta-percha, Coburn Haskell realized its potential for greater distance and thus revolutionized golf. Courses had to be lengthened and redesigned as a result.

● ADDING DIMPLING gave some consistency to the Haskell ball's unpredictable flight patterns. Research has led to up to 500 dimples covering 70 per cent of the ball's surface, based on the icosahedron pattern of 20 repeating triangles. Spalding believed more dimples would mean more lift and so increased the size of the ball to fit them on.

● TODAY THERE are two-piece, three-piece and even four-piece balls, but still the regulations state that balls must be no heavier than 46g (1.62oz) and no smaller than 427mm (1.68in) in diameter.

Did You Know?

In 1906 Goodyear introduced a pneumatic ball. In the 1907 US Open Alex Campbell punctured his ball and four-putted the mis-shapen lump. Campbell lost by three strokes, and Goodyear withdrew their ball.

Ballybunion is much loved by Americans warming up for the British Open.

BALLYBUNION

Where: County Kerry, Ireland
Par: 71
Yardage: 6,503
Opened: 1896
Designer: Lionel Hewson and Mr Smyth
Major Events Staged: None

BALLYBUNION is possibly one of the best links courses in the world and surely only its remoteness has stopped it from holding a major. Tom Watson once said, 'A man would think that the game of golf originated here.' It is a favourite course of his and he often plays there as practice for the Open.

● BASED ON THE Shannon estuary in the north of County Kerry, Old Ballybunion, as it is known, lies along a golden beach with towering cliffs. It was inaugurated in 1896, but bungled finances led to closure two years later. A Colonel Bartholomew formed the present club in 1906, this time with a banker on the committee. The editor of 'Irish Golf', Lionel Hewson, was asked to lay out nine holes, and in 1926 another nine were laid out by a Mr Smyth of a London financial company.

● IN THE 1970s Friends of Ballybunion raised £100,000 to mend eroding cliffs, and every year they spend £100,000 on protecting the course from continued Atlantic erosion.

● KILKENNY CHURCHYARD is reachable from first tee with a slice, and the graveyard lies alongside the putting area. Martin McDermott of Los Angeles loved the course so much that when he died in 1987 at the age of 43 his body was flown over to rest in the churchyard, as he had wished.

BALTUSROL

Where: Springfield, NJ, USA
Par: 70
Yardage: 7,022
Opened: 1895
Designer: Albert W Tillinghast
Major events staged: US Open 1903, 1915,
**   1936, 1954, 1967, 1980, 1993,**
**   US Amateur 1904, 1926, 1946,**
**   US Women's Open 1961, 1985,**
**   US Women's Amateur 1901, 1911**

THE COURSE is named after Mr Baltus Roll, a wealthy farmer who was murdered in front of his wife by two thieves who believed he had a fortune hidden. Socialite Louis Keller then bought his land in the 1890s and decided to build a course.

● THE SCOTTISH player Willie Anderson was the club's first professional. He won the US Open four times from 1901 to 1905 – once at Baltusrol itself.

● TODAY THERE IS an upper and lower course. In 1922 Albert Tillinghast was brought in to help with a redesign, and built two courses encompassing the existing 18 holes. The Lower is the major venue, having hosted five US Opens.

● BALTUSROL IS NOT a pretty course, but it is long and varied. Only the last two holes are par fives, and the 17th is a monster 576m (630yd) – the longest in American Championship golf. However in the 1993 US Open John Daly managed to hit it in two, as did Sandy Lyle.

● TILLINGHAST added subtle small greens with deep bunkers, and always left a low shot into the green. He used water only where it already existed and the result was a course not as harsh as many Open courses.

● THE SHORT fourth was redesigned by Robert Trent Jones in an overhaul of the lower course. There were complaints that it was too hard, but Jones went out to test it with a club official and hit a hole-in-one – whereupon the complaints stopped.

● IN THE 1980 US Open Jack Nicklaus opened with a record-equalling 63. He then went on to score a record aggregate 272, beating Aoki into second place. The record was then equalled by Lee Janzen in 1993, all four of his rounds being under 70. In that year Joey Sindelar led after 18 holes but then missed the cut.

BRIAN BARNES

Born: Addington, England – 03/06/1945
First European Tour: 1971
Highest Ranking: 4 (1971, 1974, 1975)
European Tour Wins: 10
Major Wins: 0
Ryder Cup Appearances: 6

ALTHOUGH a very competent player on the regular PGA tour, Barnes has found far more financial success on the Senior Tour than he ever did as a regular pro. In the 1995 Senior British Open at Royal Portrush, Northern Ireland, his win earned £58,330 – more than he'd ever won in a single season on the Euro tour. His best haul for one year was £51,722.

● AN ECCENTRIC, Barnes was known to smoke a pipe and swig from beer cans on

B

his rounds. He still managed to appear in every Ryder Cup team from 1969 to 1979, as well as many World Cup appearances for Scotland.

● HIS GREATEST moment came in the 1975 Ryder Cup at Laurel Valley, Pennsylvania, when he beat Jack Nicklaus twice in the same day – four and two in the morning, two and one in the afternoon.

● BARNES COULD be a fiery character. While among the leaders at the 1968 French Open, he took 12 putts at the short par three eighth for a final score of 15. Infuriated at his performance, he completely lost his cool and eventually stalked off the course.

LONG JIM BARNES

Born: Lelant, England – 08/04/1886

Career Spanned: 1910s to 1930s

Major Wins: 4 (US Open 1921, British Open 1925, US PGA 1916, 1919)

JIM BARNES, born in Cornwall, was the first winner of the US PGA in 1916, for which he won $500. He was called 'Long' on account of his length of hitting off the tee – or, alternatively, because he was 190cm (6ft 3in) tall.

● THERE WAS NO championship for the next two years because of the war, but he

Long Jim Barnes – long legs, a long drive and one of the longest golfing careers.

Brian Barnes has had more success on the Senior Tour than as a regular pro, seen here in the 1985 European Open at Sunningdale.

won again in 1919 and was a losing finalist in 1921 and 1924, losing to Walter Hagen both times. In 1921 he won the US Open by nine shots, which is still a record.

● BARNES EMIGRATED to San Francisco in 1906 and became an American citizen, but liked to return to the UK. He tied for second place in the British Open in 1922 and won in 1925, in the last Open to be played at Prestwick. Barnes had gone out earlier and avoided the crowds, and sat in the clubhouse not expecting to win. By the time Macdonald Smith went out, needing only 79 to win, there were swarms of people on the course. He hit an 82; Barnes had come from five strokes behind to achieve an unlikely victory.

● JIM BARNES'S last PGA Tour win was in 1937 at the age of 51. He remained the oldest winner until Sam Snead won it in 1965, aged 52.

ANDY BEAN

Born: Lafayette, GA, USA – 13/03/1953

First US Tour: 1976

US Tour Wins: 11

Major Wins: 0

Ryder Cup Appearances: 2 (1979 and 1987)

Tour Earnings: $3 million

BEAN'S BEST period was between 1978 and 1986, and in this eight-year period he was five times in the top seven US money-winners and accumulated all of his 11 tour wins.

● A STRONG MAN with great power and touch, he was famed for biting golf balls in half. Plagued by medical problems and back injuries, however, he had to resort to the

Nike tour and Qualifying School in 1994 because in the 19 tournaments he had entered he had made the money only three times, eventually finishing 253rd on the US Tour.

● BEAN WAS a playing partner of Hubert Green in the 1977 US Open at Southern Hills course in Oklahoma. Green had been sent a death threat that he would be shot at the 15th hole. In case a misdirected shot caught Bean, Green stayed well clear of him, but went on to complete the round and win the Open.

FRANK BEARD

Born: Dallas, TX, USA – 01/05/1939
First US Tour: 1963
Highest Ranking: 1st (1969)
US Tour Wins: 11
Major Wins: 0

A leading money-winner in 1969, despite not winning a tournament – Beard was quoted as saying, 'I can't win anything but money.'

● NEVERTHELESS, he picked up 11 titles on the US Tour between 1963 and 1971, and almost won the US Open in 1975. But after being in the lead going into the final round he hit 78, and two bogeys at the last two holes meant he missed out on a play-off by one shot.

● HE IS A businesslike and uncharismatic man, but his book 'Pro', published in 1970, is perhaps surprisingly the best account of life on a US Tour.

Frank Beard: serious about his golf.

CHIP BECK

Born: Fayetteville, NC, USA – 12/09/1956
First US Tour: 1979
Highest Ranking: 2 (1988)
US Tour Wins: 4
Major Wins: 0
Ryder Cup Appearances: 3
Tour Earnings: $6million

B ECK'S CAREER has been one of consistency with flashes of brilliance, but lately it's been consistently bad form.

● BACK IN HIS best year, 1988, Beck managed 11 top 10 finishes and two wins. He is also one of two men to record a 59 in PGA Tour history (Al Geiberger being the other), breaking 60 in the 1991 Las Vegas Invitational.

● BECK WAS also top ten in the money list for three years from 1987, and in the top 20 for the following three years. However, in 1997 he broke 70 only twice, and shot 80 five times or worse. He missed 23 cuts in a row, and made only three in the previous 32 events. Having made just over $10,000, he was 267th in the money list. It all seems a long way from that 59.

THE BELFRY

Where: Sutton Coldfield, England
Par: 72
Yardage: 7177
Opened: 1977
Designer: Peter Alliss and David Thomas
Major Events Staged: Ryder Cup 1985, 1989, 1993

T HERE ARE three courses at the Belfry: the Brabazon, which is used for Ryder Cup matches; the PGA National – the first PGA-branded National course in Europe; and the Derby Course, which is also popular. All three courses are par-72, with the Brabazon measuring 7,220 yards, the PGA National 7,100 yards and the Derby 6,009 yards.

● MENTION THE BELFRY and you immediately think of the Ryder Cup. By no means a brilliant course, the Belfry is nevertheless the British PGA HQ, and was packed for the 1985 Ryder Cup. There are a couple of dodgy holes, the flat terrain is difficult for spectators and it is not rated as a venue, but even so 27,000 people made use of nearby motorways to celebrate a famous victory.

● THE BIGGER course at the Belfry, the Brabazon, used for the Ryder Cup, was designed by Peter Alliss and David Thomas. Ironically, considering the success of the Europeans there, it is a very American course with large greens, long holes and much water play.

● AFTER MUCH complaint from most professionals, the original course architect David Thomas has been given a £2.4 million package to upgrade the course and make it a greater challenge. The third hole will become a par-five dog-leg, while the fourth will be shortened to a par-four with a new green and bunkers. There have often been grumbles about the course and it was given a face lift before the 1993 Ryder Cup. Many think that the 1989 Ryder Cup, which was tied 14–14, would have made a fitting last appearance, but the Cup will return there in 2001.

The Brabazon Course boasts American-style large greens, American-style water hazards, but as yet no American wins.

DEANE BEMAN

Born: Washington DC, USA – 24/04/1938

First US Tour: 1967

US Tour Wins: 4

Major Wins: 0

Amateur Wins: 3 (British Amateur Championship 1959, US Amateur Championship 1960, 1963)

First Senior Tour: 1994

BEMAN WAS the Commissioner (aka Chief Executive) on the PGA Tour from 1974 to 1994, providing the most successful and longest running period, in which he was effectively controlling a business with revenues of $200 million. His major achievement was turning it into a non-taxpaying organization.

● BEMAN LEFT his position to join the US Senior Tour but made little impact, although

Dean Beman was a great amateur player and a successful administrator.

Deane Beman was pushed into the Florida waters ny Jerry Pate after the 1982 Tournament Players championship.

● LLOYD MANGRUM had been the first man to hit 64 when his first round at the 1940 US Masters broke the then impenetrable 65 mark. It was another 10 years before Lee Mackey repeated the feat in the 1950 US Open, then another 14 years before a spate of 64s in the 1960s.

● JACK NICKLAUS missed a 90cm (3ft) birdie putt on the final green of the first round of the 1980 US Open at Baltusrol, which would have earned him a record-breaking 62. Even worse, Greg Norman had a 9m (30ft) putt for a 61 in the second round of the 1986 British Open. He three-putted for a 63, but went on to win the title. It was also Norman who recorded the lowest-ever 72-hole total in a major championship with a 267 in the British Open at Royal St George's in 1993. Both Colin Montgomerie and Steve Elkington then matched the total at Riviera in the 1995 US PGA. Miller's round, however, is considered by many to be the best round ever.

he finished only a shot behind Gary Player in the Senior British Open at Turnberry in 1991.

● BEMAN'S BEST golf was played as an amateur. He represented his country four times each in the Eisenhower Trophy and the Americas and Walker cups. He also won the British Amateur in 1959 and the US Amateur in 1960 and 1963.

● ONE OF THE shortest hitters to play Pro Golf, he said it toughened him up to stare at the green with a four-wood in his hands. His second tournament as a pro was at Baltusrol in the 1967 US Open, and at the first hole, playing 142m (465yd), he sank his second shot for an eagle-two.

PATTY BERG

Born: Minneapolis, MO, USA – 13/02/1918
First LPGA Tour: 1948
Highest Ranking: 1st (1954, 1955, 1957)
Tour Wins: 57
Major Wins: 5 (US Open 1946, World
  Championship 1953, 1954, 1955, 1957)

BERG REACHED the final of the US Women's Amateur Championship on her first entry in 1935. She then won it in 1938, after again finishing second the previous year. In all she won approximately 40 events

as an amateur before turning pro just before World War II.

● ALONG WITH Babe Zaharias and Betty Jameson she was one of three founder members of the US Women's Tour in 1948. In 1946 she had won the first US Women's Open (then a matchplay tournament). She then won what was called the World Championship in 1953, 1954, 1955 and 1957.

● SHE WAS leading money-winner in 1954, 1955 and 1957, and was the first woman to earn more than $100,000.

● PATTY BERG'S first tournament win came in 1941 and her last in 1962. All told, on tour, she won 57 times and in all she recorded 83 Tournament wins from the 1930s to the 1960s.

BEST ROUNDS

IT WAS 1973 before anybody recorded a 63 in a Major Championship, when Johnny Miller broke the 64 barrier in the final round of the US Open at Oakmont, winning the title by a single shot. Since then it has occurred another 17 times.

THE

BEST EVER

ROUNDS

— British Open —

63 (7 times, first by Mark Hayes at Turnberry in 1977)

Lowest 72-hole Total:
267 Greg Norman
(1993 at Royal St Georges)

— US Open —

63 (3 times, first by Johnny Miller at Oakmont, 1973)

Lowest 72-hole Total:
272 Jack Nicklaus (1980 at Baltusrol)
and Lee Janzen (1993, also at Baltusrol)

— US PGA —

63 (6 times, first by Bruce Compton, Firestone, 1975)

Lowest 72-hole Total:
267 Steve Elkington (1995 Riviera)
and Colin Montgomerie (1995 Riviera)

— US PGA US Masters —

63 (Nick Price 1986)

Lowest 72-hole Total
270 Tiger Woods (1997)

BIRDIE

AMERICAN terminology, which is now accepted worldwide, was the first to employ the word 'birdie', meaning one under par – par being the expected score for a scratch player on a hole. There are two versions of how the term was coined. The first is that in 1899 George Crump's second shot at a par four in Atlantic City hit a bird in flight and landed near the hole. The alternative is that it has developed from the phrase 'a bird of a shot'.

THOMAS BJORN

| Born: Silkeborg, Denmark – 18/02/1971 |
| First European Tour: 1996 |
| Highest Ranking: 10 (1996) |
| European Tour Wins: 1 |
| Major Wins: 0 |
| Ryder Cup Appearances: 1 (1997) |

BJORN TWICE missed out at Qualifying School, then had a poor record on the Challenge tour before eventually winning it in 1995. He made his name professionally when he won the Loch Lomond World Invitational the following year.

● BJORN IS one of the younger players hoping to succeed Faldo, Ballesteros and Woosnam, and he has strong views about being committed to the European Tour rather than going to the USA.

● AS A Ryder Cup Rookie in 1997, Bjorn marked his debut singles with a fine half against Open Champion Justin Leonard which took Europe to the brink of their victory in Valderrama, coming back from four down after four holes.

● CALM AND ANALYTICAL off the course, he is occasionally temperamental on it.

BOGEYS

BOGEY is one over par and derives from the score the mythical Colonel Bogey used to achieve – he used to make no mistakes and would therefore turn in the perfect score. Double and triple bogeys are self-explanatory.

TOMMY BOLT

| Born: Haworth, OK, USA – 31/03/1918 |
| First US Tour: 1950 |
| US Tour Wins: 11 |
| Major Wins: 1 (US Open 1958) |

BOLT WAS a great player whose career was blighted by tantrums, during which he would break his clubs over his knee or hurl them into the distance. He fell out with caddies and playing partners alike, and one playing partner, Porky Oliver, once threw Tommy's putter in a lake to stop him from throwing it further.

● NICKNAMED 'Thunder' Bolt, Tommy won 11 tour events between 1953 and 1961, including the 1958 US Open, which he won

Thomas Bjornin one of his calmer moments, after winning the 1998 Heineken Classic.

by four shots from a young Gary Player. In the 1952 US Masters he had a chance of a major and was doing well, but three-putted three of the last four greens and came third.

● WHEN BOLT played Eric Brown in a 1957 Ryder Cup match he slowed to an agonizing pace in their ill-tempered game, knowing that Brown was a quick player. At one point Brown had his caddie bring him a lounge chair from the clubhouse. Nevertheless, Brown eventually won.

Chipping in

'Always throw your clubs ahead of you – that way you don't have to waste energy going back to pick them up.'

MICHAEL BONALLACK

| Born: Chigwell England – 31/12/1934 |
| Career Spanned: 1950s to 1970s |
| Major Amateur Wins: 10 (British Amateur Champion 5 times, 1961, 1965, 1968, 1969, 1970; English Amateur Champion 5 times, 1962, 1963, 1965, 1967, 1968) |

BONALLACK WON the British Amateur Championship five times, including three in succession – a feat never repeated. It also included a win in each country of the British Isles. He also won the English title five times between 1962 and 1968.

● BONALLACK ALSO played in nine Walker Cup teams, two as captain and one of those as a victorious captain. In fact, Bonallack played 131 matches for England, including 16 years without a break from 1957 to 1972.

● POTENTIALLY the greatest English and British Amateur ever, he dominated amateur golf in the 1950s and 60s. Only John Ball and Harold Hilton are his rivals for that title. Now Sir Bonallack after his recent knighthood, he has been secretary of the Royal and Ancient since 1983.

JULIUS BOROS

Born: Fairfield, CT, USA – 03/03/1920

First US Tour: 1950

Highest Ranking: 1st (1952, 1955)

Career Wins: 18

Major Wins: 3 (US Open 1952, 1963, US PGA 1968)

Ryder Cup Appearances: 4

Tour Earnings: Over $1 million

BOROS WAS a late developer who gave up accountancy at the age of 30 to turn pro. In 1950 he was a US Open contender in his first year on tour, in 1951 he was fourth and then in 1952 he won, beating Hogan after being four shots behind after 36 holes.

● BOROS WON again in 1963. He finished with poor scores of 76 and 72 in the final two rounds, but nobody beat his average score. In an 18-hole play-off next day he beat Palmer by six shots and Jacky Cupit by three. He also won the US PGA in 1968 aged 48, and remains the oldest winner of a Major.

● JULIUS BOROS is in the top 40 of all time for tournament wins, and captured the PGA Seniors Championship in 1971. His son Guy is now on the US PGA Tour.

● A GREAT SAND PLAYER, he was told by tutor Tommy Armour, 'Aim for the bunkers and you might make it.'

Pat Bradley has won all four of the Ladies' majors during her distinguished career.

PAT BRADLEY

Born: Westford, MA, USA – 24/03/1951

First LPGA Tour: 1974

Highest Ranking: 1st (1986, 1991)

Tour Wins: 31

Major Wins: 6 (Du Maurier Classic 1980, 1985, 1986, Dinah Shore Tournament 1986, LPGA Championship 1986, US Women's Open 1981)

Solheim Cup Appearances: 3

Tour Earnings: Over $5million

BRADLEY FIRST won in 1976 and her 31st victory came in 1995. From 1976 to 1991 she was a dozen times in the top six winners, and 20 times in the top 20, experiencing just one bad year.

● HER BEST YEAR was 1991, when her 30th victory earned her a place in the Hall of Fame. She was also Rolex Player of the Year and won the Vare Trophy for best scoring average.

● BRADLEY WAS the first to go through 2, 3 and 4 million-dollar marks for earnings. Only Betsy King has earned more money. And Bradley has been in the top 10 in more than half of the 600 tournaments she has entered.

HARRY BRADSHAW

Born: Delgany, Ireland – 09/10/1913

Career Spanned: 1930s to 1950s

Major Wins: 0

Ryder Cup Appearances: 3

THE CLOSEST Bradshaw came to winning the Open was in 1949 at Sandwich. In contention after a first round 68, he hit a 77 in the second round. He recovered with a 68 and 70 to force a play-off with Bobby Locke, but lost woefully.

● HE PLAYED six times for Ireland in the Canada Cup (now World Cup) 1954–9, winning with Christy O'Connor in 1958 in Mexico City.

Did You Know?

In the second round of the 1949 Open, Harry Bradshaw's ball landed in a broken beer bottle. In those days there were no rulings on such matters and there were no officials present to make a decision, so he tried to play it and it went 18m (20yd). He could have dropped without penalty.

JAMES BRAID

Born: Fife, Scotland – 06/02/1870

Career Spanned: 1890s to 1920s

Major Wins: 5 (British Open Champion 1901, 1905, 1906, 1908, 1910)

JAMES BRAID was a reserved, powerful and placid man, and one of the Great Triumvirate. He was the first man to win five Open Championships, a figure later passed by Harry Vardon and equalled by J. H. Taylor, the other two of the Triumvirate.

B

According to legend, James Braid once hit a wind-assisted drive some 395 yards.

Between them the three dominated golf for 20 years before World War I.
● BRAID'S OPEN win in 1901 was the last won with a gutty ball, and all his Championships were won in Scotland. He also won the first PGA Matchplay Championship in 1903 and repeated the feat three more times. He finished runner-up twice, the second time in 1927 at the age of 57.
● BRAID PLAYED for Scotland against England eight times from 1903 to 1912, and for Great Britain against the USA in 1921, aged 51.
● BRAID BECAME a course designer after his retirement, designing some 200 courses, but as he abhorred travel they were rarely outside England or Scotland. Carnoustie and Gleneagles are two of his best works.

GORDON BRAND JNR

Born: Kirkcaldy, Scotland – 19/08/1958
First European Tour: 1982
Highest Ranking: 4th (1987)
European Tour Wins: 8
Major Wins: 0
Ryder Cup Appearances: 2

BRAND achieved outstanding amateur success, followed by instant fame as a pro. In his first year on the Euro Tour he won twice and finished seventh on the money list. He then suffered from trying to over-hit, but in 1984 again finished seventh after two more wins.
● HE HAS appeared in two Ryder Cup teams, in 1987 and 1989, and has also represented Scotland 10 times in the Dunhill Cup and seven times in the World Cup.

THE BRITISH AMATEUR CHAMPIONSHIP

First played: 1885 – Royal Liverpool, Hoylake
Most wins: 8 – John Ball Jnr (1888, 1890, 1892, 1894, 1899, 1907, 1910, 1912)
5 – Michael Bonallack (1961, 1965, 1968, 1969, 1970)

THE CHAMPIONSHIP was first played in 1885 when it was won by Allan McFie, who won by seven and six in the final.
● THE FINAL STAGES have always been matchplay rather than strokeplay, but various methods have been employed in the tournament. Currently there are 36 holes of strokeplay followed by the lowest 64 scorers and ties contesting a matchplay knockout phase.

British Amateur Championship
The Last 25 Winners

1972	Royal St George's	T Homer
1973	Royal Porthcawl	R Siderowf (USA)
1974	Muirfield	T Homer
1975	Royal Liverpool	M Giles (USA)
1976	St Andrews	R Siderowf (USA)
1977	Ganton	P McEvoy
1978	Royal Troon	P McEvoy
1979	Hillside	J Sigel (USA)
1980	Royal Porthcawl	D Evans
1981	St Andrews	P Ploujoux (Fr)
1982	Royal Cinque Ports	M Thompson
1983	Turnberry	P Parkin
1984	Formby	J-M Olazabal (Spain)
1985	Royal Dornoch	G McGimpsey
1986	Royal Lytham	D Curry
1987	Prestwick	P Mayo
1988	Royal Porthcawl	C Hardin (Sweden)
1989	Royal Birkdale	S Dodd
1990	Muirfield	R Muntz (Holland)
1991	Ganton	G Wolstenholme
1992	Carnoustie	S Dundas
1993	Royal Portrush	I Pyman
1994	Nairn	L James
1995	Royal Liverpool	G Sherry
1996	Turnberry	W Bladon
1997	Royal St George's	C Watson

Gordon Brand Jnr's best years came in the mid-1980s.

25

THE BRITISH OPEN

First Played: 1860 at Prestwick
(won by Willie Park)

Most Wins: 6 Harry Vardon (1896, 1898, 1899, 1903, 1911, 1914)
James Braid, JH Taylor, Peter Thomson and Tom Watson have all won five times

Lowest 72-hole Score: 267 – Greg Norman (1993 at Royal St Georges)

THE OPEN is the most famous and traditional competition in golf. Initially a strokeplay event played over 36 holes, it changed to 72 holes in 1892. Moving from course to course each year, it has only been staged among a dozen or so courses in its time, unlike the 50 that have hosted the US Open.

● THE COMPETITION was initially suggested at Prestwick Golf Club and eight players competed for a moroccan-red Championship Belt. When Young Tom Morris won the event for the third successive year in 1870 he got to keep the belt, and after the tournament paused to consider this unexpected turn of events in 1871 it returned the following year with the Claret Jug as its trophy.

● JOHN BALL was the first non-Scot to win the event, 30 years after the competition started, and then in 1922 Walter Hagen won and a period of US dominance ensued which has lasted to some extent ever since.

Justin Leonard holds the Claret Jug some 44 years after the man on his cap, Ben Hogan. If the cap fits…

The British Open – All The Winners

(36 holes until 1892)

Year	Course	Winner	Score
1860	Prestwick	W Park	174
1861	Prestwick	T Morris Snr	163
1862	Prestwick	T Morris Snr	163
1863	Prestwick	W Park	168
1864	Prestwick	T Morris Snr	167
1865	Prestwick	A Strath	162
1866	Prestwick	W Park	169
1867	Prestwick	T Morris Snr	170
1868	Prestwick	T Morris Jnr	157
1869	Prestwick	T Morris Jnr	154
1870	Prestwick	T Morris Jnr	149
1871	No Championship		
1872	Prestwick	T Morris Jnr	166
1873	St Andrews	T Kidd	179
1874	Musselburgh	M Park	159
1875	Prestwick	W Park	166
1876	St Andrews	R Martin	176
1877	Musselburgh	J Anderson	160
1878	Prestwick	J Anderson	157
1879	St Andrews	J Anderson	169
1880	Musselburgh	R Ferguson	162
1881	Prestwick	R Ferguson	170
1882	St Andrews	R Ferguson	171
1883	Musselburgh	W Fernie	159*
1884	Prestwick	J Simpson	160
1885	St Andrews	R Martin	171
1886	Musselburgh	D Brown	157
1887	Prestwick	W Park Jnr	161
1888	St Andrews	J Burns	171
1889	Musselburgh	W Park Jnr	155
1890	Prestwick	J Ball (Am)	164
1891	St Andrews	H Kirkaldy	166

Changed from 36 to 72 holes

Year	Course	Winner	Score
1892	Muirfield	H Hilton (Am)	305
1893	Prestwick	W Auchterlonie	322
1894	Royal St George's	J H Taylor	326
1895	St Andrews	JH Taylor	322
1896	Muirfield	H Vardon	316*
1897	Hoylake	H Hilton (Am)	314
1898	Prestwick	H Vardon	307
1899	Royal St George's	H Vardon	310
1900	St Andrews	JH Taylor	309
1901	Muirfield	J Braid	309
1902	Hoylake	A Herd	307
1903	Prestwick	H Vardon	300
1904	Royal St George's	J White	296
1905	St Andrews	J Braid	318
1906	Muirfield	J Braid	300
1907	Hoylake	A Massy	312
1908	Prestwick	J Braid	291
1909	Deal	JH Taylor	295
1910	St Andrews	J Braid	299
1911	Royal St George's	H Vardon	303*
1912	Muirfield	E Ray	295
1913	Hoylake	JH Taylor	304
1914	Prestwick	H Vardon	306
1915 – 1919 No Championship			
1920	Deal	G Duncan	303
1921	St Andrews	J Hutchison	296*
1922	Royal St George's	W Hagen	300
1923	Troon	AG Havers	295
1924	Hoylake	W Hagen	301
1925	Prestwick	J Barnes	300
1926	Royal Lytham	RT Jones Jnr (Am)	291
1927	St Andrews	R T Jones Jnr (Am)	285
1928	Royal St George's	W Hagen	292
1929	Muirfield	W Hagen	292
1930	Hoylake	R T Jones Jnr (Am)	291
1931	Carnoustie	T Armour	296
1932	Prince's	G Sarazen	283

1933	St Andrews	D Shute	292*
1934	Royal St George's	TH Cotton	283
1935	Muirfield	A Perry	283
1936	Hoylake	AH Padgham	287
1937	Carnoustie	TH Cotton	290
1938	Royal St George's	RA Whitcombe	295
1939	St Andrews	R Burton	290
1940 – 1945 No Championship			
1946	St Andrews	S Snead	290
1947	Hoylake	F Daly	293
1948	Muirfield	TH Cotton	284
1949	Royal St George's	AD Locke	283*
1950	Troon	AD Locke	279
1951	Royal Portrush	M Faulkner	285
1952	Royal Lytham	AD Locke	287
1953	Carnoustie	B Hogan	282
1954	Royal Birkdale	PW Thomson	283
1955	St Andrews	PW Thomson	281
1956	Hoylake	PW Thomson	286
1957	St Andrews	AD Locke	279
1958	Royal Lytham	PW Thomson	278*
1959	Muirfield	G Player	284
1960	St Andrews	K Nagle	278
1961	Royal Birkdale	A Palmer	284
1962	Troon	A Palmer	276
1963	Royal Lytham	R Charles	277*
1964	St Andrews	A Lema	279
1965	Royal Birkdale	PW Thomson	285
1966	Muirfield	J Nicklaus	282
1967	Hoylake	R de Vicenzo	278
1968	Carnoustie	G Player	289
1969	Royal Lytham	A Jacklin	280
1970	St Andrews	J Nicklaus	283*
1971	Royal Birkdale	L Trevino	278
1972	Muirfield	L Trevino	278
1973	Troon	T Weiskopf	276
1974	Royal Lytham	G Player	282
1975	Carnoustie	T Watson	279*
1976	Royal Birkdale	J Miller	279
1977	Turnberry	T Watson	268
1978	St Andrews	J Nicklaus	281
1979	Royal Lytham	S Ballesteros	283
1980	Muirfield	T Watson	271
1981	Royal St George's	W Rogers	276
1982	Royal Troon	T Watson	284
1983	Royal Birkdale	T Watson	275
1984	St Andrews	S Ballesteros	276
1985	Royal St George's	S Lyle	282
1986	Turnberry	G Norman	280
1987	Muirfield	N Faldo	279
1988	Royal Lytham	S Ballesteros	273
1989	Royal Troon	M Calcavecchia	275*
1990	St Andrews	N Faldo	270
1991	Royal Birkdale	I Baker-Finch	272
1992	Muirfield	N Faldo	272
1993	Royal St George's	G Norman	267
1994	Turnberry	N Price	268
1995	St Andrews	J Daly	282*
1996	Royal Lytham	T Lehman	271
1997	Royal Troon	J Leonard	272
1998	Royal Birkdale	M O'Meara	280*

* Play-off

THE BRITISH WOMEN'S OPEN

First Played: 1976

Most Wins: 2 – Debbie Massey USA (1980, 1981) Karrie Webb (1995, 1997)

Lowest 72-hole Score: 269 (Karrie Webb (1997)

Although it only began in 1976, the British Women's Open is nevertheless the main event on the Ladies European Tour. Only one person has won it more than once – Debbie Massey, in back-to-back wins at the start of the 1980s.

British Women's Open Winners

1976	Fulford	
	Jenny Lee Smith (am)	299
1977	Lindrick	
	Vivien Saunders	306
1978	Foxhills	
	Janet Melville (am)	310
1979	Southport & Ainsdale	
	Alison Sheard (South Africa)	301
1980	Wentworth	
	Debbie Massey (USA)	294
1981	Northumberland	
	Debbie Massey (USA)	295
1982	Royal Birkdale	
	Marta Figueras-Dotti (Spain)	296
1983	Not held	
1984	Woburn	
	Ayako Okamoto (Japan)	289
1985	Moor Park	
	Betsy King (USA)	300
1986	Royal Birkdale	
	Laura Davies	283
1987	St Mellion	
	Alison Nicholas	296
1988	Lindrick	
	Corinne Dibnah (Australia)	295
1989	Ferndown	
	Jane Geddes (USA)	274
1990	Woburn	
	Helen Alfredsson (Sweden)	288
1991	Woburn	
	Penny Grice-Whittaker	284
1992	Woburn	
	Patty Sheehan (USA) *	207
1993	Woburn	
	Karen Lunn (Australia)	275
1994	Woburn	
	Liselotte Neumann (Sweden)	280
1995	Woburn Karrie Webb (Australia)	278
1996	Woburn	
	Emilee Klein (USA)	277
1997	Woburn	
	Karrie Webb (Australia)	269

* Tournament reduced to 54 holes

What a ridiculous hat. And the lid of the British Women's Open looks equally stupid.

MARK BROOKS

Born: Fort Worth, TX, USA – 25/03/1961

First US Tour: 1983

Highest Ranking: 3 (1996)

US Tour Wins: 7

Major Wins: 1 (US PGA Championship 1996)

Ryder Cup Appearances: 0

BROOKS FELL down the rankings in 1997, after his 1996 PGA win in a play-off with Kenny Perry. The previous year he was third in the British Open, just missing play-off.

● THE TEXAN finished in the money in 23 of the 29 events entered in 1996 and was third in the money list.

● IN THE 1991 Las Vegas International at the 17th hole at 12 under par Brooks hit his tee shot into a tree. He needed to find it to avoid a penalty, so he climbed the tree and found eight other balls but not his own. He ended up with a double bogey-seven.

BUNKERS

THE BUNKER, or sand trap, is the most common hazard on a golf course. However, as bunker play is one of the most improved parts of the modern players' game, and there has also been an improvement in lofted clubs, many players would prefer to be in a bunker than in the rough or a dry, grassy lie.

● BUNKERS – the term is derived from a Scottish word – can take many forms, with either fine white sand or brown. The sand wedge, developed especially for bunkers, has more loft than a pitching wedge and a longer bottom edge. Its invention is generally credited to Gene Sarazen, one of the first players famed for his control in bunkers, while Ballesteros and Mickelson are great bunker players of the modern age.

● DAVE HILL was once fined $500 in the 1971 Colonial Invitation for throwing a ball out of a bunker. He picked it up and lobbed it onto the green after a terrible round.

JACK BURKE

Born: Fort Worth, TX, USA – 29/01/1923

Career Spanned: 1950s to 1970s

Career Wins: 15

Major Wins: 2 (US Masters 1956, US PGA 1956)

Ryder Cup Appearances: 5

BURKE HIT a streak in 1952, when he won four events in just over three weeks. He was never quite as good again, although he won two majors in 1956.

● IN THE FINAL round of the US Masters (one of his two major victories) Burke was eight strokes behind leader Ken Venturi, but in bad weather he managed a 71 while Venturi returned an 80. The same year he won the US PGA and was voted Player of the Year.

● BURKE ALSO captained US Ryder Cup teams in 1957 and 1973.

DICK BURTON

Born: Darwen, England – 11/10/1907
Career Spanned: 1920s to 1940s
Major Wins: 1 (British Open 1939)

BURTON WON the last British Open to be held before World War II. He was therefore Open Champion for seven years, the longest reign. He had to wait seven years (six of them in the RAF) to defend his trophy.

● IN THE FIRST Open after the war he finished twelfth. Asked if he felt unlucky, he said 'Unlucky? I came through the war, didn't I? That's better than many did who were there at St Andrews the day I won.'

CADDIES

CADDIE DERIVES from the French word 'cadet', the term used to describe the French noblemen who returned to Edinburgh with Queen Mary after her years in France. Scottish humour deemed it to mean porter, hanger-on or odd jobber. The word now means well-paid golf-bag carrier.

● A CADDIE'S JOB in the 20th century is to hold an umbrella to keep the golfer dry and to provide advice and sustenance when needed. A player needs to know about the wind, how far it is to the hole, which club to use and what the slope of the green is. Nick Faldo's caddie, Fanny Suneson, is perhaps the most famous modern-day caddie and one of only few female caddies on the circuit.

● WHEN FRANCIS OUIMET won the US Open in 1913 his caddie Eddie Lowery was ten years old. The logo designed for the 100th US Open in 1995 reflected this with a silhouette of the pair.

● AT THE Talamore golf course at Pinehurst, North California, golfers can rent llamas as their caddies. Four golfers can rent two llamas for $400 ($100 a bag).

● A RECENTLY published book titled '4-iron in the soul' is a brilliant insight into the world of the caddie. Ex-bass player with the Bluebells, Lawrence Donegan took a year off from his job as a political journalist with The Guardian to write the book.

MARK CALCAVECCHIA

Born: Laurel, NE, USA – 12/06/1960
First US Tour: 1981
Highest Ranking: 5 (1989)
US Tour Wins: 8
Major Wins: 1 (British Open 1989)
Ryder Cup Appearances: 3
Tour Earnings: $6,500,000

THE LATE 1980s provided the greatest success for Calcavecchia and from 1987 to 1990 he was always in the US Tour top ten. He recorded five of his eight wins in that period.

● IN THE 1989 British Open he was always in contention, but never looked like winning until a long putt at 11 and a chip in at 12 on

Mark Calcavecchia once called a putter Billy. This iron may be about to be called something less pleasant.

his final round. He eventually beat Wayne Grady and Greg Norman in a four-hole play-off.

● THE PREVIOUS year he had lost the US Masters to Sandy Lyle when expecting at least a play-off. Lyle hit to within 3m (10ft) of the hole from a bunker 128m (140yd) away, however, and with a birdie became the outright winner.

● WHEN DEFENDING his British Open title in 1990 he missed the cut, the first champion to do so in ten years. His parting shot was, 'Screw it! Golf is just a game – and an idiotic game most of the time.'

● HE ALSO headed home early after the 1991 championship, having missed the cut again – scoring 79 in the second round. This time he gave his clubs away to Jim Paton, a greenkeeper who'd had his own clubs stolen. 'Jim offered me the rake in exchange. Maybe I'd have done better playing with that,' Calcavecchia later said.

● WHEN MARK won the 1997 Greater Vancouver Open it was his first victory since 1995, and he used a putter borrowed

from Jeff Maggert to do it. For four years he has been struggling to overcome demons with his putter and perhaps breaking his own putter on the second round in Canada was the stroke of luck he needed.

CANADA

WHILE THE Canadian Open is an important tournament, no Canadian has yet won a major and the country is far from being a recognized force in world golf.

● AL BALDING was the first Canadian to win an American Tour event in 1955. He won again three times, and also helped win the World Cup for Canada in 1968 with partner George Knudson, beating Lee Trevino and Julius Boros of the US.

● FURTHER WORLD CUP wins for Canada came in 1980 (Jim Nelford and Dan Halldorson) and 1985 (Dave Barr and Halldorson again).

● CANADA also won the Dunhill Cup at

St Andrews in 1994 at long odds – they had never got past the last 16 before.
- CANADA'S PGA was founded in 1911 (five years before the US PGA), and clubs date back to (Montreal) 1873, (Quebec) 1874 and (Toronto) 1875.

Most Famous Canadian Players

Al Balding
Marlene Stewart

Top Canadian Courses

Glen Abbey
Royal Montreal

Contacts

Royal Canadian Golf Association
Golf House
RR No 2 Oakville
Ontario L6J 4Z3

THE CANADIAN OPEN

First Played: 1904
Most Wins: 4 – Leo Diegel (1924, 1925, 1928, 1929)
Lowest 72-hole Score: 263 – Johnny Palmer 1952

STARTED IN 1904, the Canadian Open is older than some of the majors. Now held at Glen Abbey every year since 1981, the course was Jack Nicklaus's first attempt at course design. Ironically, it was one of the few tournaments that he never won. The course is actually a public course and home to the Royal Canadian Golf Association.

Canadian Open – Last 25 Winners

1972	Gay Brewer	275
1973	Tom Weiskopf	278
1974	Bobby Nichols	270
1975	Tom Wieskopf	274
1976	Jerry Pate	267
1977	Lee Trevino	281
1978	Bruce Lietzke	283
1979	Lee Trevino	280
1980	Bob Gilder	274
1981	Peter Oosterhuis	280
1982	Bruce Lietzke	277
1983	John Cook	277
1984	Greg Norman	278
1985	Curtis Strange	279
1986	Bob Murphy	280
1987	Curtis Strange	276
1988	Ken Green	275
1989	Steve Jones	271
1990	Wayne Levi	278
1991	Nick Price	273
1992	Greg Norman	280
1993	David Frost	279
1994	Nick Price	275
1995	Mark O'Meara	274
1996	Dudley Hart	202*
1997	Steve Jones	275

*Tournament reduced to 54 holes

Athletics is also part of golf – Jose Maria Canizares holes the 18th to retain the Ryder Cup 1989 at the Belfry.

JOSE MARIA CANIZARES

Born: Madrid, Spain – 18/02/1947
First European Tour: 1971
European Tour Wins: 7
Major Wins: 0
Ryder Cup Appearances: 4

CANIZARES' first win on the European Tour came in 1972, but he did not win again until two victories in 1980.
- MOST OF THE Spaniard's wins came in the 1980s and he was six times in the top dozen money earners.
- WHEN HE is good he is very good, and he shares the European nine holes record. He was the first to hit 27 for nine holes when at the 1978 Swiss Open. His lowest round is 61.
- HE HAS experienced mixed fortunes in four Ryder Cup appearances. At the Belfry in 1989, he was a Ryder Cup middle order player expected to lose, but he won a great victory over Ken Green as Europe kept the trophy with a 14–14 draw. Six years earlier, though, he was one-up playing the last hole at Palm Beach only for Lanny Wadkins to secure a winning Birdie, which meant that Europe failed to halve the overall match.
- TAKING THE individual prize in the 1984 World Cup, the Spaniard has competed in four Dunhill Cup appearances and eight World Cups.

C

Tony Jacklin and Seve Ballesteros celebrating their 1987 Ryder Cup victory at Muirfield Village.

CAPTAINS

WALTER HAGEN was the first captain of the USA Ryder Cup team in 1927 and likewise the first winning captain. He also captained the USA the most times. Dai Rees, who was also a non-playing captain in 1967, captained Great Britain the most times.

● THESE DAYS, after the success of Tony Jacklin and his meticulous preparation that helped turn the Cup in Europe's favour, captains are always non-playing and very much in a managerial role.

● IAN WOOSNAM has recently announced his wish to captain the next Ryder Cup team.

Ryder Cup Captains

Most times:
United States: 6 – Walter Hagen (1927, 1929, 1931, 1933, 1935, 1937)
Europe/GB & Ireland: 5 – Dai Rees (1955, 1957, 1959, 1961, 1967)

Solheim Cup Captains

United States:
Kathy Whitworth 1990 & 1992
Joanne Carner 1994
Judy Rankin 1996
Europe:
Mickey Walker 1990, 1992, 1994, 1996

Joanne Carner's nickname has changed over the years from Great Gundy to Big Momma, both equally flattering.

ANDREW CARNEGIE

THESE DAYS it is commonplace for business deals to be done on the golf course. One of the first recorded instances, which also proved one of the biggest deals, involved the canny Scot Andrew Carnegie.

● HE WAS LOCKED in a match with financier Charles Schwab, who was trying to convince him to sell Carnegie Steel and eventually talked him into selling at the right price. Carnegie wrote £480 million on back of scorecard and passed it to him, Schwab agreed and US Steel was born.

● CARNEGIE WAS then instrumental in setting up the present-day St Andrew's club in New York, guaranteeing the mortgage for the new clubhouse. Born into poverty, Carnegie was known to quibble at the high membership prices for the club.

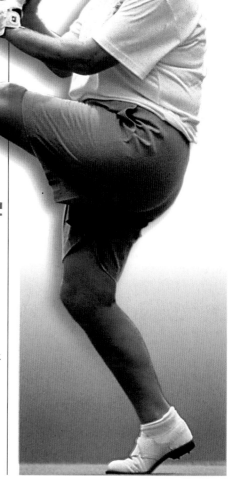

JOANNE CARNER

Born: Kirkland, WA, USA – 04/04/1939
First LPGA Tour: 1970
Highest Ranking: 1st (1976, 1982, 1983)
Tour Wins: 42
Amateur Wins: 7 (5 – US Women's Amateur Championship 1957, 1960, 1962, 1966, 1968)
Major Wins: 2 (US Women's Open 1971, 1976)
Solheim Cup Appearances: 0 (non-playing captain in 1994)
Tour Earnings: $2.5 million

NICKNAMED IN HER early days the Great Gundy (her maiden name was Gunderson), Carner was later known as Big Momma. With one of the great records in amateur golf, Carner went on to achieve even greater success as a professional.

● WINNING THE USGA Girls' title aged 17 and then five US Amateur women's titles in 1957, 1960, 1962, 1966 and 1968, she turned pro after winning an LPGA event as an amateur in 1969.

● FROM 1974 to 1984 she was always in the top ten, heading it three times. The first of her US Women's Open titles in 1971 made her the only woman to win the USGA Girls, US Women's Amateur and US Women's Open competitions.

● THE VICTORIOUS Solheim Cup captain in 1994, she was a very popular choice as captain but her last taste of individual success was when she lost a play-off to Laura Davies in the 1987 US Open at the age of 48.

CARNOUSTIE

Where: Angus, Scotland
Par: 72
Yardage: 7,272
Opened: 1842
Designer: Allan Robertson
Major Events Staged: British Open 1931, 1937, 1953, 1968, 1975, British Amateur Championship 1947, 1966, 1971, 1992, British Women's Amateur Championship 1961, 1973

IN 1999 THE OPEN will return to Carnoustie after a break of almost 25 years. Course quality has never been in doubt, but the quiet backwater lacked the suitably large hotels required to stage the massive event. Effort by the people of Angus and a new hotel scheme have helped overcome this.

● THE ten-hole course laid out in 1842 was extended to 18 holes in 1867 by Tom Morris, but James Braid altered the course in 1926 to the one we know today. A supreme test, it lacks the tradition of its Scottish partners, or the breathtaking beauty. The clubhouse has recently been demolished to make way for a new hotel.

● FLAT BUT RUGGED, with only three short holes and lots of rough, the course

US Senior Billy Casper, two-times US Open winner.

Did You Know?

The tenth hole is named South America because a member decided to emigrate around the turn of the century and held a party in the clubhouse. He was found asleep in the bunker the next morning and never actually made it abroad. The hole was named in his honour.

was described by Gary Player as 'a good swamp spoiled', and after playing there Ben Hogan said he'd have his lawnmower sent over.

● ARMOUR WAS the first to triumph there in 1931, while Hogan won in 1953 in his only Open appearance – each of his rounds was lower than the one before and he finished on a 68. When Player won in 1968 the course was the longest in Open History at 6631m (7,252yd).

JOE CARR

Born: Dublin, Ireland – 18/02/1922
Career Spanned: 1940 to 1965
Important Career Wins: 3 (British Amateur Championship 1953, 1958, 1960)
Major Wins: 0

ONE OF the greatest amateurs ever, Carr was born in the Portmarnock clubhouse, where his father was a club steward. He reached the semi-final of the US Amateur in 1961 and won the British Amateur Championship in 1953, 1958 and 1960.

● HE WAS also very successful in his own country, winning the Irish Closed Amateur Championship six times and the Irish Open Amateur Championship four times (1946, 1950, 1954 and 1956).

● CARR APPEARED in every Walker Cup team from 1947 to 1967, captaining the side on the last occasion and acting as non-playing captain in 1965. He was also

the first Irishman elected captain of the Royal and Ancient, when he served from 1991 to 1992.

BILLY CASPER

Born: San Diego, CA, USA – 24/06/1931
First US Tour: 1955
Highest Ranking: 1st (1966, 1968)
US Tour Wins: 51
Major Wins: 3 (US Open 1959, 1966, US Masters 1970)
Ryder Cup Appearances: 8
Tour Earnings: $1.6 million
First Senior Tour: 1981
Senior Tour Wins: 9
Senior Tour Earnings: $1.6 million

A CONSISTENT PLAYER, Casper won at least one tournament every year for 16 in a row on tour. On the Senior Tour his consistency has continued, with 55 top ten finishes in the 80 tournaments he's entered.

● VOTED PGA Player of the Year in 1966 and 1970, Casper was only the second golfer to pass $1million in tour earnings, and is sixth in all-time tour victories. In his stunning 1966 US Open win he made up seven strokes on Arnold Palmer over the last nine holes, then defeated him in a play-off. Casper's US Masters win was also a play-off, as was his Senior Tour Open win in 1983.

● CASPER APPEARED in eight Ryder Cup teams between 1961 and 1975 and was non-playing captain in 1979. He holds the record for the most US matches played and the most points won.

● A GREAT putter, in the 1959 US Open he single-putted 31 of the greens.

CHAMPIONSHIPS

THERE ARE NOW four major championships on the golfing calendar, the organisers of most other events calling theirs the 'the fifth major'. The four majors are the US Masters, held in April at Augusta, the US Open, which takes place in June, the British Open the following month, and the US PGA, which is in August.

● IN ADDITION to these are the British and American Amateur Championships, the Women's Championships and then numerous other European and World tour events. The nearest the men's professional game comes to a fifth major is the Players Championship, held since 1974. From 1982 this has been held at the TPC at Sawgrass, the administrative home of the PGA Tour.

THE
MAJORS

— **British Open** —
First Played: 1860

— **US Open** —
First Played: 1895

— **US Masters** —
First Played: 1934

— **US PGA** —
First Played: 1916

BOB CHARLES

Born: Carterton, New Zealand – 14/03/1936	
First US Tour: 1961	
US Tour Wins: 5	
European Tour Wins: 9	
Major Wins: 1 (British Open 1963)	
First US Senior Tour: 1986	
Senior Tour Victories: 24	
Senior Tour Earnings: $6.6 million	

THE GREATEST left-hander ever is actually naturally right-handed – he only started playing that way after borrowing his parents' club when he was a child. He is the only left-hander to have won the Open, and also the first New Zealander to do so. He won the British Open in 1963, averaging 30 putts per round, and destroyed Phil Rodgers in a play-off over 36 holes.

● CHARLES WON the New Zealand Open in 1954 but waited six years to turn professional, before achieving success both in Europe and the US. He has had further victories on the Senior Tour, where he was top of the money-winners in 1988 and 1989, including winning the Senior British Open in 1989 and 1993.

Did You Know?
Masashi Yamada was stripped of the 1995 US Amateur title after the USGA threw out his claimed handicap.

CHEATING

IN A GAME where the player is often out of sight of his or her opponent, cheating would seem easy. However, the rules of golf are such that players really only cheat themselves if they break them; as it so often does, the game of golf wins out.

● BECAUSE HONOUR plays such an important part in the game, cheating is a stigma which can lead to losing club membership. Lying about handicaps, throwing balls from bunkers, marking down wrong scores and moving balls nearer to the hole are all viewed with disgust.

Bob Charles, so good he won a major playing left-handed, the only man ever to do so.

CLARET JUG

THE TROPHY awarded for winning the British Open is a silver claret jug, of which Young Tom Morris was the first recipient when he won the 1872 British Open. It followed the original prize, a moroccan-red Championship Belt which was kept by Young Tom after a hat trick of victories.

● THERE WAS no tournament in 1871 while it was decided how to replace the Belt, but in 1872 the R & A and the Honourable Company subscribed to a cup which could never be kept outright. Smaller than many trophies, it is still a very distinctive prize.

HOWARD CLARK

Born: Leeds, England – 26/08/1954
First European Tour: 1974
Highest Ranking: 3 (1984 and 1986)
European Tour Wins: 12
Major Wins: 0
Ryder Cup Appearances: 6

HOWARD CLARK came back to form in 1994, captaining the England Dunhill Cup team, and although he currently resides just outside the top 100 on the European money list he is an outside bet to lead the Ryder Cup team as a non-playing captain.

● A TEAM PLAYER, he has been involved in six Ryder cup teams from 1977 to 1995, has played in seven Dunhill Cups and in 1985 was individual winner of the World Cup with England.

● A CONSISTENT performer from the mid-1970s to the late 1980s, his best years were 1978 and 1984 to 1986. His 12 tour wins include the PGA Championship at Wentworth in 1984.

DARREN CLARKE

Born: Dungannon, Northern Ireland –
    14/08/1968
First European Tour: 1991
Highest Ranking: 4 (1997)
European Tour Wins: 2
Major Wins: 0
Ryder Cup Appearances: 1

A BIG, POWERFUL Ulsterman, Clarke is only 29 but one of the upcoming major forces in British golf along with Lee Westwood. He ran close in the 1997 Open, leading by four shots at one point, and made a promising debut for the Ryder Cup team also in 1997, winning in the fourballs as Montgomerie's partner and losing to Phil Mickelson with a little out of luck – the American holing two chips for eagles. A previous winner of the Irish Amateur Championship, Clarke finished fourth on the European tour last year.

CLOTHING

SPONSORSHIP has long taken over in the world of golf, and designer clothes such as Farah slacks, Pringle jumpers and Lacoste T-shirts all became popular in the 1980s, and were even absorbed into popular culture by football fans and street fashion alike.

● GOLF CLOTHING has come a long way since the era of blue tailcoats, smart buckled shoes and top hats. These were superceded by tweed jackets worn with shirts and ties and by plus twos and caps. Tank tops, shirts and ties, knickerbockers and plus fours all followed.

● SINCE THEN, many players have developed their own distinctive looks. Walter Hagen wore white trousers and a bow tie, while Gary Player favoured all-

Darren Clarke – a gentle giant destined for success.

black. Roger Davis returned to traditional wear, as has Payne Stewart, and Jimmy Demaret wore many outrageous outfits.

● TODAY THE Tiger Woods look of red polo shirt and Nike cap is the most popular on the municipal courses, while on the pro circuit the most sought-after clothing is the green jacket given to winners of the US Masters.   ●

Umbrellas are a rarely overlooked item of apparel when it comes to playing an all-weather sport.

CLUBHOUSE

MOST FAMOUS is the R & A clubhouse, which stands behind the 18th green at St Andrews, tall and imposing, strong against the bleak backdrop.

● THE CLUBHOUSE is where stories are swapped over drinks at the bar, meetings are held, the day's anxieties are washed away in the locker rooms, committees are formed and expectant champions wait to see if their scores will be beaten.

● THE EMIRATES clubhouse in Dubai looks more like a space station, while recently restored Wentworth looks like a turretted white fairy castle.

CLUBS

WILSON, Ping, Callaway, Titleist, MacGregor, Cobra, Yonex, Lynx, Spalding – all are names that trip off the tongue. Golfing technology has moved on at an amazing pace and clubs are no exception. The use of graphite in clubs, woods made of metal and variations of the wedge have all been looked into in the quest for better golf.

● THE EARLY golf clubs had wooden shafts made of ash, hickory or bamboo. These were replaced by metal shafts in the 1920s, and with this came the 'set of clubs' with matching looks and a numbering system rather than individual names.

● TITANIUM WOODS with larger heads, slightly longer shafts and much lighter weight are expensive, while a set of titanium irons is quite an investment.

● AS WELL AS the advance in metal woods, many players these days carry a whole range of wedges for extra touch around the green. Some, with lofts of 55, 60 and 64 degrees, allow the ball to go virtually straight up and down. Putters have also changed, with the use of the broomstick made popular by Sam Torrance and Peter Senior. This is held under the chin and swung pendulum-style.

● PLAYERS ARE allowed to carry no more than 14 clubs. In the days of wooden clubs, six or seven were the norm. Steel clubs were legalized in the US in 1924 and then in the UK by the R & A in 1929. With extra options, players wanted more clubs and Lawson Little, winner of the British and US Amateur Championships in the 1930s, carried as many as 25. The authorities set the limit at 14 clubs in 1938.

How They Were Once Known

2 wood – Brassie
3 or 4 wood – Spoon
1 or 2 iron – Driving iron (cleek)
3 iron – Midmashie
4 iron – Mashie iron
5 iron – Mashie
6 iron – Spade mashie
7 iron – Mashie-niblick
8 iron – Pitching niblick
9 iron – Niblick

Neil Coles is the oldest man to win a European Tour event, at the age of 48.

NEIL COLES MBE

Born: London, England – 26/09/1934

Turned Pro: 1950

First European Tour: 1957

Highest Ranking: 1st (1963, 1970)

European Tour Wins: 26

Major Wins: 0

Ryder Cup Appearances: 8

NEIL COLES turned pro at 16 and made his mark in his twenties. From 1961 until 1980 he was a top ten fixture on the European Tour, twice leader and never lower than 12th.

● DESPITE TRYING for second place in 1973 after a late charge, the closest Neil Coles ever got to winning the British Open was in 1961. A leader for some of the tournament, he later dropped back to third.

● COLES MADE eight Ryder Cup appearances and has the unenviable record of the most matches lost – 21.

● HE WON the Matchplay Championship three times, the Dunlop Masters and the PGA, but never secured a major. Fear of flying kept him Britain-bound and so the British Open was his only real hope.

● SINCE JOINING the Senior Tour he has won nine times, including the British Senior title in 1987. From 1985 to 1988 he held the PGA Senior title four years running. Ironically, before he joined the Senior Tour he became the oldest winner of a European

Tour event when he won the Sanyo Open in 1982 at the age of 48.

● COLES WAS disqualified from the 1997 Seniors PGA Championship for missing his tee time by five minutes. He maintained he was told a 12.50 start, but it was in fact 11.50. Coles had only once been disqualified before, for an illegal drop from a staked tree. He vowed never return to the Belfry afterwards, although the 2001 Ryder Cup may tempt him as a spectator.

GLENNA COLLETT VARE

Born: New Haven, CT, USA – 20/06/1903

Career spanned: 1922 to 1937

Amateur Wins: 49

Major Amateur Wins: 6 (US Women's Amateur Champion 1922, 1925, 1928, 1929, 1930, 1935)

COLLETT VARE was the greatest American women's amateur ever, with six victories in the US Women's Amateur Championship between 1922– 1935. She was also runner-up in 1931 and 1932.

● IN ALL she won 49 leading amateur events, dominating the 1920s and 30s, and was the female equivalent of Bobby Jones.

● A LONG DRIVER, she once had one of her drives measured at 274m (300yd) when she was only 18.

HARRY COLT

FAMOUS AS A course designer, Colt is responsible for much of the course design at the Open courses of Muirfield and St Andrews as well as Sunningdale and Wentworth.

● AFTER TAKING a law degree at Cambridge, where he captained the golf team, he practised as a solicitor for some years before joining up with Willie Park Jnr and making golf-course architecture a profession. He laid out the Rye course (home to Oxford and Cambridge Golfing Society) when he was only 25.

● WHEN SUNNINGDALE opened in 1901 he was its first secretary, holding the post for 12 years. He expanded and lengthened Sunningdale and then went on to work on numerous courses in the UK and abroad.

● COLT WAS invited to work with George Crump, creator of Pine Valley, in 1913, just after he had created the Eden course at St Andrews. He then went on to remodel Muirfield, designed Wentworth, helped lay out Puerto de Hierro in Madrid, and also worked on courses in France, Germany and America, including Burning Tree near Washington. He was the first truly international designer.

ANDREW COLTART

Born: Dumfries, Scotland – 12/05/1970

First European Tour: 1992

Highest Ranking: 7 (1996)

European Tour Wins: 0

Major Wins: 0

Ryder Cup appearances: 0

COLTART FIRST came to light in the 1995 Dunhill Cup, when he helped Sam Torrance and Colin Montgomerie beat Nick Price and Mark McNulty's Zimbabwe team in the final. The 27-year-old Scot experienced a difficult season after his success in 1995 and 1996. Finishing 1996 at 7th in the rankings, he dropped off the pace in Ryder Cup year and just made the top 50.

COMEDIANS

FOR SOME REASON, comedians seem eternally linked to golf. In the USA Bob Hope is the most notable fan, with the Bob Hope Classic now a fixture on the US Tour.

● BEFORE HIM, Oliver Hardy was reportedly always to be found on the course, while Jack Lemmon and Bing Crosby also have strong links with the game. Bing Crosby once said of Bob Hope, 'He would rather win a golf match than an Oscar.'

● IN THE UK Jimmy Tarbuck, Bruce Forsyth and Ronnie Corbett are all vocal about their love of the sport and are often seen at pro-celebrity matches.

COMPUTERS

AS GOLF HAS developed into big business over the years, computers have become involved. They are used in three ways, the first being to evaluate the golf ball and ensure it is of a correct specification in many varied tests on its allowed velocities, size and weight, and the second being in helping to design the ultimate clubs.

● THE THIRD and most interesting way is in recording precisely the nature of people's swings and helping them to improve. By attaching marker balls to the club and a player's body in vital positions, such as hips, elbows and waist, infra-red cameras can record these as points on a computer screen which can describe the motion that the body goes through in executing a shot. This motion-capture technique has also been used to provide increased realism in video games.

Of all the golfing comedians, only Bob Hope and Bing Crosby have had tournaments named after them.

Chipping in

'If I died, it would mean I couldn't play golf. No way was I going to give up golf, so I gave up drinking.'

JOHN COOK

Born: Toledo, OH, USA – 02/10/1957	
First US Tour: 1980	
Highest Ranking: 3 (1992)	
US Tour Wins: 9	
Major Wins: 0	
Ryder Cup Appearances: 1	
Tour Earnings: $5million	

IN CONTENTION in the 1992 Open at Muirfield, Cook three-putted the 17th and then bogeyed the 18th to let Faldo back in. He was in second, four shots down on Faldo going into the last day, but pulled back to a shot behind after six holes. After a birdie at 15 and 16 he then led, but lost it at the last two holes. It is the closest he has come to a major win.

● IN 1992 he was third in the money list, which was surprising as he had barely made the top 20 in almost ten years on the tour. However, after accumulating over $5 million in total earnings he cannot complain. The Canadian Open and Mexican Open are numbered among his titles.

FRED CORCORAN

ONE OF golf's first entrepreneurs, Fred was responsible for aiding in the organization of the US Tour in its early days and ran it for some time. He then helped make the Women's Tour a more marketable commodity. He was also marketing director for Wilson Sporting Goods for some time.

● ALWAYS READY with his PR skills and ability to sell a story to the papers, he also managed Sam Snead's early career – and spun stories of Sam being a hillbilly who played barefoot and fashioned his own clubs from wood. He even got Sam to play a couple of games barefoot to reinforce the stories. He once said of his charge, 'Sam is the only man to make a million and save two million.'

SIR HENRY COTTON

Born: Holmes Chappel, England –
   26/01/1907

Career Spanned: 1926 to 1977

Major Wins: 3 (British Open 1934, 1937,
   1948)

Ryder Cup Appearances: 4

HENRY COTTON put pride back into British golf in the 1930s, breaking American dominance of the Open with his two wins. He won again in 1948, but his prime came before World War II.

● COTTON WAS from a middle-class, public-school background, and turning pro was not the norm in such circumstances. Usually middle-class players remained as amateurs as well as having a professional job.

● HE WAS ONE of the first players to be extrovert and verbose, rather than the dour, serious players that preceded him. He was one of the first sports personalities, a stylish player and person who raised the profile of the golfer. Happy to talk about his theories on golf, he was also the first to explore golfing contracts.

● NERVES PLAGUED Cotton, however, and a final round of 79 almost denied him his first Open at Sandwich in 1934. His greatest win was at Carnoustie in 1937, with all of the US Ryder Cup team in the field. However, it is his 1934 win at Sandwich which is best remembered. The best score shot in an Open had been 67 by Walter Hagen five years earlier. Cotton matched that in his first round and then shot 65 in his second. It stood as a record until 1977, when Mark Hayes hit 63 at Turnberry. The Dunlop 65 ball was named after his brilliant second round.

● COTTON CAPTAINED the Ryder Cup team that lost in 1953 and came sixth in the Open in 1956 aged 50. He made his final Open appearance in 1977 at Turnberry, and although he continued writing for the News of the World and golf magazines, he retired to Portugal. Cotton was knighted posthumously.

FRED COUPLES

Born: Seattle, Washington, USA –
   3/10/1959

First US Tour: 1981

Highest Ranking: 1st (1992)

US Tour Wins: 12

Major Wins: 1 (US Masters 1992)

Ryder Cup Appearances: 5

Tour Earnings: $8.8 million

NICKNAMED Boom Boom for the size of his drives, Couples is a volatile player with the potential to be the very best in the world.

● A FIXTURE in the Ryder Cup team since his 1989 debut, he is a great team player.

In 1995 he and Davis Love III became the first pairing to win the World Cup four times in a row.

● COUPLES CAME to the 1992 Masters on a massive run of form with $1million already in his pocket. He won by two shots, with his mentor and Ryder Cup partner Ray Floyd in second, breaking European domination of the Masters.

● CONSIDERED by many players and watchers of the game to be too laid back, he finished outside the top 50 on the US Tour in 1997, but should be back among the top ten soon. Couples is one of only a select band to have topped the world rankings.

Henry Cotton wins the British Open at Sandwich, 29 June 1934. It would be the first of three victories on home soil.

C

COURSES

FROM THE EARLY days of golf, course design has come on in leaps and bounds and these days designers such as Jack Nicklaus and Arnold Palmer can contribute to the commercial success of a course by linking their name to it. And as golf continues to boom, the search for new courses continues.

● BECAUSE OF their natural ruggedness and tradition, it is hard to imagine the links courses of England and Scotland ever being bettered. Nevertheless, newer courses such as Augusta and the Belfry have gradually gained fame.

● AS ENVIRONMENTAL concerns grow, a balance needs to be found in the future and courses will no longer simply cut swathes through land as they did at the end of the last century; instead they will blend gently with the woodland and wildlife, much as at Wentworth in Surrey, where great care is taken to maintain a natural balance.

THE TEN
MOST FAMOUS
COURSES

Augusta National, Georgia, USA
Baltusrol, New Jersey, USA
The Belfry, Warwickshire, England
Carnoustie, Angus, Scotland
Kiawah Island, Hawaii, USA
Muirfield, East Lothian, Scotland
Royal St George's, Sandwich, Kent, England
St Andrews Old Course, Fife, Scotland
Turnberry, Ayrshire, Scotland
Valderrama, Cadiz, Spain

BRUCE CRAMPTON

Born: Sydney, Australia – 28/09/1935
First US Tour: 1957
Highest US Tour Ranking: 2 (1973)
US Tour Wins: 14
Major Wins: 0
Tour Earnings: $1.3 million
First Senior Tour: 1985
Senior Tour Wins: 19
Senior Tour Earnings: $5 million

KNOWN AS an ironman for the number of tournaments he enters every year on the tour, Crampton recorded seven victories in his Rookie year on the Senior Tour.

● HE HAS NEVER won a major, although he was second on four occasions – 1972 US Masters, 1972 US Open, and 1973 and 1975 US PGAs. Jack Nicklaus was the winner each time.

Fred Couples, known as Boom Boom because of his driving ability, not his joke telling.

The *Virgin* Book Of Golf Records **37**

Gentle Ben rues hitting another shot just a little too softly.

BEN CRENSHAW

Born: Austin, Texas, USA – 11/01/1952
First US Tour: 1973
Highest Ranking: 2 (1976)
US Tour Wins: 19
Major Wins: 2 (US Masters 1984, 1995)
Ryder Cup Appearances: 4
Tour Earnings: $7 million

GENTLE BEN is regarded as one of the greatest putters on the tour. Though he was expected to follow the Palmer, Nicklaus, Watson lineage of great American champions, this never actually transpired for Crenshaw.
● HE SUFFERED one of his worst years in 1982, when he toyed with giving up the game. He returned the following year to tie for second in the 1983 US Masters and then was victorious the following year.
● ALWAYS A bridesmaid until 1984, Crenshaw was five times runner-up in majors. In 1975 he missed out on a US Open play-off by one stroke after finding water at the 17th on his final round. That was maybe a good thing as he has lost all eight play-offs he has contested in his career. He was once described as 'the best damn second- and third-place finisher in the majors the world will ever know.'
● WINNING THE 1995 Masters was very emotional for Crenshaw and the watching fans. Days earlier Crenshaw had been a pallbearer at the funeral of Harvey Penick, a great friend and his golfing mentor. After his one-stroke victory on the 18th, Crenshaw collapsed into his caddie's arms in tears.
● CRENSHAW IS tenth on the all-time money ranking and will be non-playing captain of the Ryder Cup at Boston in 1999.

CROOKED STICK

Where: Indiana, USA
Par: 72
Yardage: 7,289
Opened: 1964
Designer: Paul 'Pete' Dye
Major Events Staged: US PGA 1991, US Women's Open 1993

DESIGNED BY Paul Dye, the Indiana course witnessed its first major in 1991 when John Daly won the US PGA after being ninth reserve for a place. The event was notable for one other event, when a Mr Thomas Weaver was killed by lightning. He was only 91m (100yd) from his car when his umbrella was struck and he collapsed. He died in hospital just over an hour later.

CROWDS

GOLF'S POPULARITY as a spectator sport has grown steadily over the years since the war and now crowds of 20,000 each day are common at events such as the Opens and Ryder Cups.
● TRADITIONALLY, American crowds have been more vocal than the British and, although it is frowned upon, cheering of players missing putts in Ryder Cups is not uncommon. Now, however, the same vocal support – or lack of support – seems to have moved to the UK as well.

Valderrama 1997, and the bi-annual meeting of the Ryder Cup Appreciation Society.

BOBBY CRUIKSHANK

Born: Grantown-on-Spey, Scotland – 16/11/1894
First US Tour: 1920
Highest Ranking: 1st (1927)
US Tour Wins: 17
Major Wins: 0

A DETERMINED SCOTTISH pro, Cruikshank did well on the US Tour between the wars, winning some 17 events (putting him in the top 50 of all time). He never won a major, however, despite many near misses. Cruikshank was the runner-up in the US Open in 1923 and then again in 1932.
● IN 1934 he was in contention for the US Open, but after a lucky escape at the 11th when leading, he threw his club in the air in elation. It came down, temporarily knocking him out, and in his dizzy condition he went on to finish third.
● AFTER LOSING to Jones in the 1923 US Open, Cruikshank later bet that Jones would win the Grand Slam in 1930. He pocketed £10,000 when his prediction proved correct.
● A WAR HERO, Cruikshank was a prisoner of war who escaped through enemy lines to continue fighting.

GEORGE CRUMP

GEORGE CRUMP was responsible for only one course as a designer, but in Pine Valley, New Jersey, he created one of the world's best courses. With input from all the major designers at the time, Crump put together a perfect blend of grass, water, sand and terrain which culminated in

perhaps America's finest 18 holes. In doing so, he pumped $250,000 of his own money into the project, initially persuading 18 of. his friends to contribute $1000 each in 1912 so that he could buy the then scrubland on which the course stands.

● SIX YEARS later he died suddenly at the age of 46, with only 14 holes completed and having never played his dream course.

THE CURTIS CUP

First Played: 1932 at Wentworth (US beat GB & I by 5½ to 3½)

Wins: USA 20, Great Britain and Ireland 6, three matches halved

THE CURTIS CUP is held every two years between the best Women's Amateurs from the USA and Great Britain and Ireland. It was named after Margaret Curtis, who did everything in her powers to set up team golf between women on an international scale.

● AFTER MANY false starts and a number of friendly matches, the competition finally got under way at Wentworth in 1932, when 15,000 people turned up to see the event. The Curtis Cup, a silver Revere bowl, returned to the USA with the US ladies winning 5–3.

● THE COMPETITION has largely been dominated by the USA, including an unbroken 26-year reign. However, Great Britain and Ireland have held the trophy since 1992, when it was won back at Royal Liverpool.

CYPRESS POINT

Where: Monterey, California

Par: 72

Yardage: 6,536

Opened: 1928

Designer: Dr Alister MacKenzie

Major Events Staged: Walker Cup 1981

CYPRESS POINT is a near neighbour of Pebble Beach and although not as flirtatious with the sea, it is every bit as beautiful. A private members' club for 250 or so, it has never sought to stage a major championship or tournament.

● BOB HOPE described Cypress Point as having 'the looks of Christie Brinkley and the tenderness of Tokyo Rose,' while former USPGA president Frank Tatum called it 'the Sistine Chapel of golf.'

● THERE ARE three holes that flirt with the sea, the 15th, 16th and 17th, of which the 16th, which jets out into the ocean, is said to be one of the most photographed holes of all time. Mike Austin, when playing the 16th, attempted a three-wood to the par-three's green. He failed and hit the rocks. Four more attempts brought the same result before he made the green in 12, crying 'I knew it was the right club.'

The GB&I team celebrate winning the 1996 Curtis Cup in some great trousers.

Curtis Cup Results

Year	Venue	US	GB&I
1932	Wentworth	5.5	3.5
1934	Chevy Chase, Maryland	6.5	2.5
1936	Gleneagles	4.5	4.5
1938	Essex, Massachusetts	5.5	3.5
1948	Royal Birkdale	6.5	2.5
1950	CC of Buffalo, New York	7.5	1.5
1952	Muirfield	4	5
1954	Merion, Pennsylvania	6	3
1956	Prince's, Kent	4	5
1958	Brae Burn, Massachusetts	4.5	4.5
1960	Lindrick, Yorkshire	6.5	2.5
1962	Broadmoor, Colarado	8	1
1964	Royal Porthcawl	10.5	7.5
1966	Hot Springs, Virginia	13	5
1968	Royal Co Down, N Ireland	0.5	7.5
1970	Brae Burn, Massachusetts	11.5	6.5
1972	Western Gailes, Scotland	10	8
1974	San Francisco	13	5
1976	Royal Lytham	11.5	6.5
1978	Apawamis, New York	12	6
1980	St Pierre, Wales	13	5
1982	Denver, Colorado	14.5	3.5
1984	Muirfield,	9.5	8.5
1986	Prairie Dunes, Kansas	5	13
1988	Royal St Georges	7	11
1990	Somerset Hills, New Jersey	14	4
1992	Royal Liverpool	8	10
1994	Honors Course, Tennessee	9	9
1996	Killarney G & FC	6.5	11.5

FRED DALY

Born: Portrush, N Ireland – 11/10/1911
Career Spanned: 1941 to 1955
Career Wins: 9
Major Wins: 1 (British Open 1947)
Ryder Cup Appearances: 4

AT THE AGE of 30 Daly was big on the Irish scene but war broke out during his prime, limiting his international success. He continued to do well after the war, though, continuing his career until the 1950s.

● DALY WAS ever-present in the Ryder Cup between 1947 and 1953. The pinnacle of his success was his 1947 British Open win at Hoylake. After 73 and 70 in his opening rounds, he recorded a 78 on his third round. He then sat nervously in the clubhouse with a final 72 as the weather got worse and worse. Eventually he won by a stroke, but not without a scare. Frank Stranahan needed to eagle the final hole to tie – his second shot to the par-4 18th was pin high but just inches to the left of the hole, and despite an easy birdie it wasn't enough.

● THE FOLLOWING year Daly was second, then third in 1950. He was third again in 1952 after falling away badly when leading and gradually his career wound down.

JOHN DALY

Born: Carmichael, California – 28/04/1966
First US Tour: 1989
Highest Ranking: 17 (1991)
US Tour Wins: 4
Major Wins: 2 (British Open 1995,
   US PGA Championship 1991)
Ryder Cup Appearances: 0
Tour Earnings: $2million

JOHN DALY, the Wild Thing, is a conundrum. A brilliant player on his day and an enormous hitter, he has personal difficulties which have led to very public problems. He has won relatively few tournaments in total, but two of those have been majors, including the British Open. Daly is one of only four players to have won two majors before the age of 30.

● HIS FIRST MAJOR win was a strange tale, as he was ninth reserve for a place at the US PGA Championship in 1991. Failing to win a place through qualifying rounds, through a combination of many former champions not playing and other international players turning down invites due to injury or circumstance, Daly drove overnight to the tournament, having been told that a late withdrawal had given him a place in the field, then played without having had a practice round. He won by three strokes.

● DALY WON the 1995 British Open, beating Costantino Rocca in a four-hole play-off, after coming into the tournament at St Andrews with only one victory to his name and standing 57th in the world rankings.

● A CROWD favourite, the portly blond

has struggled with alcohol and gambling addictions. His marriages split up and an alleged assault followed. Daly then went into rehab and is trying to rebuild his career.

● WHEN WINNING the Bell South Atlanta Classic in 1994 he admitted, 'This is the first time I've won sober and knowing I can do it sober means a lot.'

● A COMPETITION was set up in 1993 which pitted Daly against Jim Dent, the biggest hitter on the Senior Tour. A crowd of almost 10,000 turned up to watch the event. Daly hit his first drive 293m (321yd), but said, 'I didn't hit that one that well.' He then hit another 311m (340yd). Dent said he just enjoyed watching Daly hit. After the competition, Daly said he hoped he was hitting the ball as well when he was 54. Then, referring to the rest of his life, he added, 'I just hope I live to be 50.'

EAMONN DARCY

Born: Delgany, Ireland – 07/08/1952
First European Tour: 1971
Highest Ranking: 2 (1976)
European Tour Wins: 4
Major Wins: 0
Ryder Cup Appearances: 4

THE IRISHMAN with the odd swing has achieved more success as a team player than as an individual, playing in four Ryder Cups, seven World Cups with Ireland and three Dunhill Cups.

● AS AN INDIVIDUAL, he never got close to a major. But in Britain he came second to Arnold Palmer in the 1975 PGA Championship and then lost in a play-off to Neil Coles the following year.

● HE RECORDED five overseas wins to go with his

*The Wild Thing
John Daly about to
unleash another
huge drive.*

Did you know?

John Daly took 18 at one hole
in a recent tournament.

four European victories, and finished third and second on the European money list in 1975 and 1976 respectively. By 1981 he had slumped to ninth on the list, but still earned his third Ryder Cup place.

● HIS ONLY really decent Ryder Cup contribution, however, came in his last appearance in 1987, when he came back to hole a memorable putt at the last at Muirfield Village against Ben Crenshaw to win the match. When later asked about his thoughts as he took the putt, he admitted they were 'Don't effing miss.'

Some would say that this is the closest Eamonn Darcy ever came to Jack Nicklaus in a tounament.

LAURA DAVIES MBE

Born: Coventry, England – 05/10/1963
First LPGA Tour: 1989
Highest Ranking: 1st (1994, 1996)
Tour Wins: 15
First European Tour: 1985
European Tour Wins: 27
Highest Ranking: 1st (1985, 1986, 1992, 1996)
Major Wins: 4 (Women's US Open 1987, US Ladies PGA 1994, 1996, Du Maurier Classic 1996)
Solheim Cup Appearances: 4
Tour Earnings: $2million

LAURA DAVIES is the modern British Ladies golfer who conquered America. An unorthodox, powerful player, she has been likened to John Daly of the LPGA.

● FOUR TIMES leader of the European Women's Order of Merit (in 1985, 1986, 1992 and 1996), she has 27 European Tour wins to her name, including the 1986 British Open. She also recorded wins at Junior and Amateur levels before becoming a pro.

● DAVIES WON the US Open in 1987 before becoming a member of the US LPGA Tour, and has since gone on to register three more classic wins in the 1990s, including two in 1996. In the 1992 Solheim Cup she was inspirational, winning all three of her matches.

● HER FAVOURITE event on the LPGA Tour must be the Standard Register Ping, which she won for the fourth time in a row in 1997.

RODGER DAVIS

Born: Sydney, Australia – 18/05/1951
First European Tour: 1977
European Tour wins: 7
Major Wins: 0

AFFABLE Australian Rodger Davis was best known on the European Tour during the 1970s and 80s for his distinctive long socks and plus twos.

● AFTER RECORDING 19 wins in New Zealand and Australia, he was also successful in seven European Tour events including the PGA Championship in 1986 and the Volvo Masters in 1991. He never won a major, but held the lead in the 1979 Open with five holes to play before eventually losing to a young Ballesteros.

● IN THE 1987 British Open he started and finished well but had dodgy middle rounds at Muirfield and eventually tied for second with Azinger a stroke behind Faldo.

DEFENDING CHAMPIONS

CHAMPIONS can fall from grace very quickly and while there are many instances of champions defending their title successfully, there are quite a few who have failed miserably – notably Seve Ballesteros, who both times missed the cut in the years following his US Masters victories.

● THERE ARE also people who have simply not defended their titles. A car crash meant that Ben Hogan could defend neither the US Open nor the US PGA in 1949, while one of his predecessors, Walter Hagen, had refused to defend his US PGA tournament because he preferred playing in an exhibition match.

Defending Champions Who Have Missed The Cut

— British Open —
Tom Watson	1976
Mark Calcavecchia	1990

— US Open —
Johnny Farrell	1929
Sam Parks Jnr	1936
Craig Wood	1946
Jack Fleck	1956
Jack Nicklaus	1963
Julius Boros	1964
Ken Venturi	1965
Lee Trevino	1969
Orville Moody	1970
Tony Jacklin	1971
Jerry Pate	1977
Hubert Green	1978
Larry Nelson	1984
Tom Kite	1993
Lee Janzen	1994
Ernie Els	1995

— US Masters —
Jack Nicklaus	1967
Tommy Aaron	1974
Seve Ballesteros	1981
Seve Ballesteros	1984
Sandy Lyle	1989

— US PGA —
Bob Rosburg	1960
Jerry Barber	1962
Larry Nelson	1982
Paul Azinger	1994

A gambler on and off the course, Laura Davies weighs up the odds of sinking her putt.

JIMMY DEMARET

Born: Houston, Texas – 10/05/1910
First US Tour: 1938
Highest Ranking: 1st (1940)
US Tour Wins: 31
Major Wins: 3 (US Masters 1940, 1947, 1950)
Ryder Cup Appearances: 3

DESPITE WINNING over 30 US Tour events, three majors and being undefeated in three Ryder Cup matches, Jimmy Demaret was most noted for his flamboyant clothes. He was always resplendent in tam-o'-shanter, vivid shirt and garish trousers, and owned more shoes than Imelda Marcos.

● ONE OF THE first players to favour a fade over a draw, he was the first golfer to win the Masters three times. His first win at Augusta in 1940 was by four strokes, then a record.

● HIS ONLY OTHER flirtation with majors was the US Open in 1948, when he came second to Ben Hogan.

● WITH A personality to match his outrageous dress sense, Demaret became a popular TV presenter, who has gradually tried to rein in his spontaneous outbursts. Commentating at the 1953 World Championship, when Lew Worsham holed out from 91m (100yd) for a winning eagle, Demaret shouted, 'The son of a bitch holed it.'

BRUCE DEVLIN

Born: Armidale, Australia – 10/10/1937
Turned Pro: 1961
US Tour Wins: 8
Major Wins: 0
US Senior Tour Wins: 1

DEVLIN TURNED pro in 1961 after winning the Australian Open and recorded eight US tour wins in the 1960s and 70s. He also did well in Europe, being leading money-earner in 1966.

● THE CLOSEST to a major he ever came were the two fourths he recorded in the Masters and two sixths in the US Open.

LEO DIEGEL

Born: Detroit, USA – 27/04.1899

Career Spanned: 1920s and 30s

Career Wins: 30

US Tour Wins: 11 (5 in one year)

Major Wins: 2 (US PGA 1928, 1929)

Ryder Cup Appearances: 4

ONE OF America's big names around the 1920s along with Gene Sarazen and Walter Hagen, Diegel should have won more trophies but the young player suffered from nerves and had problems with his putting, experimenting with many different styles.

● INDEED DIEGEL was in contention for the 1920 US Open but nerves failed him, and as late as 1933 he was still suffering. Needing a par four at the relatively easy 18th of St Andrews for the Open, he was let down again by his putting.

● NEVERTHELESS, Diegel recorded 11 US Tour wins, but only his two US PGAs were majors, when he broke Walter Hagen's run of four consecutive victories. Unfortunately Hagen had lost the trophy and Diegel had to have a replacement from the PGA. The original trophy was later found in a Detroit factory, and ironically the PGA have since lost the replacement.

● DIEGEL WON four Canadian Opens, and recorded the biggest winning margin by an American over 36 holes in a Ryder Cup singles match when he defeated Abe Mitchell 9 and 8 in 1929. However, a year later he was the bridesmaid again, losing to Bobby Jones in the British Open in Jones' Grand Slam year.

Chipping in

'They keep on trying to give me the Championship, but I just won't take it.'

THE DINAH SHORE TOURNAMENT

First played: 1972

Most wins: 3 – Amy Alcott (1983, 1988, 1991), Betsy King (1987, 1990, 1997)

Lowest 72-hole Score: 273 Amy Alcott (1991), Betsy King (1997)

TWELVE YEARS after it was first played, the Dinah Shore became a major in 1983. It is a 72-hole strokeplay event held at the Mission Hills Country Club in California. The tournament celebrates the late Dinah Shore, the only non-player to be elected to the LPGA Hall of Fame.

● AFTER HER THIRD win in the Dinah Shore tournament, Amy Alcott (the only player to record three wins) jumped into the lake with Dinah to celebrate.

Dinah Shore Last 25 Winners

1972	Jane Blalock
1973	Mickey Wright
1974	JoAnne Prentice (after play-off)
1975	Sandra Palmer
1976	Judy Rankin
1977	Kathy Whitworth
1978	Sandra Post (after play-off)
1979	Sandra Post
1980	Donna Caponi
1981	Nancy Lopez
1982	Sally Little
1983	Amy Alcott
1984	Juli Inkster (after play-off)
1985	Alice Miller
1986	Pat Bradley
1987	Betsy King
1988	Amy Alcott
1989	Juli Inkster
1990	Betsy King
1991	Amy Alcott
1992	Dottie Mochrie (after play-off)
1993	Helen Alfredsson
1994	Donna Andrews
1995	Nanci Bowen
1996	Patti Sheehan
1997	Betsy King

DOG-LEGS

THIS DESCRIBES a hole where the fairway is partly straight, but then angles off either to the left or right. Often as a result, the hole will involve hitting over trees, or fading or drawing a shot round a bend. It can be used as a verb, as in 'this hole dog-legs left to right.'

FLORY VAN DONCK

Born: Terveuren, Belgium – 23/06/1912

Career Spanned: 1930s to 1970s

THE FINEST golfer Belgium has ever had, van Donck won the Belgian Championship 16 times across four decades, and in 1979 at the age of 67 he was still representing his country in the World Cup – an event he played in regularly from 1954 to 1970. He was individual winner of the trophy in 1960.

● VERY MUCH at ease on the continent, he also won the Belgian and Dutch Opens five times each, the Italian four times, the French three times, and the Swiss and German Opens twice.

● DESPITE FIVE victories in the UK and over a decade of top ten finishes in the Open, he never won a major.

DRAW

A DRAW IS A SHOT which spins from right to left for the right-hander. By closing the stance and gripping round the shaft, you can make the ball turn round an obstacle for a better lie. You only want to move the ball a few yards right to left, as anything more

than that could turn into a dangerous hook. The opposite is a fade, when you open the stance and let the ball drift left to right.

● FOR LEFT-HANDERS, a draw spins the ball in the opposite direction, making it travel from left to right.

DRIVE

THE SAYING GOES, 'Driving for show, putting for dough', but there is no doubt that crowds love a big-hitter such as John Daly, and the explosive first shot in golf is one of the most exciting aspects of the sport. The unleashing of power at the beginning of a hole is almost the complete opposite of a controlled putt to finish.

● THE DRIVER, or one wood, is the club with the least loft and is used for striking off the tee. Traditionally made of wood, drivers have latterly been made of metal and graphite. In the past there have been variations on the driver, with the driving cleek, driving iron, driving mashie and even driving putter all being used to start a hole.

● JOHN DALY is the longest driver on the US Tour and possibly the world, averaging around the 263m (288yd) mark – 1.8m (2yd) longer than anyone else. His average of 264m (289yd) in 1995 was the longest average since the tour started keeping records in 1980.

John Daly: a driven man?

● OTHER BIG hitters in the US include Fred Couples and Davis Love III who both average over 261m (285yd), while in Europe Ian Woosnam and Colin Montgomerie are two of the most powerful hitters.

● THE LONGEST drive recorded, however, was by Carl Hooper in the 1992 Texas Open. When he badly sliced a shot at the 3rd at Oak Hills, his ball hit a slope designed for letting water run away, but which did not constitute out of bounds. His drive eventually finished 720m (787yd) away from the tee. He made a double-bogey six after playing his way back.

● THE LONGEST drive by a senior player is 471m (515yd), by Mike Austin in 1974. In the 1974 Seniors US Open the then 64-year-old landed a ball 59m (65yd) past the 411m (450yd) par 4 fifth, aided by a 56kmh (35mph) tail wind.

DRUGS

DRUGS HAVE never been a problem in golf, although there are players who have been known to indulge in alcohol to excess. John Daly once alleged that players on tour snort cocaine, but his claims were largely ignored.

● WHETHER DRUGS are taken as performance enhancers, however, is not known as professional golfers are not subject to drug tests (even though amateurs are). There have been allegations that painkillers and beta-blockers are part of the pro-circuit, with players such as Sam Torrance and Nick Price admitting to using them in the past. Mac O'Grady, who briefly

coached Ballesteros, said in 1994 at the Masters that 'seven of the top 30 golfers in the world are on beta-blockers'. For now, however, there remains no testing and the allegations are largely discounted.

THE DUBAI DESERT CLASSIC

THE EMIRATES course in Dubai was opened in 1988 and the Dubai Desert Classic has been a part of the European Tour since 1989, although it was not played in 1991.

● THE COURSE, set 20 minutes outside Dubai, is literally an oasis in the desert, with an almost space-age clubhouse made from marble and glass but in the style of Bedouin tents. Winners of the Desert Classic have included Ballesteros, Couples, Els and Montgomerie, although the 1997 Classic was won by virtual unknown, Richard Green.

THE DU MAURIER CLASSIC

First Played: 1973 (Earned major status in 1979)

Most Wins: 3 (Pat Bradley 1980, 1985, 1986)

Lowest 72-hole Score: 272 Jody Rosenthal (1987)

THIS 72-HOLE strokeplay tournament is the only women's major to be held outside the USA, staged at various courses throughout Canada.

● PAT BRADLEY has recorded the most

The Emirates Golf Club has somehow established itself as part of the European Tour.

wins in the event with three successes in the 1980s, while Ayako Okamoto is perhaps the unluckiest competitor as she was three times runner-up in four years from 1984 to 1987.

Du Maurier Classic – Last 25 Winners

1973	Jocelyne Bourassa
1974	Carole Jo Callison
1975	JoAnne Carner
1976	Donna Caponi (after play-off)
1977	Judy Rankin
1978	JoAnne Carner
1979	Amy Alcott
1980	Pat Bradley
1981	Jan Stephenson
1982	Sandra Haynie
1983	Hollis Stacy
1984	Juli Inkster
1985	Pat Bradley
1986	Pat Bradley (after play-off)
1987	Jody Rosenthal
1988	Sally Little
1989	Tammie Green
1990	Cathy Johnston
1991	Nancy Scranton
1992	Sherri Steinhauer
1993	Brandie Burton (after play-off)
1994	Martha Nause
1995	Jenny Lidback
1996	Laura Davies
1997	Colleen Walker

GEORGE DUNCAN

Born: Methlick, Scotland – 16/09/1883
Career Spanned: 1900s to 1920s
Major Wins: 1 (British Open 1920)
Ryder Cup Appearances: 3

DUNCAN CAME young onto the scene and was in the Scotland team by the age of 23. Dubbed the Flying Scotsman because of his brisk and stylish play, he was a lively personality with plenty to say who emerged to challenge the Great Triumvirate. In 1913 he beat Braid in the final of the Matchplay Championship on his home course of Walton Heath.

● A HERO OF the early Ryder Cups, Duncan was the only singles winner in the inaugural contest for Great Britain and Ireland, and as captain in the next, he then beat the mighty Walter Hagen. His victory ten and 8 remains the biggest singles winning margin in the history of the competition.

● WINNING THE 1920 British Open – the first played after World War I – Duncan trailed by 13 strokes after 36 holes. He eventually won by two strokes after clawing his way back with two steady rounds in poor conditions.

THE ALFRED DUNHILL CUP

First Played: 1985
Most Wins: 3 (USA 1989, 1993, 1996)
Lowest Score: 62 Curtis Strange USA vs Greg Norman Australia 1987 (3rd place play-off)

HOSTED AT St Andrews, the Dunhill Cup is contested by 16 three-man teams, until 1991 on a knockout basis, but since 1992 as four groups of four in round robin, with the the four winners playing semi-finals.

● THE THREE PAIRS play medal matchplay format, with the player with lowest single 18-hole score in each pairing the winner. If one match is won each and there is a draw in the last, it goes to a play-off – in 1991 Sweden beat South Africa when Lanner beat Gary Player at the first play-off hole.

● THE CUP'S biggest shock came in 1993, when the unknown Paraguay team defeated the Scottish side of Sam Torrance, Colin Montgomerie and Gordon Brand Jnr on home soil in the first round, Montgomerie and Torrance both losing in windy Scottish conditions. Paraguay, with only four clubs, had fewer than St Andrews, let alone Scotland. They also beat Wales 2–1, but lost to USA 2–1 and failed to make the knockout stage.

Dunhill Cup Winners

1985 Australia (Norman, Marsh, Graham) beat USA (M O'Meara, R Floyd, C Strange)

1986 Australia (Davis, Graham, Norman) beat Japan (T Ozaki, N Ozaki, T Nakajima)

1987 England (Faldo, Brand, Clark) beat Scotland (Lyle, Torrance, Brand Jnr)

1988 Ireland (Smyth, Rafferty, Darcy) beat Australia (Davis, Graham, Norman)

1989 USA (Calcavecchia, Kite, Strange) beat Japan (Meshiai, N Ozaki, Suzuki)

1990 Ireland (Walton, Rafferty, Feherty) beat England (James, Boxall, Clark)

The brilliant South African trio of Els, Frost and Goosen at St Andrews in 1997.

1991 Sweden (Forsband, Johansson, Lanner)
beat South Africa (Bland, Frost, Player)

1992 England (Richardson, Spence, Gilford)
beat Scotland (Lyle, Montgomerie, Brand Jnr)

1993 USA (Stewart, Couples, Daly)
beat England (James, Faldo, Baker)

1994 Canada (Barr, Gibson, Stewart)
beat USA (Kite, Strange, Couples)

1995 Scotland (Coltart, Torrance, Montgomerie)
beat Zimbabwe (Johnstone, McNulty, Price)

1996 USA (O'Meara, Mickelson, Strickes)
beat New Zealand (Nobilo, Turner, Waite)

1997 South Africa (Goosen, Frost, Els)
beat Sweden (Parnevik, Johansson, Haeggman)

David Duval wonders if he's having the mickey taken at the 1997 Disney Golf Classic.

DAVID DUVAL

Born: Jacksonville, USA – 09/11/1971
First US Tour: 1995
Highest Ranking: 2 (1997)
US Tour Wins: 3
Major Wins: 0
Ryder Cup Appearances: 0
Tour Earnings: $3.8million

THE SON of Bob Duval, who competes on the US Senior Tour, David Duval has been a consistent player on the tour over the past three years. He exploded onto the scene in 1995, making the top ten as a Rookie after numerous second places.

● DUVAL SET a record for earnings as a Rookie, winning $881,436, and also made the quickest climb into the Sony rankings, climbing from 437 into the top 50.

● HE THEN went quiet until last year, when he won three events in a row on the US Tour, the first player to do so since Nick Price in 1993, and finished second to Tiger Woods in the money list.

● YET TO WIN a major or compete in the Ryder Cup, 1998 could be Duval's big year.

PAUL 'PETE' DYE

DYE HAS BEEN described as the Picasso of modern golf course design, with his innovative, artistic ideas. Courses had become somewhat predictable in the 1960s and Dye decided to put some strategy, skill and fun back into them.

● AN INSURANCE salesman and a fine amateur golfer from Ohio, Dye retired in 1959 at the age of 34 and designed his first course that year. Early works include Crooked Stick in Indiana, where John Daly had his famous US PGA win in 1991.

● DYE'S TRADEMARKS were the use of deep bunkers and vast roughs, together with bumpy fairways and tiny greens. Generally he tried to restore the values of the traditional old Scottish courses to America. This was captured at the very difficult Tournament Players Course at Sawgrass in Florida, and the Ocean course at Kiawah Island.

EAGLES

AN EAGLE is a score two strokes below par for a hole. While hole-in-ones are very rare in golf, and two shots at a par-four are possible for long-hitters, it is three shots at a par-five which provide the most common opportunity for an eagle.

● ONE OF THE first ever eagles seen on television was Lew Worsham's winning shot in the 1953 World Championship of Golf. This lucrative tournament was the first golf competition to be broadcast coast-to-coast in America, and when Worsham's 91m (100yd) wedge shot span back into the eighteenth hole, robbing Chandler Harper of victory, it caused novice commentator Jimmy Demaret to make his famous gaffe.

● IN 1997 the ten players averaging the most eagles on the US PGA Tour were as follows:

1 Tiger Woods
2 Steve Lowery
3 Tim Herron
4 Fred Couples
5 David Berganio Jnr
6 Mark Calcavecchia
7 John Daly
8 Vijay Singh
9 Ken Green
10 Bill Ray Brown

EARNINGS

GOLFERS HAVE always made good money, but today the sport's top earners are among the richest sportsmen in the world. In 1997, only Michael Schumacher, Michael Jordan and three of the world's top boxers earned more than Tiger Woods, with Greg Norman, Arnold Palmer and Jack Nicklaus not far behind. Woods' earnings are bolstered by contracts with Nike, Rolex, Titleist and American Express, while there are rich rewards to be found on tour, especially in America.

● IN 1997, 18 players on the US Tour earned more than a million dollars, and all of the top 40 earned over $500,000. Even a relatively poor year for Fuzzy Zoeller, down in 148th place, saw him pick up $134,776 from a mere 16 events.

● IN EUROPE the rewards are not so great. Colin Montgomerie won almost £800,000, making him Europe's top earner for the fifth successive year. But with a total of less than £30 million to be won, European tournaments compare poorly with the States. It all seems a far cry from the estimated £2,000 that the great Triumvirate of Braid, Vardon and Taylor amassed between them for their 16 Open wins. And even further from former three-times Open Champion, Jamie Anderson, who died penniless in a poorhouse.

The Top Ten European Tour Earners in 1997

1	Colin Montgomerie	£798,947
2	Bernhard Langer	£692,398
3	Lee Westwood	£588,718
4	Darren Clarke	£537,409
5	Ian Woosnam	£503,562
6	Ignacio Garrido	£411,479
7	Retief Goosen	£394,597
8	Padraig Harrington	£388,982
9	Jose Maria Olazabal	£385,648
10	Robert Karlsson	£364,542

The Top Ten US Tour Earners in 1997

1	Tiger Woods	$2,066,833
2	David Duval	$1,885,308
3	Davis Love III	$1,635,953
4	Jim Furyk	$1,619,480
5	Justin Leonard	$1,587,531
6	Scott Hoch	$1,393,788
7	Greg Norman	$1,345,856
8	Steve Elkington	$1,320,411
9	Ernie Els	$1,243,008
10	Brad Faxon	$1,233,505

The Top Ten Earners Ever

1	Greg Norman	$11,910,518
2	Tom Kite	$10,286,177
3	Fred Couples	$8,885,487
4	Nick Price	$8,794,431
5	Mark O'Meara	$8,506,774
6	Davis Love III	$8,470,982
7	Payne Stewart	$8,465,062
8	Tom Watson	$8,307,277
9	Corey Pavin	$8,130,356
10	Scott Hoch	$7,899,250

JOHN DOUGLAS EDGAR

Born: Newcastle-upon-Tyne, England – 30/09/1884

Career Spanned: 1910s to 1921

Significant Career Wins: 3 (French Open 1914, Canadian Open 1919, 1920)

Major Wins: 0

THE GREAT Scotsman Tommy Armour referred to JD Edgar as 'the best golfer I ever saw,' and the great Bobby Jones was also a fan of the Newcastle-born player who won successive Canadian Opens. Edgar also romped away from the legendary Harry Vardon in the 1914 French Open, finally winning by six strokes.

● IN 1921, however, he died in gruesome circumstances which have never been explained. Apparently the victim of a mugger, Edgar was found on the streets of Atlanta, Georgia, having bled to death from a deep wound to his thigh.

DWIGHT EISENHOWER

US President 1952 – 1960

ALTHOUGH A number of US Presidents have been associated with golf, including Nixon, Kennedy and Ford, it is President Eisenhower with whom the sport is most identified, not because of his abilities, but because of his sheer passion for the game.

● A FRIEND and playing partner of the great Bobby Jones, Eisenhower was a longtime member of the Augusta course which Jones helped design, while Jones in return helped the Eisenhower campaign in the 1951 Presidential Elections.

● THE PRESIDENT employed a certain degree of latitude in his interpretation of the rules, often turning a ball over with his club to identify its make, giving himself a better lie in the process. People did not want to argue with the President. However, he admitted to losing a lot more games after his Presidential term had ended.

● FAMED FOR having a putting green installed in the White House grounds, and practising his putting in the Oval Office, Eisenhower always insisted that despite his celebrated life, his happiest moment occurred at the Seven Lakes Country Club at Palm Springs, when he holed a nine-iron for a 95m (104yd) hole-in-one.

● PERHAPS HIS greatest disappointment as a statesman was failing to get the oak tree on the 17th fairway at Augusta removed, after many complaints to the committee. It was an obstacle he could never overcome, despite being the most powerful man in the world during the 1950s.

Steve Elkington celebrates his exemption from US tour qualification until 2007, after winning the 1997 Players Championship.

THE EISENHOWER TROPHY

THE EISENHOWER TROPHY, named in recognition of President Eisenhower's contribution towards the sport, was first presented at St Andrews in 1958. It is awarded to the winner of the World Amateur Team Championship, the first tournament to be governed by the World Amateur Golf Council.

● THE TOURNAMENT was contested over four rounds, by teams of four of the best Amateurs from 29 countries. The team with the lowest aggregate score were deemed the winners, and in 1958 Australia recorded 918 along with America – the Australians going on to win a play off. The American team was captained by a non-playing Bobby Jones, at Eisenhower's request.

LEE ELDER

Born: Dallas, TX, USA – 14/07/1934

First US Tour: 1967

US Tour Wins: 4

Major Wins: 0

Ryder Cup Appearances: 1

LEE ELDER is most famous for being the first black golfer to take part in the US Masters. Traditionally an invitation-only event, the introduction of qualifying in 1974 allowed Elder to compete in the hitherto all-white field. He qualified by winning the Monsanto Open, beating Peter Oosterhuis in a play-off.

● ELDER WAS, rather appropriately considering his name, also successful in Senior competitions during the 1980s. His 61 in the opening round of one of his eight Senior Tour victories remains a Senior Tour record.

STEVE ELKINGTON

Born: Inverell, Australia – 08/12/1962

First US Tour: 1987

Highest Ranking: 5 (1995)

US Tour Wins: 8

Major Wins: 1 (US PGA 1995)

Tour Earnings: $6.3 million

AUSTRALIAN Steve Elkington had his best ever year in terms of earnings in 1997, picking up a cool $1,320,411. He finished eighth on the US Tour Money List, only three places down from his best-ever placing and recorded two tournament wins – the Doral-Ryder Open and The Players Championship.

● ELKINGTON's greatest moment came in the 1995 US PGA, when he came from six shots behind on the final day. Trailing Ernie Els at breakfast, he overtook the South African and finished on 64 to force a play-off with Colin Montgomerie, who had also recovered well. Elkington won after sinking a beautiful 7.5m (25ft) birdie putt at the only play-off hole. The scores of 267 which both players recorded were the lowest in a US Major Championship.

● ELKINGTON HAS also won the Players Championship twice, in 1991 and 1997. Winning this tournament, ranked just below that of the four US majors, guarantees US Tour qualification for ten years, and so Elkington should be around well into the next century.

ERNIE ELS

Born: Johannesburg, South Africa – 17/10/1969
First US Tour: 1994
Highest Ranking: 9 (1997)
US Tour Wins: 5
Major Wins: 2 (US Open 1994,1997)
Tour Earnings: $3,750,000

IT IS EASY to forget that the talented Els is still only in his twenties, and were it not for a certain Tiger Woods he would undoubtedly be the best young player in the world.

● ELS EXPLODED onto the world stage in 1994 when he was Rookie of the Year on the US Tour, making the US Top 20 money earners and winning the US Open in the same year. He picked up almost £2 million in earnings worldwide that year and was winner of the Johnnie Walker World Championship and the World Matchplay event at Wentworth. Not bad for a 25-year-old, the first bachelor to win the US Open since Sam Parks in 1935.

● ELS CAME to the attention of his home country in 1992, when at the tender age of 23 he equalled Gary Player's record of winning the South African Open, South African PGA and the South African Masters all in the same year.

● IN 1994, Els finished in the top 20 on four of the world's Tours – those in the US, Europe, Australasia and South Africa. Since then his game has become one of the most complete in the world and he has kept up his form, winning the Dubai Desert Classic and three successive World Matchplay titles, a feat never previously achieved.

● YET TO WIN a British Open, Els was runner-up in 1996. In the 1993 British Open he became the first player in the tournament's history to record four rounds in the 60s.

● 1997 WAS YET another great year: he finished ninth in the US rankings, won a second US Open, and also won the Johnnie Walker Classic.

THE ENGLISH GOLF UNION

THE ENGLISH GOLF UNION is the governing body for golf clubs in England, and the male amateurs who play at them. It has over 1,700 affiliated clubs, and at any one time there will also be another 100 courses under construction, and up to 500 with planning permission.

● HAVING RECENTLY moved from its previous HQ in Leicester, the EGU is now based at Woodhall Spa in Lincolnshire. With the help of £2 million from National Lottery funds, the Union has embarked on an ambitious £8 million scheme to develop its picturesque base. A second Championship course has been built, complemented by a training academy, short game practice area, administrative offices and conference centre. The intention is that Woodhall Spa will become to English amateur golf what The Belfry is to the PGA.

Contact

English Golf Union, The Broadway, Woodhall Spa, Lincs LN10 6PU

ENVIRONMENT

IN THE 1980s, new golf courses were being constructed in Britain at an alarming rate. A recent report suggested that within ten years there could be as many as 10,000 courses in Europe (four times the number at the time of the report) if the trend continued.

● IN THE 1990s, however, environmental concerns have come to the fore, and now up to a tenth of the expenditure on a new course can be spent on finding out how it can co-exist happily with nature.

● AN EXAMPLE of such harmony is at Wentworth, where the third course (originally to be the South Course, but finally named the Edinburgh course) is testament to what can be achieved when clubs work closely with environmental scientists.

ETIQUETTE

IN GOLF, etiquette is vital, and respect for your playing partners is valued more than in almost any other sport. As well as the standard rules of golf, there are a number of additional 'rules' which form an extra code of conduct and are maintained by golfers throughout the world. These include the fact that total silence must be maintained while a playing partner is taking their shot. Not only must you not talk, but you must not move either, or stand too close to the person playing.

● PACE OF a golfer's play is important as well, and while a group cannot play until the players in front are clear, equally they must allow faster players to overtake and 'play through'.

● LEAVING THE green as soon as the hole is finished is a must, as is replacing any divots and smoothing out bunkers.

● WHEN PUTTS are being taken, you must not step on a player's line and any marks you make on the green must be repaired. Dropping clubs on the green is also an offence.

Ernie Els is threatening to take over Tiger Woods' mantle as the best golfer in the world.

EUROPE

AS GOLF has become more international, Europe is now mentioned in the same breath as the US in the way that Great Britain was earlier in the century. The move by the US to embrace Europe as a golfing continent has largely been a slow one, with the Order of Merit only taking in European events as late as the 1970s. It was not until 1979 that the European Ryder Cup team included players from the rest of Europe, rather than just those from Great Britain and Ireland.

● THE EUROPEAN game has largely developed from resort courses created by the British wanting golfing holidays abroad – examples being Pau in the French Pyrenees and a course at Biarritz established in 1888. These in turn planted seeds of interest in the local inhabitants, and today nations such as Sweden and Spain are very strong.

● PLAYERS SUCH as Bernhard Langer and Seve Ballesteros have done much to bridge the gap between Britain and the rest of Europe, and Ballesteros' captaincy of the Ryder Cup team marked a high point of this relationship. Of the top 20 in the European Money List in 1997, only eight were from Great Britain or Ireland, while less than half of the 1997 Ryder Cup team were from the British Isles.

THE EUROPEAN TOUR

THE EUROPEAN TOUR was founded in 1972, when European tournaments were added to British events under the aegis of the PGA. It was not until 1979 that the tournament was known as the PGA European Golf Tour.

● WHILE Seve Ballesteros currently tops the list for the most wins, with six,

Colin Montgomerie achieved a record-breaking five in a row in 1997 and could well make it six this year. His prize money failed to top the £1,220,540 that Nick Faldo won in 1992, but the £798,947 he earned was still way in excess of the £18,538 that Bob Charles earned at the tour's inception in 1972.

● SINCE THEN the total prize money has risen from some £250,000 to way over the £20 million mark. Today the European Tour also takes in South Africa, Australia and some Asian countries.

Leading European Money Earners Since 1972

1972	Bob Charles	£18,538
1973	Tony Jacklin	£24,839
1974	Peter Oosterhuis	£32,127
1975	Dale Hayes	£20,507
1976	Seve Ballesteros	£39,504
1977	Seve Ballesteros	£46,436
1978	Seve Ballesteros	£54,348
1979	Sandy Lyle	£49,233
1980	Greg Norman	£74,829
1981	Bernhard Langer	£95,991
1982	Sandy Lyle	£86,141
1983	Nick Faldo	£140,761
1984	Bernhard Langer	£160,883
1985	Sandy Lyle	£254,711
1986	Seve Ballesteros	£259,275
1987	Ian Woosnam	£439,075
1988	Seve Ballesteros	£502,000
1989	Ronan Rafferty	£465,981
1990	Ian Woosnam	£737,978
1991	Seve Ballesteros	£790,811
1992	Nick Faldo	£1,220,540
1993	Colin Montgomerie	£798,145
1994	Colin Montgomerie	£920,647
1995	Colin Montgomerie	£1,038,718
1996	Colin Montgomerie	£1,034,752
1997	Colin Montgomerie	£1,583,904

Rumours that Colin Montgomerie is the new Messiah have been greatly exaggerated.

CHICK EVANS

Born: Indianapolis, IN, USA – 18/07/1890
Career Spanned: 1900s to 1950s
Major Wins: 1 (US Open 1916)

CHICK EVANS was the greatest amateur in the USA until Bobby Jones arrived on the scene, and his tally of wins included eight Western Amateur titles, the French Amateur title in 1914, the US Amateur Championships in 1916 and 1920, and the US Open in 1916.

● A GREAT EARLY exponent of the short game, Evans almost robbed Walter Hagen of his US Open title in 1914. Needing an eagle at the last to tie, and with the crowd willing him on, his second shot finished 30cm (1ft) to the left of the hole.

● EVANS HAD many attempts at the US Amateur title, competing in a record 50 consecutive US Amateur competitions. He lost at the semi-final stages in three successive years from 1909, then lost in the final in 1912. His win in 1916 was accompanied by a US Open win, the first time such a double had been achieved.

● HE WAS competing in the US Amateur tournament as late as 1953 at the age of 63, and played his last nine holes of golf in 1978 at the age of 88.

FADE

A SHOT THAT curves from left to right, thus avoiding an obstacle. To play a fade, a right-handed golfer must open his stance, and while the clubface aims at the centre of the fairway, the body must aim to the left. The ball should be teed low, and well forward in relation to the stance, and the ball will start left before spinning to its desired lie. For left-handers, the directions are reversed.

FAIRWAYS

NORMALLY UP TO 46m (50 yd) wide, and starting 23m (25 yd) from the tee, the fairway is the close-cut grass along the centre of a hole. Golfers always aim to hit the fairway with their drives as it provides the best surface from which to play. In winter the ball sits up beautifully on the lush fairway grass, while in summer the ball bounces and runs on the hard, dry ground.

● SOME PLAYERS such as Ballesteros seem to show no regard for hitting the fairways and can recover from any position. Others like Faldo and Price rely on their accuracy of drive to hit the fairway more often than not, and produce steady rounds.

Hitting The Fairways

On the 1997 US Tour, these were the men hitting the fairways most regularly:

1	Allen Doyle	6	Nick Faldo
2	Fred Funk	7	David Edwards
3	Larry Mize	8	Loren Roberts
4	Nick Price	9	John Morse
5	Jim Furyk	10	Olin Browne

NICK FALDO MBE

Born: Welwyn Garden City, England –
18/07/1957

First European Tour: 1976

Highest Ranking: 1 (1983, 1992)

European Tour Wins: 26

European Tour Earnings: £3,746,626

First US Tour: 1979

US Tour Wins: 6

Highest Ranking: 12 (1996)

US Tour Earnings: $4,372,259

Major wins: 6 (British Open 1987, 1990,
1992, US Masters 1989, 1990, 1996)

Ryder Cup Appearances: 11 (A record for
both European and US players)

NICK FALDO is probably the most single-minded and determined golfer that Britain has ever produced. Despite having an average swing at the start of his career, Faldo's dedication has helped him to withstand the pressures of big competitions, and to keep his head in any crisis. With more Ryder Cup appearances than any other golfer, six majors and a healthy record on both sides of the Atlantic, Faldo is one of the all-time greats.

● FALDO FIRST came to prominence in 1975 when he won the British Youths Amateur and English Amateur Championships, but he was always destined to be a notable sportsman. A good cricketer, swimmer and cyclist from an early age, it is reputed that on the first hole of the first round of golf that Faldo played, aged 15, he hit the green of a 411m (450 yd) par-four with two shots.

● FALDO TURNED professional in 1976 and was Rookie of the Year in 1977. That same year saw Faldo compete in his first Ryder Cup match (the first of 11 record-breaking appearances), achieving a remarkable singles victory over Tom Watson.

● BY 1983 he had topped the European PGA Tour, won three PGA Championships, and was winning regularly on the European Tour. However, his single-minded ambition was to win a major, and after missing out when well placed in both the Open and the Masters, he turned to David Leadbetter to rebuild a swing which would cope under severe pressure.

● THREE YEARS in the golfing wilderness followed: Faldo dropped out of Europe's top 40 rankings, and only retained his beloved Ryder Cup berth as a wild card in 1985 – losing both his matches as Europe won at the Belfry.

● THEN IN 1987 it all came right. Faldo made 18 straight pars in the final round at Muirfield to win the British Open, one of the greatest victories in golfing history. And over the next five years, Faldo was the dominant force in majors, only finishing outside the top 20 in one of 20 major events.

● IN 1990 he did even better. Not only did he equal his idol Jack Nicklaus's feat of two consecutive Masters titles, but he also won the British Open in the same year, missed out on a play-off in the US Open by one shot,

Chipping in

'I think if I'd had some coaching I could have played County cricket as a bowler. Luckily I didn't have any coaching.'

and was the first foreign golfer to be given the US PGA Player of the Year award.

● WHEN FALDO won his third British Open, at Muirfield in 1992, it was the first time a British golfer had won the trophy three times since Henry Cotton had completed his trio of wins in 1948.

● ALTHOUGH HIS Masters win in 1996 was his first major for four years, Faldo remains a strong force in world golf and

One of the rare occasions when Nick Faldo loses his head. And a leg too by the look of it.

has indicated that the US Open is his prime target for the future.

● HAVING JOINED the ranks of those very few sportsmen awarded the MBE, Faldo has been recognised quite rightly as one of the greatest sportsman that Britain has ever produced.

THE FAR EAST

FOUNDED IN 1962, the Far Eastern Circuit was for years administered by amateurs and dominated by foreign professionals. In 1994, however, the Asian PGA started the Omega Tour, with 18 events paying out a combined $5 million, and the Order of Merit was topped by players from Taiwan and Thailand.

Top Far Eastern Competitions

Epson Singapore Open
Volvo Chinese Open
Sabah Masters
Dunhill Masters (at Royal Hong Kong)
Myanmar Open

Five Famous Far East Players

Mr Lu
Wook-soon Kang
Hong Chia-yuh
Lin Keng-Chi
Boonchu Ruangkit

JOHNNY FARRELL

Born: White Plains, NY, USA – 01/04/1901
Career Spanned: 1920s to 1930s
Career Wins: 22
Major Wins: 1 (US Open 1928)
Ryder Cup Appearances: 3

DESPITE WINNING only one major, Farrell was a dominant force in golf at the time of Bobby Jones and Walter Hagen. Farrell's 22 wins put him in the Top 25 winners of all time. In 1927 he recorded eight victories in only one year, seven of them in consecutive tournaments.

● IN 1928 Farrell won the US Open and the following year was runner up in both the British Open and the US PGA Championship. He played in three consecutive Ryder Cups from 1927, before his career tailed off in the 1930s.
● A GREAT PUTTER, occasionally dogged by nerves, Farrell's greatest moment was undoubtedly the 1928 US Open when he beat the great Bobby Jones by one shot in a 36-hole play-off. A 2.1m (7ft) putt at the last hole secured Farrell's victory.

MAX FAULKNER

Born: Bexhill, England – 29/07/1916
Career Spanned: 1930s to 1950s
European Wins: 16
Major Wins: 1 (British Open 1951)
Ryder Cup Appearances: 5

MAX FAULKNER was perhaps one of the first Tour professionals, in that he was never attached to a club as a pro. Instead he was assistant to Henry Cotton, just like his father Gus had been to James Braid.
● FAULKNER was renowned for his eccentric range of clubs, most of them self-made. In winning the British Open in 1951 – a feat which would not be repeated by another Brit until Tony Jacklin in 1969 – he played with a very light and thin putter, no doubt fashioned by his own hands.
● ALSO WELL KNOWN for his garish outfits, the ex-RAF man sported bright plus-twos, and together with his scruffy caddie Mad Max they made an interesting pair.
● FAULKNER's most famous story involves his 1951 Open triumph. On the final round, a spectator asked Faulkner to autograph a ball for his son. Faulkner farsightedly signed it '1951 Open Champion'.

Max Faulkner was known for making his own clubs. It looks like this one works just fine.

BRAD FAXON

Born: New Jersey, USA – 01/08/1961
First US Tour: 1983
Highest Ranking: 8 (1992, 1996)
US Tour Wins: 5
Major Wins: 0
Ryder Cup Appearances: 2
Tour Earnings: $5,842,620

BRAD FAXON comes from a long line of golfers: his father taught him the game, on a course owned by his grandmother. A family man himself, Faxon left the course during the second round of a US Tour event in 1995 to witness the birth of his third child.
● A RELATIVELY short player off the tee, Faxon's steady putting has kept him in the top ten money earners over the last two years. Yet to win a major, Faxon's 1993 Australian Open triumph is his biggest win to date. Faxon finished tenth on the US Tour in 1997, with one win and $1,233,505 in earnings.

DAVID FEHERTY

Born: Bangor, Northern Ireland – 13/08/1958
First European Tour: 1979
Highest Ranking: 8 (1990)
European Tour wins: 5
European Tour Earnings: £1,662,287
First US Tour: 1994
US Tour Wins: 0
US Tour Earnings: $178,501
Major Wins: 0
Ryder Cup Appearances: 1

DAVID FEHERTY has always had reasonable success on the European Tour, never winning a major but always finishing in the money. A long hitter and decent putter, it is more for his words than his deeds that Feherty is known, due to his part-time career as a commentator in the States.

● WHEN ASKED if he could win the 1994 British Open, when in contention at Turnberry, Feherty replied 'I think I can win, I've got nothing better to do this weekend.'

BOB FERGUSON

ALTHOUGH Young Tom Morris is the only man to win four consecutive British Opens, Bob Ferguson came very close in 1883. Having completed a hat-trick of wins at St Andrews the previous year, Ferguson recovered from a ten at one hole to force a play-off with Willie Fernie. Fernie – who later went on to design Turnberry – had been runner-up to Ferguson at St Andrews in 1882. One shot up at the final hole, Ferguson holed a par four to put victory within sight. After driving the green, however, Fernie holed a long putt for an eagle-two and took the title.

VINCENTE FERNANDEZ

Born: Corrientes, Argentina – 05/04/1946
First European Tour: 1971
European Tour Wins: 5
Highest Ranking: 6 (1974)
Major Wins: 0
First Senior Tour: 1996
US Senior Tour Wins: 2

A CONSISTENT PLAYER on the European PGA Tour since the 1970s, Fernandez lies just behind Roberto de Vicenzo as the best South American player of all time. Fernandez has won the Argentine Open eight times and the Brazilian Open on three occasions, as well as five tournaments in Europe.
● FERNANDEZ WON the Murphy's English Open as recently as 1992, when he holed a putt of over 24m (80ft) on the three-tiered final green at The Belfry.

An explosive shot from Vicente Fernandez.

● TURNING 50 in 1996, Fernandez started on the US Senior Tour and in his first season earned over $500,000 and exemption from qualification the following year.

FILMS

GOLF HAS BEEN the subject of some major feature films, and there are many others in which the sport has played a major role.

THE BEST GOLF FILMS EVER

Babe! (1975)
Intelligent made-for-TV biopic of Babe Zaharias.

The Caddy (1953)
Dean Martin and Jerry Lewis in slapstick fairway pranks.

Caddyshack (1980)
Bill Murray and Chevy Chase in silly but occasionally hilarious form.

Dead Solid Perfect (1988)
Randy Quaid as a Tour pro with drinking and women problems.

Follow The Sun (1951)
The story of Ben Hogan's return from a near-fatal car crash to win the US Open.

Tin Cup (1996)
Kevin Costner, Rene Russo and Don Johnson in a golfing *ménage-à-trois*.

HAROLD FINCH-HATTON

HAROLD FINCH-HATTON is a little-known character, but is apparently responsible for the design of Royal St David's, despite having little experience in the world of golf.
● SO THE STORY GOES, Finch-Hatton was spotted by a Mr WH More playing with a boomerang on land which was later to become the course. The next day Finch-Hatton, who had recently returned from Australia, was out playing with golf clubs. He convinced Mr More that the area was ideal for a links course, despite the fact his new friend knew nothing of the sport. Together they built the Harlech course and Mr More was the secretary for the next 40 years.

Ray Floyd 'found golf easy as a kid.' Now at 56, he's finding it slightly harder.

DOW FINSTERWALD

Born: Athens, GA, USA – 06/09/1929

First US Tour: 1952

Highest Ranking: 2 (1956)

US Tour Wins: 12

Major Wins: 1 (US PGA 1958)

Ryder Cup Appearances: 4

A CONSISTENT – one might even say boring – player, Finsterwald once held the record for the most cuts (72) made successively in tournament play. He was admired for his ability to fade and draw the ball accurately at will.

● A GOOD team player in his day, with four Ryder Cup appearances to his name, Finsterwald was a non-playing Ryder Cup captain in 1977 at the age of 48.

● FINSTERWALD's win in the 1958 US PGA was the first in the competition's history as a strokeplay event. His only other major Championship chance came in the 1962 US Masters when he lost to Arnold Palmer in a three-way play-off with Gary Player. Palmer stroked a 68 to win by three shots from Player. Finsterwald trailed in with a 77.

JACK FLECK

Born: Bettendorf, IA, USA – 08/11/1921

First US Tour: 1952

US Tour Wins: 3

Major Wins: 1 (US Open 1955)

JACK FLECK was a little-known pro, both before and after his great moment in golfing history. In the 1955 US Open, Ben Hogan sat in the clubhouse receiving congratulations for his record-breaking fifth US Open. Only one player out on the course had a mathematical chance of catching him, but five strokes behind, an outsider from the municipal courses of Iowa without a tour win to his name wasn't going to pose any problems.

● WHEN JACK FLECK birdied the 18th, however, he took Hogan to a play-off. Amazingly, Fleck went on to win by three shots over 18 holes the following day. He achieved his great feat using a set of Ben Hogan Signature Clubs.

RAY FLOYD

Born: Fort Bragg, NC, USA – 04/09/1942

First US Tour: 1963

Highest Ranking: 2 (1981, 1982)

US Tour Wins: 22

Tour Earnings: $5,277,329

Major Wins: 4 (US Open 1986, US Masters 1976, US PGA 1969, 1982)

First Senior Tour: 1992

Senior Tour Wins: 13

Senior Tour Earnings: $5,000,000

Ryder Cup Appearances: 8

RAY FLOYD has had, and now on the Senior Tour continues to have, a remarkable career. He won his first of 22 Tour events at the tender age of 20.

● SINCE THEN he has won all but one of the four majors. He has represented the USA in Ryder Cup competitions more times than anyone else, and in his final appearance in 1993 became the competition's oldest competitor, aged 51.

● ALONG WITH Sam Snead, Floyd is one of only two players to have won a PGA Tour event in each of four decades, and in 1992 he became the first player to win on both the PGA Tour and the Senior PGA Tour in the same year. His PGA win that year, the Doral Ryder Open, made him the oldest Tour winner at the time, aged 49 years and six months. It came two weeks after his home in Miami had burnt to the ground.

● ALL HIS majors have been won as a front-runner, winning both the US PGA in 1982 and the US Masters back in 1976 having led from start to finish.

● THE ONLY major that Floyd has missed out on is the British Open. The closest he came was tying for second in the 1976 tournament, finishing two shots behind Jack Nicklaus.

● STILL A brilliant player, Floyd is one of golf's great names. He represented the Ryder Cup team as recently as 1993, four years after captaining the team to a draw at The Belfry. Even at the age of 56 you wouldn't bet against Floyd capturing that elusive British Open.

Chipping in

'The game was easy for me as a kid, and I had to play a while to find out how hard it is.'

Paraguay's Carlos and Angel Franco.

DOUG FORD

Born: West Haven, CT, USA – 06/08/1922

First US Tour: 1950

Highest Ranking: 2 (1955)

US Tour Wins: 19

Major Wins: 2 (US Masters 1957, US PGA 1955)

Ryder Cup appearances: 4

DOUG FORD was one of the great players of the 1950s, and although he won two majors, it is for his final shot at the 1957 Masters that he is best remembered. At the 72nd hole, leading by one, he hooked into a bunker. With a difficult lie, things looked bleak, but a remarkable shot saw his ball pitch 3m (10ft) from the hole and roll in for a birdie-three.

● VOTED PGA Player of the Year in 1955, he was never off the Ryder Cup team in the next four matches, and indeed never out of the top ten money earners during the whole of the 1950s. Although Ford's success continued into the 1960s, he was just too old to reap the financial benefits of the Senior Tour.

FORE!

'FORE!' is the warning called out to other golfers when the ball is heading their way. It is said that the word derives from the phrase 'beware before' yelled out by British soldiers when a volley of cannonballs were about to be fired.

FOURSOMES

IN FOURSOMES two players compete against two others, each side playing one ball. Partners play tee-shots at alternate holes, thereafter playing alternate shots. (Playing out of turn costs the hole in matchplay, and two shots in strokeplay.)

FOUR-BALLS

IN FOUR-BALL GOLF, two play against two, with each side playing the ball from the better of the two drives. In four-ball stroke play, both players play a complete hole, and the lower score of the partners is their score for the hole.

● IN RYDER CUP Tournaments, both four-balls and foursomes are played. On each of the first two days, there are four foursomes in the morning, and four four-balls in the afternoon.

FRANCE

FRANCE BOASTS the oldest club in mainland Europe at Pau, founded in 1856 for Britons on holiday. However, golf is still a minority sport in France, and there are few well known French golfers. Only 200 courses were in place during the 1980s, but this number has now more than doubled. Some, such as the Golf National and Chantilly, are among the best in Europe.

Top French Courses

Golf National, Paris
Chantilly, Chantilly
Morfortaine, Morfortaine
Fontainebleau, Paris
Seignosse, Biarritz

Contact

French Golf Federation, 69 Avenue Victor Hugo, 75783 Paris, Cedex 16

FRANCO BROTHERS

The Franco brothers make up a quarter of Paraguay's golfing professionals. The six brothers are among the country's top 20 players, and Carlos and Angel have both topped the South American Order of Merit.

David Frost looking cold as he tries to rescue a bunkered shot in the 1998 South African Open.

DAVID FROST

Born: Cape Town, South Africa – 11/09/1959

First European Tour: 1983

Highest Ranking: 11 (1984)

European Wins: 1

First US Tour: 1983

Highest Ranking: 5 (1993)

US Tour Wins: 10

Major Wins: 0

US Tour Earnings: $6,300,000

AFTER TURNING PRO in 1981, Frost played two years in Europe, making the top 11 in his second season, 1984, and recording his only win. The following season he started on the US Tour, and by 1993 was in the top five money earners.

● IN ADDITION to his ten wins in the US and his sole success in Europe, Frost has also won in Hong Kong and South Africa, including three wins in the Sun City Challenge.

● FROST HAS never won a major, but his win in the 1989 World Series of Golf gave him a ten year exemption from qualification for the US Tour. Back-to-back wins in 1993 included a 259 aggregate for 72 holes.

● FROST's last three seasons have seen him finish around the top 50 mark, but he has a lot of potential and could still register that elusive major win.

JIM FURYK

Born: Westchester, PA, USA – 12/05/1970

First US Tour: 1993

Highest Ranking: 4 (1997)

US Tour Wins: 2

Major Wins: 0

Ryder Cup Appearances: 1

Tour Earnings: $3,200,000

JIM FURYK had his best year in 1997 and continues to go from strength to strength, despite the scarcity of his wins. So far he has only the Hawaiian Open and Las Vegas International to his name; he has, however, won over $3 million in prize money.

● AN UNORTHODOX player, Furyk favours a cross-handed putting style and a very loose swing. While the putting seems to work and he is often high up the averages, his driving can be somewhat wayward.

BERNARD GALLACHER

Born: Bathgate, Scotland – 09/02/1949

First European Tour: 1968

Highest Ranking: 1 (1969)

European Tour Wins: 14

Major Wins: 0

Ryder Cup Appearances: 8

BERNARD GALLACHER exploded onto the scene in the late 1960s, and was Rookie of the Year in 1968, a year after turning pro. A year later he led the European Order of Merit.

● GALLACHER's Ryder Cup fortunes have been very mixed. His first appearance in 1969 at the age of 20 made him the youngest ever competitor at that time. He went on to make eight appearances, beating Jack Nicklaus and Lee Trevino along the way, and was vice-captain to Tony Jacklin when the European team experienced success in the 1980s.

● HE ALSO tasted defeat, however, as captain of the European team in 1991, when Bernhard Langer missed his putt in the final pairing at Kiawah Island. It was almost a repeat of the 1983 Ryder Cup when Gallacher himself missed his putt on the final green of the PGA National Club.

ROBERT GAMEZ

Born: Las Vegas, NV, USA – 21/07/1968

First US Tour: 1989

Highest Ranking: 27 (1990)

US Tour Wins: 2

Major Wins: 0

Ryder Cup Appearances: 0

Tour Earnings: $2,318,290

ROBERT GAMEZ had a great start to his professional career, winning his first ever Tour event, the Northern Telecom Open. In 1990 he was voted Rookie of the Year, and won a stunning victory over Greg Norman at the Nestle Invitational, when he sank a 160m (176yd) iron shot at the final hole for an eagle two.

● DISAPPOINTINGLY, Gamez has never finished in the top ten for a major tournament, and has faded from the rankings since his early success.

G

Left: 1990 Rookie of the Year Gamez has faded as the 1990s have progressed.

Above: Bernard Gallacher becomes the first British Ryder Cup captain to win on US soil, in 1995 at Oak Hill.

ROBERT GARDNER

Born: Scotland – 1909

A CONTEMPORARY of Bobby Jones and Chick Evans, Bob Gardner recorded two wins in the US Amateur Championship, the first in 1909, the second in 1915. He also competed in Walker Cup competitions, but failed to impress in Tournament play in Britain, losing at the 37th hole to Cyril Tolley in the final of the 1920 British Amateur at Muirfield.

● AFTER HIS 1915 win, Gardner was stopped for speeding on the freeway. Holding up his gleaming trophy for the traffic cop, he asked to be let off and was duly sent on his way.

IGNACIO GARRIDO

Born: Madrid, Spain – 27/03/1972

First European Tour: 1992

Highest Ranking: 6 (1997)

European Tour Wins: 1

Major Wins: 0

Ryder Cup Appearances: 1

Tour Earnings: £796,064

IT WAS a great year for Garrido in 1997, one in which he truly emerged from his Ryder Cup-playing father Antonio's shadow. Not only did he help Europe to Ryder Cup success on his home soil, but he also climbed from 47th to 6th in the European Tour Money List.

● GARRIDO ALSO recorded his first victory in 1997, winning the German Open in his fifth year on Tour, earning almost a million pounds in prize money.

AL GEIBERGER

Born: Red Bluff, CA, USA – 01/09/1937

First US Tour: 1960

US Tour wins: 11

Tour earnings: $1,256,548

Major wins: 1 (US PGA 1966)

First Senior Tour: 1987

Senior Tour Wins: 11

Tour Earnings: $3,843,368

Ryder Cup appearances: 2

AL GEIBERGER is known as 'Mr 59' for the obvious reason that he was the first player to card a score of less than 60 in a PGA Tour event. When winning the 1977 Danny Thomas Memphis Classic his brilliant second round included 11 birdies and one eagle. Strangely, he failed to break 70 in any of his other three rounds.

● GEIBERGER's biggest win came in the 1966 US PGA Championship, but he has also collected trophies for the Tournament of Champions and Tournament Players Championships. He is now playing successfully on the Senior Tour.

Did You Know?

Al Geiberger always carries a peanut butter sandwich in his bag. When asked why it was always peanut butter he replied, 'Have you ever smelt your golf bag after carrying a tuna sandwich around in the sun all day.'

GERMANY

BY FAR THE country's most successful player, Bernhard Langer has done much to increase interest in the sport in Germany. It is ironic that German golf has only recently enjoyed a renaissance, as the word golf actually derives from a German word, 'kolbe,' meaning club.

● PLAYERS SUCH as Sven Struver are now coming through gradually, and German golf is gaining credibility due to the influence of courses such as the Sporting Club, Berlin, designed by Nick Faldo.

German Competitions

Volvo German Open
Deutsche Bank Open TPC of
  Europe
Linde German Masters

Top German Courses

Sporting Club, Berlin
Club Zur Vahr, Bremen
Golf Resort Bad Griesbach, Bayern
Falkenstein, Hamburg
Schloss Nippenburg, Stuttgart

DAVID GILFORD

Born: Crewe, England – 14/09/1965

First European Tour: 1986

Highest Ranking: 7 (1994)

European Tour Wins: 6

Major Wins: 0

Ryder Cup Appearances: 2

Tour Earnings: £1,687,862

FINISHING JUST outside the top 30 European money earners, David Gilford is best known for his unlikely win in the 1995 European Ryder Cup triumph at Oak Hill, New York. After wayward play, Gilford looked like halving a match in which he was one up at the final hole. A tough putt managed to salvage a bogey five, and the normally reliable Brad Faxon had a reasonable putt for par and a share of the match. Somehow Faxon missed and Gilford contributed towards Europe's sensational victory.

GIMME

IN MATCHPLAY, a gimme is a very short putt which will be conceded to a player without him or her having to play the stroke, which would be extremely embarrassing if missed.

● IN SOME circumstances, the length of a gimme may be increased by generous partners, one such example being Jack Nicklaus's concession of a 60cm (2ft) putt to Tony Jacklin to halve the Ryder Cup in 1969.

After a great year in 1997, Ignacio Garrido could be the Spaniard that tops even Ballesteros.

BILL GLASSON

Born: Fresno, CA, USA – 29/04/1960
First US Tour: 1984
US Tour Wins: 7
Major Wins: 0
Tour Earnings: $4,206,807

BILL GLASSON finished just outside the top 20 US Tour money earners in 1997, but in many ways did well to finish in the money at all. He recorded his seventh victory, in the Las Vegas Invitational, despite numerous medical problems that have hampered his career. These include back, elbow and knee problems all requiring surgery, a detached muscle in his forearm, a shoulder injury and four sinus operations.

GLENEAGLES

Where: Perthshire, Scotland
Par: 70
Yardage: 6,503
Opened: 1919
Designer: James Braid

THERE IS NOWHERE quite like Gleneagles anywhere else in the world. Set in beautiful surroundings with a magnificent hotel, and with more than one testing course, it is a mecca for the amateur golfer. It has never staged a major event, but professional tournaments such as the Scottish Open and Curtis Cup have taken place there.

● DONALD MATHESON, General Manager of the Caledonian Railway Company, founded the Perth-based Gleneagles complex as competition for Turnberry on the Ayrshire Close. He commissioned James Braid to design the courses, and in conjunction with CK Hutchinson he created the 18-hole King's Course and the nine-hole Queen's Course.

● WORK WAS started in 1908, but with the intervention of war the courses were not opened until 1919. By then the Queen's Course had expanded to 18 holes and another nine-hole course had been added – the Wee Course, comprised soley of par 3 holes.

● THE COURSE-BUILDING did not stop there, however, and in 1974 the Wee Course also grew to 18 holes. In 1980 the Glendevon course was added, and then in 1993 the latter two courses were joined and became the Monarch course – the first designed by Jack Nicklaus in Scotland.

● NOT QUITE testing enough for professionals, the big greens and wide fairways are loved by amateur golfers the world over.

Bill Glasson picks up a couple of lovelies in the 1997 Las Vegas Invitational.

Heavens above, what a view. For golfers Gleneagles is heaven on earth.

G

GLOVES

MOST GOLFERS wear a glove on their leading hand (left hand for right-handed golfers) to help with their grips. On hot days, sweat can effect the hold you have on a club and so a soft, tight-fitting leather glove is employed for driving and iron shots.

● RECENTLY, developments have been made in marking gloves to aid amateur players in how they hold the club.

BOB GOALBY

Born: Belleville, IL, USA – 14/03/1929
First US Tour: 1957
US Tour wins: 11
Major wins: 1 (US Masters 1968)
Ryder Cup appearances: 1

BOB GOALBY turned pro in 1956, and was Rookie of the Year on the following year's Tour. He recorded 11 wins in his career, and was a fixture on the Money List, always consistent despite an erratic swing. As well as his Masters win, he was a runner-up in both American majors – the Open in 1961, and the PGA the following year.

● IT IS THE circumstances of his Masters win for which he is best remembered, however. In the heat of the final round Roberto de Vicenzo's card was filled in wrongly, his playing partner giving him a par at the 17th rather than the birdie he achieved. Having signed the card, Vicenzo's score had to stand, and Goalby took the Green Jacket by a single shot. It was bad luck on both players; for Vicenzo because he missed the chance of a play-off, but also for Goalby because his title was always tainted by 'what if?' thoughts.

JOHNNY GOODMAN

WHEN Johnny Goodman won the US Open in 1933, it was the last time an Amateur player would win one of the four golfing majors. A Walker Cup regular in the 1930s, Goodman was also a US Amateur Champion in 1937.

RETIEF GOOSEN

Born: Pietersburg, South Africa – 03/02/1969
First European Tour: 1992
Highest Ranking: 7 (1997)
European Tour Wins: 2
Major Wins: 0
Tour Earnings: £963,607

GOOSEN grew up with Ernie Els in South Africa, and after turning pro recorded six wins in his first five years. He was also voted Rookie of the Year on the Sunshine Tour. His biggest win to date has been the 1995 South African Open, although a top ten finish in 1997 in the European Money List suggests that big things lie ahead for Goosen.

Retief Goosen keeps his eye on the ball at all times, as he shows how to get ahead in the 1997 Compaq European.

WAYNE GRADY

Born: Brisbane, Australia – 26/07/1957
First US Tour: 1984
Highest Ranking: 21 (1990)
US Tour Wins: 2
Major Wins: 1 (US PGA 1990)
Tour Earnings: $1,963,769

AFTER JOINING the US Tour in 1984, it was five years before Wayne Grady picked up a win, the Westchester Classic. Grady had already been German Open Champion in 1984 and went on to win the Australian PGA twice. He had a successful year in 1989, and took the US PGA Championship in 1990, but this was the last time he was to present a challenge in a major.

DAVID GRAHAM

Born: Windsor, Australia – 23/05/1946
First US Tour: 1971
US Tour Wins: 8
Major Wins: 2 (US PGA 1979, US Open 1981)

INSPIRED PUTTING has seen David Graham win tournaments in every corner of the world. Although he has concentrated mostly on the US Tour, he has also won in Australia, France, Japan, Mexico, Thailand and New Zealand.

● BOTH GRAHAM's major successes have been in America, but he almost added the British Open as well in 1985, losing out to Sandy Lyle at Royal St Georges by two shots.

● AFTER A TOUGH upbringing, followed by a few harsh lessons in business at an early age, Graham found himself on the verge of European and US success in his early twenties.

● GRAHAM won the Japanese Open in 1971, his first US event in 1972, and the Australian Open five years later, but it was not until 17 years after turning pro that a major success came his way. His brilliant putting won Graham a play-off in the US PGA against Ben Crenshaw, when ironically it had looked as though his putting in the final holes might even deny him that play-off spot.

● IN 1981, Graham added the US Open to his list of trophies, becoming the first Australian to win the tournament.

Chipping in

'To be in contention for three or four days is better than sticking a needle in the arm.'

THE GRAND SLAM

A GRAND SLAM in golf can have two different meanings. Traditionally it meant winning a full sweep of major tournaments. While nobody has ever won the British Open, US Open, US Masters and US PGA in one season, Bobby Jones did secure all the major trophies to be had in 1930 – a feat never likely to be repeated. He completed his clean sweep of British Amateur, US Open, British Open and US Amateur with a spectacular victory at Merion. Jones decided to retire shortly afterwards.

● TODAY, the Grand Slam of Golf is a yearly competition between the winners of the four majors, which in 1997 was won by Ernie Els, beating Tiger Woods by 3 strokes with a 65 in a rain-soaked second round.

GREAT BRITAIN

L ONG BEFORE the Ryder Cup became a competition between the USA and Europe, it was contested between America and a team of players from Great Britain and Ireland. While England, Scotland, Ireland and Wales have their own sections elsewhere in this book, it is also worth documenting the achievements of Great Britain as a team.

● THE FIRST Ryder Cup in 1927 was actually won by America, but two years later the Great Britain and Ireland team won back the cup, at Moortown, Leeds.

● WHILE THE individual countries of the UK have always competed in The World Cup and the Alfred Dunhill Cup, players in the World Matchplay Championship have always competed under the banner of Great Britain and Ireland. Indeed, in amateur golf the Walker Cup and Curtis Cup are still fought for by teams from the USA and Great Britain and Ireland.

David Graham, graduate of the University of Life.

HUBERT GREEN

Born: Birmingham, AL, USA – 28/12/1946

First US Tour: 1970

US Tour Wins: 19

Major Wins: 2 (US Open 1977,
    US PGA 1985)

Tour Earnings: $2,591,959

Ryder Cup Appearances: 3

IT IS AMAZING that Hubert Green won anything with his bizarrely unorthodox swing, but he did, winning 19 events on the US Tour. This would have been 20 – and a clean sweep of US majors – but for a poor final putt at the 1978 US Masters.
● A YEAR LATER, Green missed out on the opportunity to add the US Masters to his collection. He missed a short putt at the last hole and lost by one shot to Gary Player, who had finished with a superb 64.

Chipping in

'I owe everything to golf. Where else could a guy with an IQ like mine make this much money?'

Hubert Green survived death threats to win the 1977 US Open. He was lucky that the match didn't go to a sudden death play-off.

Did You Know?

Hubert Green's biggest win came in the US Open in 1977, when he played out the last four holes of his win under threat of death. A woman had phoned the FBI to warn them that a contract was out on Green and that he would die at the Southern Hills Club in Tulsa. Two pars, a birdie and a bogey at the last were enough for Green, who later joked that the assassin was probably an ex-girlfriend!

GREENS

THE GREENS are the putting areas, where the tense drama often unfolds. As those employed to tend golf courses are called greenkeepers, however, greens can be taken to mean the whole course.
● GOLFERS will often refer to greens as being fast or slow. If the grass has been heavily watered, or it has rained, then the ball will tend to slow up. In hot weather the hard ground often allows the ball to move faster. As a result, greens tend to be quicker in America than in Britain. The greens also tend to be larger in America, although some British courses such as The Belfry have adopted larger greens.
● GRASS ON greens is kept very short, and it is on greens that the etiquette for looking after the course is most observed. With the subtle slopes and 'borrow' needed to sink a putt on undulating ground, it is vital that there are no obstacles to the ball moving uninterrupted.
● ONCE ON the green, the person whose ball is furthest from the hole will putt first, and this continues until everybody has putted-out.

GRIPS

THE POSITION of the hands on the club is vital, and over the years many suggestions have been made, including the overlapping and interlocking grips, the Vardon grip – made popular by the great Harry Vardon – and even the baseball grip.
● FIRST USED in the early 1900s, the Vardon grip – in which the little finger of the right hand is crooked over the index finger of the left hand – is named after Harry Vardon, but it was actually Scottish Amateur Johnny Laidlay that first employed the grip. Vardon described it as the hands being 'wed'.
● THE VARDON grip mutated into the overlapping grips used today. The split-handed baseball grip that was used in early golfing circles – especially in the States – is now almost obsolete.

JAY HAAS

Born: St Louis, MO, USA – 02/12/1953
First US Tour: 1976
Highest Ranking: 13 (1982)
US Tour Wins: 9
Major Wins: 0
Ryder Cup Appearances: 2
Tour Earnings: $6,400,000

JAY HAAS was an early starter, winning his first trophy, The National Pee Wee Championships, at the age of seven.

● HAAS HAS been on the US Tour now for over 20 years, and although a consistent money earner, he has never made the top ten. His highest ranking came in 1982, but it was 1995 in which he earned the most cash, picking up a cool $822,259.

● HAAS MUST feel the US Tour is a home-from-home, as his brother Jerry was previously on the Tour, his brother-in-law, Dillard Pruit, is a Tour member, and former US Masters winner Bob Goalby is Haas's uncle.

● THE TWO appearances Haas has made in the Ryder Cup have been 12 years apart. In 1983 he lost both his singles matches. Then, having waited 12 years for his second appearance, Haas was the man that conceded a short putt at the 18th to Philip Walton as the 1995 European team were victorious in the States.

JOAKIM HAEGGMAN

Born: Kalmar, Sweden – 28/08/1969
First European Tour: 1989
Highest Ranking: 15 (1993)
European Tour Wins: 2
Major Wins: 0
Ryder Cup appearances: 1
Tour Earnings: £1,137,338

HAEGGMAN was the first Swede to play in a Ryder Cup when he made his only appearance in 1993. A keen ice hockey player, a broken rib sustained during a match in 1994 has put him off his second sport. Not yet having fulfilled his potential, Haeggman has time very much on his side.

Haeggman was the first Swede to represent Europe in the Ryder Cup, but definitely not the last.

The *Virgin* Book Of Golf Records **63**

Hagen, a party-loving golfer, was a swinger in more ways than one.

Did You Know?

Walter Hagen had a $50 bet with Joe Kirkwood after the Tijuana Open in 1928 that he could hit his ball back to the hotel in less shots than him. Although Hagen reached the hotel first, it was Kirkwood who won the bet as he was the first of the two to chip his ball into the toilet bowl – which they'd decided would be the hole.

WALTER HAGEN

Born: Rochester, NY, USA – 21/12/1892
Career Spanned: 1913 to 1935
Career Wins: 40
Major Wins: 11 (British Open 1922, 1924, 1928, 1929, US Open 1914, 1919, US PGA 1921, 1924, 1925, 1926, 1927)
Ryder Cup Appearances: 5

IN MUCH the same way that Henry Cotton advanced the standing of golf in Britain, so Walter Hagen was a great ambassador for American golf. The first American to win the British Open, Hagen was a flamboyant character, and the first touring professional in the sense we know today.

● HAGEN WAS a colourful personality on and off the course. Always cool and relaxed under pressure, yet an extrovert in his dress sense and the way he dealt with people, he led a lavish lifestyle, often partying well into the early hours – even during tournaments. It didn't seem to affect his play though.

● ALTHOUGH HIS total of 40 victories on the PGA Tour puts him only seventh on the all-time winners list, his total of 11 majors is bettered only by Jack Nicklaus and Bobby Jones. Hagen dominated golf in the first two decades of this century and was literally unbeatable in the PGA Championship for four years: Hagen won 22 consecutive PGA matches (a record) as he won the Championship for four successive years from 1924 to 1927.

● HAGEN's first major win came in the 1914 US Open at the age of 21, which prompted him to turn to golf as a career. Were it not for the outbreak of war, he would no doubt have added to his total of titles immediately. Indeed, he won the US Open in 1919 as soon as it resumed. Had he played in as many tournaments as Nicklaus, he could have been undisputedly the best golfer of all time.

● NOT A GREAT striker of the ball, it was Hagen's short game which was impressive. Very much in the style of Ballesteros, he would recover a wayward drive with a deft touch around the green and a steady putter.

● HAGEN supplemented his income as a touring professional by playing exhibition matches, often against Joe Kirkwood. Hagen played in all but one of the first six Ryder Cups, but captained the USA on all six occasions. America were victorious four times under his leadership.

● WELL KNOWN for his clashes with authority, Hagen was very much his own man, and would not accept second best. He would arrive at tournaments in a limousine and use the car as his changing room – at the time, professionals were not allowed to use clubhouses for such purposes.

Chipping in

'I didn't want to be a millionaire. I just wanted to live like one.'

HANDICAPS

A PLAYER's handicap is, in principle, an assessment of his or her ability to play to the Standard Scratch Score of a course. It is, in effect, the number of shots above or below par he or she should generally play the course.

● IT WAS DEVELOPED so that players of varying skills could play competitively against each other. Professionals, by and large, should play the course to par or better, and are therefore regarded as scratch players with a handicap of zero.

● THE MAXIMUM handicap varies, but in Britain it is 28 for men and 36 for women. A player's handicap is judged by a club's handicap committee, who assess the player's scorecards. The handicap might then be adjusted up or down depending on subsequent competition performances. However, if a player's home club considers that a handicap is too high or too low, and does not reflect their current playing ability, the handicap committee is duty bound to adjust it accordingly.

BOB HARLOW

B OB HARLOW has one of the strongest claims for being the founder of the US PGA Tour. Harlow was a newspaper journalist who in 1929 brought order to the chaos surrounding the PGA tour and was instrumental in setting up sponsorship deals, gaining publicity, and organizing events properly.

● HARLOW INTRODUCED an Order of Merit for the first time, and tee times for designated pairs of players – previously it had been organised on a first-come first-served basis. Harlow also doubled the purse for prizes in his first year, but was sacked by the PGA in 1932 for spending too much time on other interests.

● THE PGA reinstated Harlow in 1933 after experiencing organisational difficulties, and he returned with ideas for exemption from qualification and minimum purses. Harlow was also Walter Hagen's manager when the PGA Tour was set up, and so had plenty to gain from the ensuing financial success of its players.

PADRAIG HARRINGTON

Born: Dublin, Ireland – 31/08/1971

First European Tour: 1996

Highest Ranking: 8 (1997)

European Tour Wins: 1

Major Wins: 0

Ryder Cup appearances: 0

Tour Earnings: £674,006

I N ONLY HIS second season on the European Tour, the young Irishman finished eighth on the Money List, picking up £388,982 in prize money. He has so far failed to win a tournament, but has been consistently amongst the money.

● HE ALSO topped the birdies leaderboard, with 402 birdies in his 106 rounds over the year. His score of 125 also put him in fifth place on the overall leaderboard, behind such stars as Montgomerie, Clarke and Olazabal.

HATS

H ATS AREN't essential to golf, but you wouldn't believe that considering the number of players that wear them. Early players sported the fashionable headgear of the day, from the top hats of the late 18th century to the fedoras favoured by Leo Diegel, and of course the tam o'shanter.

● TODAY, sponsored headwear is everywhere in professional golf and, among the many peaked baseball caps worn by today's players, it is perhaps Tiger Woods' Nike cap that is the most recognisable.

THEODORE HAVEMEYER

T HEODORE HAVEMEYER was the inaugural President of the United States Golf Association when it was formed in 1894. Known as the Sugar King because of his vast sugar empire, his first move was to donate a trophy for the first US Amateur Championship, held in 1895 and won by Charles MacDonald. Unfortunately the trophy was destroyed by fire in 1925.

● HAVEMEYER WAS also one of the first men to fight racism in the golfing world. When a black player, John Shippen, was admitted to the 1896 US Open field, many of the players – mostly immigrants from Britain – threatened not to play. Havemeyer told them that the competition would take place with or without them, and Shippen remained in the competition.

Padraig Harrington at the Canon European Masters in 1997.

Now that's what I call a water hazard; the famous Turnberry Lighthouse hole.

HAZARDS

WHEN GOLFERS talk of hazards, they are referring to the bunkers and water hazards encountered on a round. Play from these hazards are normally restricted in some way. For instance when playing out of a bunker, you cannot ground your club before playing your shot.

● WATER HAZARDS can include rivers, lakes and ponds, and even oceans and seas. If the ball lands in water, the player may, under penalty of one stroke, (a) play another ball from as near as possible to the spot where the original stroke was played, (b) drop another ball behind the water hazard in line with the trajectory of the original ball, or (c) drop a ball on the margin of the hazard, as long as it is not nearer the hole than where the ball entered the hazard. Phew!

SANDY HERD

Born: St Andrews, Scotland – 22/04/1868
Career Spanned: 1892 – 1939
Major Wins: 1 (British Open 1902)

SANDY HERD was a contemporary of the Great Triumvirate, and despite never emulating their great success he did manage to get the better of them individually on occasion. He certainly outlasted them in career terms, having played as a pro for 47 years before the Second World War.

● HERD WAS one of the first British players to use a modern Haskell ball instead of the old gutta percha. In 1902 at the age of 35, Sandy Herd was becoming a perennial contender in the British Open. The day before the 1902 competition, Herd played a practice round with the great amateur John Ball using the Haskell ball. He liked the ball so much that he bought all of the pro shop's remaining stock. The next day he claimed his one and only Open win.

● IN 1926 at the age of 58 Herd won the News of the World Matchplay Championship (second only to the Open at the time), and he was still playing professionally at the age of 71.

HAROLD HILTON

Born: West Kirby, England – 12/01/1869
Career Spanned: 1880s to 1910s
Major Amateur Wins: 5 (British Amateur Championship 1900, 1901, 1911, 1913, US Amateur Championship 1911)
Major Wins: 2 (British Open 1892, 1897)

HAROLD HILTON is the only British Amateur player to have held the British and US Amateur Championship titles at the same time. And he is the only British amateur to have won the British Open twice – surprisingly, before he had ever recorded a win in the Amateur Championship. Hilton won his first Open in 1892 at Muirfield after finishing with a 72 and 74 – a brilliant score for the time. His second Open victory in 1897 came on his home ground of Hoylake.

● HILTON's first British Amateur win came at Sandwich in 1900, and he won three more Amateur titles. While British Amateur Champion in 1911 he went to America and claimed the US Amateur title in the same year – a feat never repeated by a Brit.

● REPUTED TO like a drink, Hilton also smoked up to 50 cigarettes in a round. He wrote extensively on the game and was the first editor of *Golf Monthly*.

HISTORY

A brief guide to the landmarks in golfing history:

1363 An edict from Edward III banned a number of leisurely pursuits including 'cambuca', an early forerunner of golf

1457 James II specifically bans the game of golf

1502 James IV takes up golf

1600 Feathery ball introduced

1608 First club in England founded at Blackheath

1637 Boy hanged in Scotland for stealing golf balls

1744 Company of Gentlemen Golfers formed at Leith. A set of rules is introduced for the first time

1786 Playing of golf first recorded in the USA

1834 St Andrews becomes the Royal and Ancient

1848 Gutta percha ball introduced

1861 Willie Park wins first British Open

1872 Claret Jug becomes British Open prize

1885 First British Amateur Championship

1893 Ladies Golf Union formed

1894 British Open moves to England, United States Golf Association formed

1895 First US Open

1898 Haskell ball introduced

1916 PGA of America founded

1922 Inaugural Walker Cup competition

1927 First Ryder Cup match takes place

1934 First US Tour

1947 US Open is the first golfing event to be televised live

1951 USGA and R&A meet to clarify rules

1958 Arnold Palmer wins his first major

1962 Jack Nicklaus wins his first major

1971 European PGA Tour conceived

SCOTT HOCH

Born: Raleigh, NC, USA – 24/11/1955
First US Tour: 1980
Highest Ranking: 6 (1997)
US Tour Wins: 8
Major Wins: 0
Ryder Cup Appearances: 1
Tour Earnings: $7,900,000

SCOTT HOCH had his best year to date on the US Tour in 1997, finishing sixth in the Money List and earning over a million dollars for the second year running. Hoch also made his first Ryder Cup appearance in 1997 and was the USA's most effective player, winning two matches and halving the third.

● HOCH IS BEST known, however, for failure in a major rather than success. In the 1989 US Masters play-off against Nick Faldo, Hoch had a simple putt to secure victory after Faldo had holed out from a bunker to save a bogey. Hoch missed and Faldo won at the next play-off hole.

● AS WELL AS eight wins on the US Tour, Hoch has had a number of international victories including the Dutch and Korean Opens.

BEN HOGAN

Born: Dublin, TX, USA – 13/08/1912
Career Spanned: 1930s–1960s
US Tour Wins: 63
Major Wins: 9 (British Open 1953,
    US Open 1948, 1950, 1951, 1953,
    US Masters 1951, 1953,
    US PGA 1946, 1948)
Ryder Cup Appearances: 2

BEN HOGAN easily ranks as one of the top five golfers of all time, and perhaps even the greatest. He won nearly every major available to him and had a truly remarkable life as well as a spectacular career.

● HE TURNED PRO at the age of 17, but it wasn't until 1946 that Hogan won his first major, the 1946 US PGA Championship. Between 1948 and 1953, Hogan was virtually unbeatable, winning eight of the eleven majors that he entered.

● WHAT MADE the five year period from 1948 even more remarkable was that in 1949 Hogan was in a severe car crash. After his car was struck head-on by a Greyhound bus, Hogan lay unconscious for an hour before an ambulance arrived. He survived, despite doubts that he would ever walk again. Remarkably, he returned to competitive golf in 1950, and immediately won the US Open.

● THREE YEARS later at the age of 40, Hogan produced the greatest season of golf that had ever been seen, and which has never been bettered. He won the 1953 British Open, US Open and US Masters, and was only denied the chance of the Grand Slam because the dates of the British Open and the US PGA coincided. Hogan chose to play at Carnoustie, and duly won his only British Open. It is unlikely, however, that

Hogan would have competed in the US PGA, as he never took part in the competition after his car crash – the 36 holes in one day would have been too much for his legs to take.

● HOGAN DECIDED not to play on the Senior Tour as his career wound down, but he was still competing at the highest level to a good age. Hogan was also non-playing captain of the winning American Ryder Cup team in 1967. That same year he scored a 66 in the US Masters aged 54, including a back nine of 30.

● HOGAN'S LIFE was dramatised in the film 'Follow the Sun,' in which Glenn Ford played the part of Hogan.

● HOGAN WAS held as a hero by many golfers. In 1992, one of them, Nick Faldo, asked him the secret of winning the US Open. 'Shoot a lower score than anybody else,' was his reply. Thinking he was joking, Faldo asked again. 'Just score lower than anybody else,' repeated Hogan.

Chipping in

'If I miss one day's practice I know it, if I miss two days the spectators know it, and if I miss three days the world knows it.'

Ben Hogan, a truly remarkable golfer and a truly remarkable man.

HOLE-IN-ONES

ALSO KNOWN as an 'ace', the hole-in-one is pretty much self-explanatory. A hole-in-one occurs most commonly at a par three, but occasionally they have been recorded at short par fours.

● IT IS ESTIMATED that a golfer has to hit on average 12,000 tee shots to record a hole-in-one. What odds then, on the feat Margaret Waldron achieved at the Long Point Golf Course, Florida in 1990. 74 years old and legally blind, Margaret scored a hole-in-one. And then did the same thing the following day at the same hole with the same ball.

● HAVING LOST both arms in a childhood accident, Jim Taylor took up golf in 1986 using special rubber aids. Since then Taylor has scored eight hole-in-ones.

Did You Know?

The longest hole-in-one ever recorded was 409m (447 yd), achieved by Robert Mitera in 1965 at the tenth hole of the Miracle Hills Golf Club, Nebraska, USA.

HONG KONG

GOLF FIRST came to Hong Kong at the end of the nineteenth century when Britain had a military presence in the country. The first club, later to become the Royal Hong Kong, initially had no holes, and golfers finished a 'hole' when their balls hit a designated piece of granite. The authorities were concerned that holes would provide a danger to the military horses stabled adjacent to the course.

● THE HONG KONG Open is played annually over a composite of the Royal Hong Kong club's three courses. Previous winners have included Greg Norman and Ian Woosnam, and the development of the Asian Tour has increased the competition's prestige.

Contact

Hong Kong Golf Association, Suite 1420, Princes Building, 10 Chater Road, Hong Kong

Always the bridesmaid? Not any more. Tommy Horton never came higher than second on the European tour, but 30 years later he came top of the Seniors.

HOOKS

WHEN A DRAW goes out of control, it is then considered a hook. By pulling the club too far across your body, the ball will move viciously from right to left (for the right-hander) and will often result in a penalty or lost ball.

TOMMY HORTON

Born: St Helens, England – 16/06/1941	
First European Tour: 1964	
Highest Ranking: 2 (1967)	
European Tour Wins: 7	
Major Wins: 0	
Ryder Cup Appearances: 2	
Tour Earnings: £242,321	
First Senior European Tour: 1991	
Senior Tour Earnings: £487,236	

TOMMY HORTON was one of several British players groomed by Max Faulkner to win the British Open in the 1970s. Although Horton was the leading British player in the 1976 and 1977 Opens, he never came close to winning them.

● HORTON WAS nevertheless a

successful player, and as well as winning the Dunlop Masters he was also a Ryder Cup player in two consecutive matches and the PGA Captain in 1978.

● NOW A successful Senior Tour player, Horton topped the European Seniors Tour Money List in 1997, with £158,427. He has now earned twice as much money in six years on the Senior Tour as he did in 20 on the regular PGA Tour.

HOYLAKE ROYAL LIVERPOOL

Where: Merseyside, England

Par: 72

Yardage: 6,780

Opened: 1869

Designer: Not known

Major Events Staged: British Open 1897, 1902, 1907, 1913, 1924, 1930, 1936, 1947, 1956, 1967,

British Amateur Championship 1885, 1887, 1890, 1894, 1898, 1902, 1906, 1910, 1921, 1927, 1933, 1939, 1953, 1962, 1969, 1975, 1995

Walker Cup 1983

Curtis Cup 1992

HOYLAKE's history is closely entwined with that of The British Open, and its clubhouse is a shrine to British Golf. The first British Amateur Championship was staged at Hoylake in 1885, and the British Open moved to Hoylake in 1897. Hoylake is also famous for staging the first English Amateur Championship, and the first international between Britain and America in 1921.

● IN ANOTHER first, Hoylake also witnessed the first British Open winner to use a Haskell ball, when Sandy Herd won an elusive major victory in 1902.

● THE BRITISH OPEN has not been staged at Hoylake since 1967, when Roberto de Vicenzo outplayed Nicklaus and Player. It is unlikely that the event will ever return to Liverpool, not because of the course's quality – top Amateur events are still staged there – but because it cannot cope with the large crowds that the Open now attracts.

JOCK HUTCHISON

Born: Scotland – 1884

Career Spanned: 1910s – 1920s

US Tour Wins: 8

Major Wins: 2 (British Open 1921, US PGA 1920)

AS WELL AS his US PGA win, Scottish-born Hutchison was also a losing finalist in the US PGA and was four times in the top three of the US Open.

● HUTCHISON's greatest win, the British Open, was a controversial one as his clubs were marked with lines, which were thought to add backspin. Such trickery was immediately banned, but has now become an integral part of golf club design.

INDIA

ALTHOUGH THERE are few Indian golfers on the international scene, golf has a long history in India. The Royal Calcutta course dates from 1829 and is the oldest club outside the British Isles. The Royal Bombay club was also founded early in the nineteenth century – both clubs were built to provide sporting relief for the administrators of the British Empire.

Contact

Indian Golf Union, Tata Centre (Third Floor), 43 Chowringhee Road, Calcutta 700071

INTERNET SITES YOU SHOULD VISIT

http://golf.com/
Results of almost every tournament on the PGA, LPGA and Nike tours.

http://www.golfonline.com/
News, tips and ads, this is a great on-line golfing magazine.

http://www.traveller.com/golf
Ideal for golfers planning holidays in the USA.

http://www.golf.com/tour/lpga
The best site for women's golf on the Internet.

IRELAND

GOLF WAS relatively late coming to Ireland, not arriving until the 1890s. First established in Northern Ireland, the game later moved to the South.

● AS A NATION, Ireland has provided some fine players. They were winners of the World Cup in 1958, and have twice won the Alfred Dunhill Cup – beating Australia in 1988 and England in 1990. The Irish Open is always a popular event on the European Tour, with Colin Montgomerie the current Champion.

Major Irish Competitions

Murphy's irish Open

Most Famous Players

Harry Bradshaw
Joe Carr
Eamonn Darcy
Padraig Harrington
Christy O'Connor Snr
Christy O'Connor Jnr

Top Irish Courses

Ballybunion, County Derry, Ireland
Lahinch, County Clare, Ireland
Portmarnock, Dublin, Ireland

Contact

Irish Golf Union, Glencar House, 81 Eglinton Road, Donnybrook, Dublin 4

IRONS

IRONS WERE previously known as cleeks, and an approach club (the forerunner of the wedge) was known as a jigger. Today irons range from the one-iron to the wedge. More accurate than a wood, but without the power, they are used mainly from fairways, or from the tee when accuracy is required, or when the hole is a par three.

● IRONS ARE graduated by degrees, so that the same swing can produce a shot of varying length.

Even at the age of 53, it is a rare sight to actually see Hale Irwin in a bunker.

HALE IRWIN

Born: Joplin, MO, USA – 03/06/1945
First US Tour: 1968
Highest Ranking: 3 (1976)
US Tour Wins: 20
Tour Earnings: $5.6 million
Major Wins: 3 (US Open 1974, 1979, 1990)
First Senior Tour: 1995
Senior Tour Wins: 13
Highest Ranking: 1 (1997)
Senior Tour Earnings: $4,758,308
Ryder Cup Appearances: 5

A VERY STEADY player, Hale Irwin was consistently amongst the money on the US Tour, and once played 86 consecutive tournaments without missing a cut – an achievement which has only been bettered twice.

● IRWIN's three US Open wins are the only major successes he has achieved. The closest he got to adding to the haul in other competitions was the 1979 British Open when he lost over the last four holes to Seve Ballesteros. The complete antithesis of Ballesteros, Irwin was amazed at his playing partner's inaccuracy, saying that he'd 'never seen somebody miss so many fairways and win.'

● IRWIN's third US Open win in 1990 was at the age of 45, making him the oldest ever winner of the tournament. And his gap of sixteen years between wins is only bettered in major golf by Jack Nicklaus.

● TURNING TO the Seniors Tour in 1995, Irwin was Rookie of the Year, and in his second year he finished second after four tournament wins. In 1997 there were

another nine wins, and Irwin continues to go from strength to strength.

Did You Know?

One of Hale Irwin's most memorable golfing moments came in a US Tour event in 1973, when Irwin's shot landed in a spectator's bra. Technically he was allowed to retrieve the ball, but it was decided that the lady could remove it herself.

ITALY

ITALY HAS never been a major force in world golf, and Constantino Rocca is probably the most famous golfer that the country has produced. Italy did finish third in the World Cup in 1968, however, and again in 1982. Rocca has become a favourite in Europe as a result of his emotions in the Ryder Cup – he burst into tears after his 1993 defeat.

Top Italian Courses

Biella, Biella
Castelconturbia, Conturbia
I Roveri, Turin
Milano, Monza
Villa D'Este, Como

Contact

Italian Golf Federation, Viale Tiziano 74, 00196 Rome

TONY JACKLIN

Born: Scunthorpe, England – 07/07/1944
First European Tour: 1963
Highest Ranking: 5 (1966)
European Tour Wins: 14
First US Tour: 1967
US Tour Wins: 3
Major Wins: 2 (British Open 1969, US Open 1970)
Ryder Cup Appearances: 7

AT THE END of the 1960s and the beginning of the 1970s, Jacklin was the darling of British golf. In retrospect his record does not look stunning – and in many ways he never reached his true potential – but for golfers of two different generations he will be remembered for two things: winning the British and US Opens in the 1960s and 1970s, and transforming the Ryder Cup in the 1980s.

● JACKLIN WON the British Open in 1969 with a textbook final hole at Royal Lytham, a beautifully-played par four seeing him home by two shots from New Zealander Bob Charles.

● IN 1970 Jacklin briefly held both US and British Open titles. His US Open win in 1970 made him the first English US Open winner for 50 years. He achieved it with remarkable statistics as well, leading by one shot after the first round, by two on the second day, by three on the third, and eventually triumphing by seven strokes.

● IT WAS his last major triumph, as Jacklin never really fulfilled his promise. In 1972 Jacklin fought a great battle with Lee Trevino at Muirfield, and many believe this unlucky

defeat signalled the start of his decline.
● FOR ALL OF Jacklin's potential, he never finished better than fifth in the European Order of Merit. This is because he concentrated on the US Tour, in the belief that the experience would aid him in his major challenges.

● TO MODERN golf fans it is Jacklin's exploits as the Ryder Cup captain for which he is best known. Having competed in seven successive Ryder Cups as a player from 1967, Jacklin took over as a non-playing captain in 1983. After meticulous preparation, the European team lost by a

single point at the National Golf Club in Florida. Two years later they won the title amidst historic scenes at The Belfry, and they retained the cup at Muirfield Village in 1987. And in 1989, after halving the return match at The Belfry, they kept the trophy once more.

Tony Jacklin has provided two of British golf's proudest moments, one as a player, another as a captain.

JOHN JACOBS

Born: Lindrick, North Yorkshire – 1925

IT IS DIFFICULT to know where to pigeonhole John Jacobs. He was a tournament player for some time, and competed in the Ryder Cup. He was also a writer and coach, but he is best known as the man who set up the European Golf Tour in 1972, becoming Director General as the tour took shape under his guidance.

● FROM THERE, he went on to design golf courses, including the Edinburgh at Wentworth, with the help of Gary Player.

● JACOBS is not to be confused with his namesake who played on the US Tour from 1968 until 1980 without recording a victory.

PETER JACOBSEN

Born: Portland, OR, USA – 04/03/1954

First US Tour: 1977

Highest Ranking: 7 (1995)

US Tour Wins: 6

Major Wins: 0

Ryder Cup Appearances: 2

Tour Earnings: $4,969,691

AMIABLE PETER JACOBSEN is a true character in American golf, and his ability to imitate players' mannerisms and swings is legendary.

● IN A CAREER that has been hampered by injury, Peter Jacobsen's best years have been a decade apart. His best year on tour was in 1984, when he finished tenth, and he played in the Ryder Cup the following year. Ten years on, however, he again played in the Ryder Cup and this time finished seventh in the Money List, winning over a million dollars.

● KNOWN FOR his sense of fun, Peter Jacobsen once bet playing partner Scott Simpson in a practice round that his caddie could beat Simpson on a hole – the eighth at the Hazeltine National Golf Club. His caddie's drive landed 2.4m (8 ft) from the flag, nearer than Simpson's. The pro holed out for a two, however, and the caddie missed his putt. Jacobsen lost the bet and had to carry his own clubs over the hole.

MARK JAMES

Born: Manchester, England – 28/10/1953

First European Tour: 1976

Highest Ranking: 3 (1979)

European Tour Wins: 18

Major Wins: 0

Ryder Cup Appearances: 7

Tour Earnings: £2,486,754

DEADPAN and serious on the course, Mark James is, along with fellow Brits Woosnam and Torrance, one of the most convivial and gregarious players on tour when he reaches the clubhouse.

● A GREAT team player, James has appeared in seven Ryder Cup teams. He previously represented Great Britain and Ireland in the Walker Cup, after a distinguished amateur career which included winning the English Amateur Championship and reaching the final of the British Amateur Championship.

● CONSISTENT on the European Tour without ever really threatening to land a major, James again made the top 20 money earners in 1997, and recorded his 18th victory by winning the Spanish Open.

BETTY JAMESON

Born: Norman, OK, USA – 19/05/1919

First LPGA Tour: 1948

Tour Wins: 10

Major Wins: 1 (US Open 1947)

Tour Earnings: $91,740

AFTER A successful career as an amateur, Jameson was one of the three women players (along with Patty Berg and Babe Zaharias) who started the LPGA Tour in 1948. She was one of the foremost players in America throughout the 1940s and 1950s.

● AS AN AMATEUR, Jameson won the US Women's Amateur Championship in 1939 and 1940. In 1947 she added the US Women's Open, having finished as runner-up the previous year. It was the only major that Jameson managed, although she was again runner-up in the US Open in 1948 and 1952, and also won the Western Open (then considered a major championship) in 1954.

Peter Jacobsen has almost $5 million in earnings, so he can afford to smile.

1993 US Open winner Lee Janzen wonders where his next win is coming from.

JAPAN

GOLF CAME to Japan in 1903 when Arthur Groom started a course at the spectacular Mount Rokko. Japan is absolutely crazy about golf and their own lucrative Japanese Tour means that few players venture abroad. Only Tommy Nakajima, 'Jumbo' Ozaki and Isao Aoki have made any sort of impact on the world stage.

● LACK OF suitable space means that the number of Japanese courses is limited and membership very expensive as a result. One ingenious solution to this is two-tiered floodlit driving ranges, which can house hundreds of practising golfers at any one time.

● TODAY GOLF is one of Japan's most popular sports and famous players are treated like royalty.

Major Japanese Competitions

Japan Open
Sumitomo Visa Taiheyo Masters
Dunlop Phoenix

Five Famous Japanese Players

Isao Aoki
Tommy Nakajima
Masashi 'Jumbo' Ozaki
Tomekichi Miyamoto
Torakicki (Pete) Nakamura

Top Japanese Courses

Biwako
Kasumigaseki
Ryugaski
Saitama Pref
Shimonoseki

Contact

Japan Golf Association, 606 6th Floor, Palace Building, Marunouchi, Chiyoda-ku, Tokyo

DON JANUARY

Born: Plainview, TX, USA – 20/11/1929
First US Tour: 1956
US Tour Wins: 10
Major Wins: 1 (US PGA 1967)
Ryder Cup appearances: 2
Tour Earnings: £1,140,925
First Senior Tour: 1980
Senior Tour wins: 22

NOW APPROACHING his 70th year, Don January is still a fixture on the Senior Tour, despite competing in fewer events. He is still capable of a top ten finish, but his days of winning a tournament appear on the wane. January was, however, the first man to win a Senior Tour event, when he bagged the 1980 Atlantic City Senior International. In 1990, January became eligible for the Super Seniors (for players 60 and over) and has won a record 33 victories.

Chipping in

'I like to smoke and drink, and I'm lazy. It's past time for me to train. I enjoy doing absolutely nothing and I'm pretty darn good at it.'

LEE JANZEN

Born: Austin, MN, USA – 28/08/1964
First US Tour: 1989
Highest Ranking: 3 (1995)
US Tour Wins: 7
Major Wins: 2 (US Open 1993, 1998)
Ryder Cup Appearances: 2
Tour Earnings: $5,337,930

WHEN JANZEN won the 1993 US Open in a straight battle with Payne Stewart at Baltusrol, his score of 272 equalled Jack Nicklaus's all-time low for the major. And despite criticism of the Baltusrol course as being too easy, his win was still a magnificent achievement.

● IN 1995, Janzen had his best year, and perhaps also his worst. Despite finishing the Tour in third place and winning $1,378,966 – then one of the ten highest totals in history – he was sensationally left out of the Ryder Cup team.

● SINCE 1995, Janzen has failed to win a single Tour event, but was recalled for the 1997 Ryder Cup, where he beat Olazabal in his singles match. His debut in 1993 had not been so sweet, losing at a crucial time to Europe's Colin Montgomerie.

● THIS YEAR, however, Janzen came from nowhere to win a second US Open.

THE JAPAN OPEN

First Played: 1927
Most Wins: 6 – Tomekichi Miyamoto
(1929, 1930, 1932, 1935, 1936, 1940)
Lowest 72-hole score: 270 –
Masashi 'Jumbo' Ozaki 1994

STARTED IN 1927, the Japan Open is dominated by the home nation, with only back-to-back wins by Seve Ballesteros in 1977 and 78 and Craig Parry's win in 1997 breaking Japanese dominance in the last 20 years.

Last 20 Winners

Year	Winner	Score	Year	Winner	Score
1977	S Ballesteros	284	1987	I Aoki	279
1978	S Ballesteros	281	1988	M Ozaki	288
1979	K Chie-Hsiung	285	1990	T Nakajima	281
1980	K Kikuchi	296	1991	T Nakajima	290
1981	Y Hagawa	280	1992	M Ozaki	277
1982	A Yabe	277	1993	S Okuda	281
1983	I Aoki	281	1994	M Ozaki	270
1984	K Uehara	283	1995	T Izawa	277
1985	T Nakajima	285	1996	P Teravainen	282
1986	T Nakajima	284	1997	C Parry	286

PER ULRIK JOHANSSON

Born: Uppsala, Sweden – 06/12/1966
First European Tour: 1991
Highest Ranking: 11 (1997)
European Tour Wins: 5
Major Wins: 0
Ryder Cup Appearances: 2
Tour Earnings: £1,533,231

THE GOOD-LOOKING Swede continued his strong form in 1997 by finishing just outside Europe's top ten money winners, the English and European Opens contributing towards his 11th place.

● IN 1995 Johansson became only the second Swede ever to take part in the Ryder Cup, and his victory over Davis Love III in 1997 has probably secured his place in the 1999 team.

● HIS GIRLFRIEND also attracted attention at the tournament, with her painted finger nails, displaying the Swedish flag, often held over her mouth in trepidation.

THE JOHNNIE WALKER WORLD CHAMPIONSHIP

First Played: 1991
Most wins: 2 – Fred Couples (1991, 1995)
Lowest 72-hole score: 266 – Larry Mize 1993

THE JOHNNIE WALKER was played between 1991 and 1995 and was a highlight on the Tour calendar, mainly because of the quality of the field. Normally 28 players took part, with players qualifying either by winning one of the designated tournaments, or by invitation. It was held at Tryall, Jamaica, but was discontinued in 1995.

Roll of honour

1991	Fred Couples	281
1992	Nick Faldo	* 274
1993	Larry Mize	266
1994	Ernie Els	268
1995	Fred Couples	* 279

* after play-off

BOBBY JONES

Born: Atlanta, GA, USA – 17/03/1902
Career Spanned: 1916 – 1930
Major Amateur Wins: 6 (British Amateur Championship 1930, US Amateur Championship 1924, 1925, 1927, 1928, 1930)
Major Wins: 7 (British Open 1926, 1927, 1930, US Open 1923, 1926, 1929, 1930)

BOBBY JONES is possibly the greatest golfer of all time. Only Jack Nicklaus has won more majors, and that in a career over twice the length. Jones entered just over fifty tournaments before his retirement in 1930 at the age of 28, and won almost half of them. In 1930 he became the only player, before or since, to have won both the British and US Amateur Championships and the British and US Opens.

● JONES' first success came at the age of 14, when he qualified for the US Amateur Championship. Eight years later at the age

Chipping in

'You have to study it, and the more you study, the more you learn. The more you learn, the more you study it.'

Bobby Jones wins the 1927 British Open with a record score at St Andrews.

of 22 he won the tournament. By then he had already won the US Open, a tournament he was to win another three times.

● JONES's first British Open win came in 1926. He first appeared as a nineteen-year-old in 1921, but ripped up his card after some disastrous scoring. He only returned in 1926 because he was on tour with the Walker Cup side. A year later he returned to St Andrews under his own steam and defended his title successfully.

● HIS GREATEST success came in 1930 when he completed his unique Grand Slam by winning the US Amateur at Merion. He then retired to play golf for fun and enjoy his summers in Atlanta.

● JONES SUFFERED terribly in later years from a disease which affects the spinal column. He died at the age of 69, brave until the very end. Jones was a remarkable player and a remarkable man.

STEVE JONES

Born: Artesia, NM, USA – 27/12/1958
First US Tour: 1982
Highest Ranking: 8 (1989)
US Tour Wins: 7
Major Wins: 1 (US Open 1996)
Ryder Cup appearances: 0
Tour Earnings: $3,902,392

STEVE JONES is one of the only US Open winners in recent times not to have taken part in the Ryder Cup, mainly due to circumstance and timing. In 1989, Jones recorded three wins in his best-ever season, finishing eighth on the Money List. In 1991 his form had dropped off somewhat, before a dirt bike accident effectively put him out of the game for three years.

● THE ACCIDENT meant that Jones could no longer grip a club in the normal way and so he had to implement an overlapping grip normally used for putting. The 1996 US Open was his first major since the 1991 British Open. He won it, beating playing partner Tom Lehman on the final green at Oakland Hills.

● JONES CONTINUED his rehabilitation in 1997 when he finished 20th on the US Tour, winning the Canadian and Phoenix Opens.

ROBERT KARLSSON

Born: St Malm, Sweden – 03/09/1969
First European Tour: 1991
Highest Ranking: 10 (1997)
European Tour Wins: 2
Major Wins: 0
Ryder Cup Appearances: 0
Tour Earnings: £1,069,720

KARLSSON CAME to prominence in 1992 when he came fifth in the British Open at the age of 22. Two months later he finished second to Nick Faldo in the European Open at Sunningdale.

Steve Jones with the four most important things in his life – US Open trophy, wife and kids.

● KARLSSON HAD his greatest year to date in 1997, winning the BMW International and finishing tenth on the European Money List with £364,542. Still only 27, there looks to be a big career ahead for the huge Swede.

KASUMIGASEKI

Where: Japan
Par: 72
Yardage: 6,959
Opened: 1929
Designer: Kinya Fujita
Events Staged: Canada Cup 1957 (now World Cup)

KASUMIGASEKI was designed by Kinya Fujita, and Hugh Alison, famous for his work in the Far East, was called in to make a few changes. It has not staged a Japanese Open in over 25 years, but is still the pride of Japanese golf, with over 2000 members and a history steeped in national pride.

● IN 1957, Kasumigaseki was host to the Canada Cup – later to become the World Cup – and Japan announced their intentions as a major force in world golf by winning. Torakichi Nakamura and Koichi Ono were the Japanese pairing which beat, amongst others, Americans Sam Snead and Jimmy Demaret.

● THE COURSE has a very European feel to it, with little water and much surrounding woodland. The East course is famous for its tenth hole, which has two tees and two greens, which are used alternately between summer and winter. A second West course has recently been added to cope with the increased demand for membership.

K

KIAWAH ISLAND

Where: South Carolina, USA
Par: 72
Yardage: 6,552
Opened: 1998/1991
Designer: Tom Fazio/Pete Dye
Events staged: Ryder Cup 1993

KIAWAH ISLAND in South Carolina has two courses: Osprey Point, which was opened in 1988 and designed by Tom Fazio; and The Ocean Course, designed by Pete Dye and opened in 1991.

● KIAWAH ISLAND is ten miles long by a mile and a half wide, and every hole has the Atlantic Ocean on one side and marshland on the other. Dye assembled a links-style course which was one of the greatest achievements in American course design for years. It was not appealing to everyone, however, and many golfers have criticised the severe greens. David Feherty commented that is was 'not like something from Scotland or Ireland, more like something from Mars.'

● IT WAS OPENED in 1991 and staged the Ryder Cup that year – the so-called 'War on the Shore'. It was a thrilling encounter, with the US winning the cup by a single point. Bernhard Langer missed a putt against Hale Irwin at the final hole and the European team, captained by Bernard Gallacher, relinquished their title.

If Betsy King ever contemplated giving up golf, dancing could be the next move.

BETSY KING

Born: Reading, PA, USA – 13/08/1955
First LPGA Tour: 1977
Highest Ranking: 1 (1984, 1989, 1993)
Tour Wins: 31
Major Wins: 6 (US Open 1989, 1990, US LPGA 1992, Dinah Shore 1987, 1990, 1997)
Tour Earnings: $5.3 million

BETSY KING is one of the greatest female golfers the world has ever seen, and certainly one of the richest. In 1995 she became the first female professional to pass the $5 million mark in earnings. She has also topped the Ladies Money List three times, in 1984, 1989 and 1993, as well as finishing second another three times. From 1984 until 1995 she was never out of the top ten earners.

● KING CAME to prominence with her top ten finish in the 1976 US Open. She turned professional a year later, but it was 1981 before she won on the Tour. She then rebuilt her swing, with the help of Ed Oldfield, and it was 1984 before things came right for her again. She has been amongst the top ten women professionals in the world ever since.

● IN 1987, King won the Dinah Shore, and at the beginning of the 1990s her career moved into a higher gear. King won the Dinah Shore again in 1990, and then won the US Open two years running. Stuck on 29 US Tour wins, she finally gained entry to the Hall of Fame with her 30th win in 1995.

● IN 1997, ten years after her first major win, King won the Dinah Shore for the third time, thus equalling Amy Alcott's achievement.

TOM KITE

Born: Austin, TX, USA – 09/12/1949
First US Tour: 1972
Highest Ranking: 1 (1981, 1989)
US Tour Wins: 19
Major Wins: 1 (US Open 1992)
Ryder Cup Appearances: 7
Tour Earnings: $10.2 million

AFTER YEARS of being described as the best player never to win a major, Tom Kite finally won the US Open in 1992 at Pebble Beach 20 years after joining the US Tour.

● UNTIL HE WAS passed by Greg Norman in 1995, Kite was the biggest money winner of all time. Were it not for a back condition diagnosed in 1993, he might still have been ahead. Since then, however, he has failed to win a tournament, but with the Senior Tour imminent, the gateway to further riches must be tempting.

● KITE IS A consistent player, amassing his great wealth with relatively few victories compared to the great champions. Not a big man, Kite has never relied on his driver, but is great with a wedge, often carrying a selection in his bag.

● IN ADDITION to his US wins, Kite also won the European Open in 1980, and has

L

racked up numerous other honours, including Rookie of the Year in 1973 and PGA Player of the Year in 1989.

● PERHAPS HIS greatest honour, however, was captaining the US Ryder Cup team at Valderrama in 1997, following his seven Ryder Cup campaigns as a player.

LADIES PGA

THE LPGA Tour was first run in 1950, almost six years after Betty Hicks founded the Women's Professional Golfers' Association, the forerunner of the LPGA. The prize money at the time totalled $50,000 – less than one twentieth of the money Karrie Webb alone received last year. The first winner of the Tour was Babe Zaharias, who won over a quarter of the total prize money on offer.

● THESE DAYS the LPGA budget for Tour prizes is over £$30 million, and players compete in 30 tournaments. In 1996, Karrie Webb was the first to break the $1 million barrier in a season – previously the record had been the $863,578 which was earned by Beth Danial in 1990.

● LAURA DAVIES was the first European winner in 1994, and she was followed in 1995 by the Swede, Annika Sorenstam. Kathy Whitworth has finished at the top of the Ladies Money List on eight occasions, a record. From 1965 until 1973, she only missed out on the top spot once, in 1969.

LPGA Last 16 Leading Money Winners

1982	JoAnne Carner	1990	Beth Daniel
1983	JoAnne Carner	1991	Pat Bradley
1984	Betsy King	1992	Dottie Mochrie
1985	Nancy Lopez	1993	Betsy King
1986	Pat Bradley	1994	Laura Davies
1987	Ayako Okamoto	1995	Annika Sorenstam
1988	Sherri Turner	1996	Karrie Webb
1989	Betsy King	1997	Annika Sorenstam

JOHNNY LAIDLAY

JOHNNY LAIDLAY should perhaps be a more famous figure than he actually is, as he was responsible for inventing what came to be known as the Vardon grip. This method, later adopted by the more famous Harry Vardon, involves the little finger of the right hand riding over the index finger of the left.

● LAIDLAY WAS himself no mean player, however, winning the British Amateur Championship twice, in 1889 and 1891. Indeed, between the years of 1887 and 1895, either John Ball or himself were always in a British Amateur Final. There has been some suggestion that Laidlay actually learnt the grip from Harry Vardon, but as Laidlay was ten years senior to Vardon, and adopted the grip as a 20-year-old, this is extremely doubtful.

Greg Norman may have overtaken him in the money list, but with over $10 million in the bank, Tom Kite can afford to miss the odd putt.

BERNHARD LANGER

Born: Anhausen, Germany – 27/08/1957

First European Tour: 1974

Highest Ranking: 1 (1981, 1984)

European Tour Wins: 37

Major Wins: 2 (US Masters 1985, 1993)

Ryder Cup Appearances: 9

Tour Earnings: £4,816,882

BERNHARD LANGER is considered to be one of the best golfers in the world. The first golfer from Germany to have succeeded at a major level, he has done much to increase the profile of the sport in his own country. He finished second to Colin Montgomerie on the 1997 European Tour and was instrumental in Europe's Ryder Cup victory at Valderrama.

● LANGER IS a very philosophical golfer, and it is this which has perhaps helped him overcome three complete breakdowns in his putting ability. He has experimented with various clubs and grips over the years and has recovered to become one of the most consistent players in the world. Indeed Langer was the number one player in the world when the Sony rankings were first introduced in 1986.

● LANGER HAS won tournaments in many countries, but his greatest triumphs have come in the US Masters at Augusta. In 1985, a bogey five was enough to take the title at the final hole. Eight years later his margin of victory was more impressive. He won the 1993 US Masters by four strokes and three-putted only twice. He again bogeyed the final hole, but it was one of only six he made all week.

● PERHAPS Langer's worst moment came in 1991 in the Ryder Cup tournament at Kiawah Island. Langer missed the putt from 2.4m (8 ft) which gave America the trophy. It was an incredibly difficult putt, but one which many put down to Langer's

Bernhard Langer at Wentworth in the 1997 Volvo PGA Championship.

occasional putting problems. Langer remains one of the world's greatest players, and it is perhaps surprising that he has not competed more on the US Tour.

DAVID LEADBETTER

THE TALL and imposing Leadbetter was a player on the European Tour in the 1970s. He failed to make an impression of any note, but it is as a coach that he has made his mark in the world of golf, notably with his star pupil Nick Faldo.

● LEADBETTER had already had some success coaching Nick Price when Faldo turned to him after losing under pressure in the majors. They decided that Faldo's swing should be remodelled, and so Leadbetter prepared his now famous practice routines, having filmed Faldo and studied his swing for faults. As a result, Faldo became the greatest British player of his generation.

LEFT-HANDERS

THERE ARE only really two left-handed players that have achieved success on the world golfing stage, Bob Charles and Phil Mickelson.

● BOB CHARLES is probably the greatest left-handed player of all time, although he is actually right-handed. He only started playing golf left-handed because his parents' left-handed clubs were the only ones available.

● CHARLES REMAINS the only left-hander to have won a major, although Phil Mickelson will surely change that one day. The brilliant young American was second on the Money List in 1996 and has already appeared in two Ryder Cups. A second major triumph for left-handers cannot be far away.

TOM LEHMAN

Born: Austin, MO, USA – 07/03/1959	
First US Tour: 1983	
Highest Ranking: 1 (1996)	
US Tour Wins: 4	
Major Wins: 1 (British Open 1996)	
Ryder Cup Appearances: 2	
Tour Earnings: $5,826,271	

AFTER PLAYING on the mini tours for years, Lehman finally made his breakthrough on the PGA Tour with a win in 1994. By 1996 he was the leading money winner on the Tour, and the first American to win the British Open at Royal Lytham since Bobby Jones in 1926.

● LEHMAN LED the 1994 Masters going into the last round, before losing out to Olazabal, and also led the US Open in 1995 and 1996 going into the final round.

● IN 1996, Lehman was not only the top US money winner, he also finished second to Greg Norman in the World Rankings, and won the Vardon Trophy for best scoring averages, together with the Player of the Year trophy.

Lehman in great spirits as he holes out in the 1997 Ryder Cup. His joy was short-lived.

TONY LEMA

Born: Oakland, CA, USA – 25/02/1934	
First US Tour: 1957	
Worldwide Wins: 16	
Major Wins: 1 (British Open 1964)	
Ryder Cup Appearances: 2	

KNOWN AS Champagne Tony, Lema got his nickname after winning a small tournament, the Orange Country, in 1962. On the third day, he promised everyone at the club he would buy them champagne if

they won. And despite the low prize money he was true to his word. The press picked up on the champagne party, and from then on wherever Lema won, the champagne would flow.

● TONY LEMA's only major success came in the 1964 British Open. His win at St Andrews by five strokes from Nicklaus was remarkable, as Lema had never played in the British Open before, and it was his first time at St Andrews, having never played a links course.

● IF THAT WAS Lema's most famous victory, his most famous defeat is even more well documented. Seven holes up with 17 holes to play in the World Matchplay Championship in 1965, Lema managed to lose to Gary Player.

● TONY LEMA died in a plane crash between tournaments in 1966.

JUSTIN LEONARD

Born: Dallas, TX, USA – 15/06/1972

First US Tour: 1994

Highest Ranking: 5 (1997)

US Tour Wins: 3

Major Wins: 1 (British Open 1997)

Ryder Cup Appearances: 1

Tour Earnings: $3,419,877

AT ONLY 26 years of age, Leonard is one of the next wave of young American golfers who look set to sustain the US as the world's strongest golfing nation well into the 21st century.
● IN 1996 Leonard made his name on the world stage when he won the British Open, winning a lot of friends with his dignified play and easy manner. Leonard made his Ryder Cup debut in 1997 and looks destined to become one of the world's greatest players.

BRUCE LIETZKE

Born: Kansas City, KS, USA – 18/07/1951

First US Tour: 1975

Highest Ranking: 4 (1981)

US Tour Wins: 13

Major Wins: 0

Ryder Cup Appearances: 1

Tour Earnings: $5.8 million

SINCE LIETZKE, by his own admission, discovered something more interesting than golf – his wife – his interest in golf has waned, and he devotes as much time as possible to his family life. He enters tournaments whenever he feels they are necessary, and his last win came in 1994. In 1996 he was 150th on the Money List, dropping outside this last year.
● IT WAS during his early years that Lietzke was at his best, with his biggest career win coming in 1982, the Canadian Open. The closest he has come to a major was in 1991 when he lost by three strokes to John Daly in the US PGA.

LIGHTNING

IN 1975, LEE TREVINO was one of three golfers struck during the Western Open. Trevino suffered a back injury and was out of the game for some time. One of his playing partners Jerry Heard was less fortunate, and his career was virtually ended.
● ALL OF THEM were relatively fortunate, however, compared to the two spectators

who died at golf tournaments in 1991. One spectator was killed at the Hazeltine National Golf Club as the US Open took place, and then two months later another died after a strike while watching the US PGA at Crooked Stick.
● IN 1964, Tottenham footballer John White was killed by lightning while sheltering under a tree on his local golf course.

LINKS

A LINKS COURSE is one which is laid out in an elongated shape, along the coast, on the land between the sea and cultivated land.

Bruce Lietzke must surely be a keen gardener when he's not on the course.

LAWSON LITTLE

Born: Newport, RI, USA – 23/06/1910

First US Tour: 1935

US Tour Wins: 7

Major Wins: 1 (US Open 1940)

Major Amateur Wins: 4 (British Amateur Championship 1934, 1935, US Amateur Championship 1934, 1935)

A LEADING AMATEUR in the 1930s, little was pretty much unbeatable in 1934 and 1935. He won the Amateur Championships on both sides of the Atlantic in 1934, and successfully defended both titles the following year. Such prodigious play convinced him to turn pro, and five years later he won the US Open, beating Gene Sarazen in a play-off.

GENE LITTLER

Born: San Diego, CA, USA – 21/07/1930

First US Tour: 1954

US Tour Wins: 29

Tour Earnings: $1.5 million

First Senior Tour: 1981

Senior Tour Wins: 8

Senior Tour Earnings: $2,044,991

Major Wins: 1 (US Open 1961)

Ryder Cup Appearances: 7

GENE LITTLER had an almost perfect swing, and had it been coupled with any sort of ambition he may well have become a player of the calibre of Nicklaus or Palmer – as it was he was content to be merely a great player.
● LITTLER WAS US Amateur Champion in 1953, and won a US Tour event as an amateur the following year, prompting him to turn professional. He then won another four Tour events in his first year and was runner-up in the 1954 US Open.
● GENE THE MACHINE, as Littler was known, went on to win almost 30 events

on the PGA Tour, but his 1961 US Open win was his only major. He was a poor play-off golfer, losing ten out of the 14 he contested in his career, including play-offs in the 1970 US Masters and 1977 US PGA against Billy Casper and Lanny Wadkins respectively.

● AFTER RECOVERING from cancer in 1972, Littler regained a place on the US Tour and has had a successful career on the Senior Tour, which he helped form. Now aged 68, Littler's last win came in the 1989 Aetna Challenge.

BOBBY LOCKE

Born: Germiston, South Africa – 20/11/1917
First US Tour: 1947
Highest Ranking: 2 (1947)
US Tour Wins: 11
Major Wins: 4 (British Open 1949, 1950, 1952, 1957)

BOBBY LOCKE was the first South African to make his mark on international golf. Born Arthur D'Arcy Locke, he took the name Bobby after his hero Bobby Jones. Like Jones he insisted on hooking every shot he played, but had great control over the ball. He was also a supremely confident putter.

● ALWAYS a man out of step with his peers, Locke wore grey or navy plus-fours when the fashion was for bright colours. He was called Old Muffin Face by the Americans and his dry wit was not always endearing. Eventually the USA banned him from the tour, allegedly for no other reason than that he was a foreigner winning their money!

● HE THEN turned to Europe, becoming four-times Open Champion. In twelve years playing in the Open, he was six times in the top two. His last win came at St Andrews in 1957, when he denied Peter Thomson the championship which would have given him four titles in a row.

● DURING THE 1940s and 1950s, Locke was successful throughout the world, winning the South African Open nine times. He also took on the American Champion

Sam Snead in a series of matches in his home country, winning 12 of the 16 encounters.

● VISITING his wife after the birth of their child, Locke's car was hit by a train on a level crossing, and he was unconscious for several days, eventually losing his sight in one eye. Locke nevertheless returned to golf, but his competitive career was over.

LOCH LOMOND

Where: Luss, Stirling, Scotland
Par: 71
Yardage: 7,060
Opened: 1995
Designer: Tom Weiskopf and Jay Morrish
Events staged: Standard Life Loch Lomond every year since 1994

THE COURSE at Loch Lomond was designed by the successful partnership of Jay Morrish and Tom Weiskopf. Based on the banks of the Loch, it is a stunning course, and a favourite of players the world over.

● SINCE 1996 it has hosted the Standard Life Loch Lomond Tournament (now the Gulfstream World Invitational), which has rapidly become one of the most important on the European golf calendar. The event is held the week before the British Open and

in 1997 was won by Tom Lehman.

● IN THE 1998 tournament there is an additional prize for winning both the Loch Lomond and the British Open. As well as the two first prizes of £141,666 and £300,000 respectively, a double winner would pick up a bonus of $1 million which has been underwritten by the event's sponsors.

NANCY LOPEZ

Born: Torrance, CA, USA – 06/01/1957
First LPGA Tour: 1977
Highest Ranking: 1 (1978, 1979, 1985)
Tour Wins: 47
Major Wins: 3 (US LPGA 1978, 1985, 1989)
Tour Earnings: $4 million

NANCY LOPEZ is not the most successful female golfer ever, but she is certainly one of the most famous. She was always likely to be a great golfer, having won a state championship at the age of 12. She then won the USGA Junior Girls Championship twice, and while still a senior at high school tied for third in the US Women's Open.

● IN HER 20 years on Tour, Lopez has recorded 47 victories and has only missed out on a trophy for four of those years, one of which was spent having a baby.

● NANCY LOPEZ has won the US LPGA three times, but despite coming close has never won the US Women's Open. She was voted Rolex Player of the Year in 1978, 1979, 1985 and 1988.

● CURRENTLY RESIDING just inside the Top 30, Lopez now devotes much of her time to family life, but is still capable of tournament victories.

Nancy Lopez must have a bad lie if she's looking for her ball in this shot.

Bobby Locke at the 1962 World Matchplay.

DAVIS LOVE III

Born: Charlotte, NC, USA – 13/04/1964

First US Tour: 1986

Highest Ranking: 2 (1992)

US Tour Wins: 12

Major Wins: 1 (US PGA 1997)

Ryder Cup Appearances: 3

Tour Earnings: $8,470,982

DAVIS LOVE had a great year in 1997, finishing third on the Money List, winning over $1.6 million, and the US PGA Championship. Love also made his third Ryder Cup appearance on the trot – but lost all of his four matches.

● LOVE TURNED pro in 1985, and won his first Tour event in 1987. In 1992 he won three events and finished second on the money list.

● ALWAYS caddied for by his brother Mark, Davis Love III is one of the biggest drivers in the game. Along with Fred Couples he has won the World Cup title a record four successive times.

My other home is a castle, says Davis Love III.

SANDY LYLE

Born: Shrewsbury, England – 09/02/1958

First European Tour: 1978

Highest Ranking: 1 (1979, 1980, 1985)

European Tour Wins: 17

Major Wins: 2 (British Open 1985, US Masters 1988)

Ryder Cup Appearances: 5

THE 1990s have not been kind to Lyle. In 1988 he was second in the Sony World Rankings and had just won the US Masters. He also won three times on the US Tour, and defeated Nick Faldo in the final of the World Matchplay Championship at Wentworth, having beaten Seve Ballesteros in the semis.

● A YEAR EARLIER, Lyle had become the first European player to win the Players Championship at Sawgrass, and had made his fifth Ryder Cup appearance. Lyle burst onto the scene as a young man when, at 17, he was the youngest ever winner of the Brabazon Trophy (the English Open Amateur Strokeplay Championship).

● HE PLAYED in the Walker Cup in 1977 and turned pro the same year. Nick Faldo

became his natural rival, and although Lyle was the first to secure victory in the majors, Faldo has since overtaken him.

● LYLE WON his Open at St Georges in 1985 – he was the first British winner since Tony Jacklin in 1969.

● SINCE HIS success in the 1980s, Lyle's best golf seems to be behind him, his win in the 1992 Volvo Masters at Valderrama being his last notable success.

MARK McCORMACK

NOW ONE OF golf's most powerful agents, creative business visionary and entrepreneurial workaholic Mark McCormack formed a small promotions company in the early 1960s with less than $1000. Today he runs a sports and entertainment promotion and media conglomerate worth billions.

● MCCORMACK's first big coup was to form a partnership with Arnold Palmer and act as his agent. He followed that by managing Nicklaus and Player, and between them it seemed that McCormack's 'Big Three' won every tournament going during the 1960s.

● MCCORMACK WAS a reasonable golfer

himself, qualifying for a handful of US Amateur Championships and even once qualifying for the US Open, but it was on the fringes of the sport that the Yale law graduate has made his mark. As his company IMG (International Management Group) has grown, he has continued to concentrate his efforts on golf – IMG manages Montgomerie, Langer and Woosnam, and promotes events such as the Toyota World Matchplay Championship and various tournaments on the PGA European Tours.

MARK McCUMBER

Born: Jacksonville, FL, USA – 07/09/1951
First US Tour: 1978
Highest Ranking: 3 (1994)
US Tour Wins: 10
Major Wins: 0
Ryder Cup Appearances: 1
Tour Earnings: $6 million

MARK McCUMBER is a veteran of some 20 US Tours, has appeared in the Ryder Cup, and won the World Cup for the US with Ben Crenshaw in 1988.

● MCCUMBER's US Tour wins have spanned some 17 years, from his first in 1979 to the latest in 1994. That year he won three tournaments and came third on the Money Winners list with some $1,208,209. Although he has never won a major, he has been successful in other ways, running a course design business with his brothers.

● In 1984 he won a car for his hole-in-one at the Honda Classic, commenting: 'They ought to give away the car for hitting the green at all.'

JOHNNY McDERMOTT

Born: Philadelphia, PA, USA – 1891
Career Spanned: 1909 – 1915
Major Wins: 2 (US Open 1911, 1912)

JOHNNY McDERMOTT's story is short, and anything but sweet. An intense young man, McDermott would practise endlessly. He apparently used to try to stop his ball on an open newspaper placed on the driving range – and rumour has it he would be annoyed if it landed on the wrong paragraph!

● AS AN 18-year-old, he lost the US Open in a play-off, but the following year became the tournament's youngest, and first American-born, winner. He retained the trophy in 1912, and in 1913 beat Harry Vardon by some 13 shots in another US tournament.

● IN 1914 he headed home after a disastrous British Open in which he missed his tee-off time. The ship he was travelling on collided with another, and although a lifeboat saw McDermott to safety, he was deeply affected by the accident. He never won another tournament, and indeed spent the rest of his life in and out of rest

They say the best deals are done on the golf course. Mark McCormack should know.

homes after suffering a complete mental breakdown.

CHARLES MACDONALD

Born: Niagara Falls, NY, USA – 1856
Major Amateur Wins: 1 (US Amateur Championship 1895)

BORN IN AMERICA, Charles MacDonald developed his love of golf while studying at university in St Andrews. Upon returning to America he realised that

enthusiasm for the sport in America did not match his love of the game, and set about changing things – in many ways he was one of the most important figures in shaping the game in the US.

● AS A PLAYER he was accomplished, but not brilliant. He was the first winner of the US Amateur Championship, but that was as much due to circumstance and the lack of decent opposition as to his own abilities.

● HIS GREATEST contribution to golf was as an architect, and he was responsible for one of the earliest courses in America, built in Chicago. His lasting monument is the National Golf Links at Long Island.

● A GRUFF MAN, his courses were as testing as his personality. He was especially fond of bunkers and the way they penalised a player, and he often said that he would rather have a herd of elephants run through a bunker than have it raked.

PAUL McGINLEY

Born: Dublin, Ireland – 16/12/1966
First European Tour: 1992
Highest Ranking: 15 (1996)
European Tour Wins: 2
Tour Earnings: £918,620

FORMER Irish Amateur Champion and Walker Cup player, McGinley turned pro in 1991 and has since earned almost £1m. With two European wins to his name, the last coming in 1997, McGinley is one to watch in the future.

Together with Padraig Harrington, Paul McGinley won the World Cup for Ireland.

Like his recent form, Mark McNulty looks wobbly during the 1997 British Open.

DR ALISTER MACKENZIE

DR ALISTER MACKENZIE was a multi-talented man, who made his mark on the world of golf as a course architect. Born in Yorkshire to Scottish parents, Dr Mackenzie became a practicing GP after serving as a surgeon in the Boer War.

● HE FIRST turned to golf as a hobby, and his ideas for greens and fairways were sparked by his interest in camouflage techniques, cultivated while serving in South Africa. When Harry Colt stayed with Mackenzie at his local club, Alwoodley in Leeds, he was so impressed with his work that he invited Mackenzie to join him in course design.

● MACKENZIE's medical career was put on a back burner, and finally abandoned after the doctor won first prize in a competition set up by his contemporary, Charles MacDonald, to design a two-shot hole at the Long Island course.

● IN THE 1920s, Mackenzie became a prolific designer. His work includes the Eden course at St Andrews, Royal Troon, Lahinch, Royal Melbourne and Cypress Point. In many ways, Mackenzie was the first international designer, and many of the principles set down in his book Golf Architecture are still adhered to today.

● MACKENZIE's final project, in partnership with Bobby Jones, was the design of the Augusta National course. Unfortunately he died just before its completion in 1934.

Chipping in

'A good golf course is like good music. It is not necessarily a course that appeals the first time you play it.'

MARK McNULTY

Born: Bindwa, Zimbabwe – 25/10/1953	
First European Tour: 1978	
Highest Ranking: 2 (1987, 1990)	
European Tour Wins: 15	
Major Wins: 0	
Tour Earnings: £2,621,557	

McNULTY IS AN old school friend of Nick Price, but has never equalled the feats of his fellow Zimbabwean. Success in the US has not been forthcoming, despite reasonable results on the European Tour, and the closest McNulty has come to a major was a second place to Nick Faldo in the 1990 British Open.

● McNULTY's wins, most of which were in the mid-1980s, include the Volvo Masters, South African Open and the Million Dollar Challenge. Last year, McNulty finished outside the top 50 in Europe and was without a win.

M

JEFF MAGGERT

Born: Columbia, MO, USA – 20/12/1964
First US Tour: 1986
Highest Ranking: 9 (1994)
US Tour Wins: 1
Ryder Cup Appearances: 2
Tour Earnings: $4,411,032

NEVER A THREAT in the majors, Maggert has nevertheless been a consistent performer, earning almost $5 million and competing in the two most recent Ryder Cups. Now in his 30s, a major may not yet have passed him by.

MAJORS

THERE ARE FOUR majors: the British Open, the US Open, the US Masters and the US PGA Championship. In terms of prestige, the British and American Opens are probably the most important competitions, followed by the US Masters and the US PGA. The Players Championship at Sawgrass is often referred to as the fifth major, but it has not yet officially attained that status.

The Major Competitions

British Open – First played 1860
US Open – First played 1895
US Masters – First played 1934
US PGA Championship – First played 1916

LLOYD MANGRUM

Born: Trenton, NJ, USA
First US Tour: 1940
Highest Ranking: 1 (1951)
US Tour Wins: 36
Major Wins: 1 (US Open 1946)
Ryder Cup Appearances: 5

LLOYD MANGRUM was a brave, determined man, both in golf and life. Injured in the Battle of the Bulge, he was awarded two Purple Hearts in 1944. This came a few years after he had made his mark on the world of golf with a round of 64 in the US Masters at Augusta, a record at the time.

● AFTER HE RETURNED from convalescence at St Andrews, he won his only major championship, the 1946 US Open. That was something of a battle in itself. Tying with Byron Nelson and Vic Ghezzi, all three were still square after an 18-hole play-off. Mangrum went on to win the second 18-hole play-off by a single shot.

● MANGRUM never repeated a major triumph, despite often coming close, but he remained near the top of the Tour list, and indeed topped it in the early 1950s.

● ANOTHER marathon play-off for Mangrum occurred three years later in the 1949 Motor City Open. In a sudden-death play-off with Gary Middlecoff, both were declared joint winners after bad light stopped them when level after 11 holes.

Did you know?

Lloyd Mangrum suffered an unlucky fate in the 1950 US Open when he spotted an insect on his ball. He picked the ball up and brushed off the insect, only to be penalised two shots. Mangrum finished second behind the eventual winner Ben Hogan.

BIGGEST VICTORY MARGINS

— 13 —
Tom Morris Snr –
1862 British Open
Prestwick
— 12 —
Tom Morris Jnr – 1870 British Open
Prestwick
Tiger Woods – 1997 US Masters Augusta
— 11 —
Willie Smith – 1899 US Open Baltimore
— 9 —
Jim Barnes – 1921 US Open Columbia

Since 1945
— 9 —
Jack Nicklaus – 1965 US Masters Augusta
— 8 —
Ray Floyd – 1976 US Masters Augusta
— 7 —
Cary Middlecoff – 1955 US Masters Augusta
Tony Jacklin – 1970 US Open Hazeltine National
Jack Nicklaus– 1980 US PGA Oak Hill
— 6 —
Ben Hogan – 1953 US Open Oakmont
Arnold Palmer – 1962 British Open Troon
Arnold Palmer – 1964 US Masters Augusta
Johnny Miller – 1976 British Open Royal Birkdale
Nick Price – 1994 US PGA Southern Hills

DAVE MARR

Born: Houston, TX, USA – 27/12/1933

AN INTELLIGENT and thoughtful golfer, Dave Marr won the US PGA Championship in 1965. He was a successful Ryder Cup player and non-playing captain of the US team, but it was as a commentator for American TV that Marr was best known, until his untimely death in 1997.

Despite a consistently successful career and almost $5 million in earnings, Jeff Maggert remains largely a man of mystery,

GRAHAM MARSH

Born: Kalgoorlie, Australia – 14/01/1944
European Tour Wins: 13
European Tour Earnings: £210,000
US Tour Wins: 1
Major Wins: 0
First Senior Tour: 1994
Senior Tour Wins: 3
Senior Tour Earnings: $2,366,041

NICKNAMED SWAMPY by his fellow players, Graham Marsh is the quieter brother of Australian cricketer Rodney.
● DESPITE NEVER having won a major championship, Marsh has been a winner all over the world. He has won 24 tournaments on the Japan PGA Tour, 15 events in Australasia, and another 16 in the US and Europe. His biggest wins have come in the European Open and World Matchplay Championships.
● IN 1994 Marsh started competing on the

Graham 'Swampy' Marsh shows the sort of emotion more usually seen in his brother Rodney.

US Senior Tour, winning three tournaments and finishing second in the US Senior Open. He is already one of the top 30 earners on the Senior Tour after only three years, and seems to have many more lucrative years ahead of him.

MATCHPLAY VS. STROKEPLAY

THE SIMPLE difference between matchplay and strokeplay is that in matchplay the result is based on the number of holes won, while in strokeplay the winner is the player who gets the lowest overall score over 18 holes. This means that a matchplay match does not always last for 18 holes. If, for instance, a player wins the first ten holes, then that is the end of the match, because the total cannot be bettered.
● IN THE MODERN era, strokeplay has replaced matchplay in the major championships, with the US PGA making the transition to strokeplay in 1958. Wentworth still hosts the World Matchplay Championship, however, and the Ryder Cup is still a matchplay competition.

WILD BILL MEHLHORN

WILD BILL MEHLHORN was not a hard-drinking, gun-slinging cowboy, as his name suggests, but an excellent golfer from the 1920s who supplemented his tournament play by teaching golf and selling subscriptions to golfing magazines.
● HE IS memorable not only for his name, but because of his brush with glory, losing to Walter Hagen

in the 1925 US PGA Championship. Perhaps he could have guessed it would not be his day when, in the final, Hagen's first tee shot dropped in for a hole-in-one.

MERION

Where: Philadelphia, PA, USA
Par: 70
Yardage: 6,544
Opened: 1912
Designer: Hugh Wilson
Major Events Staged: US Open 1934, 1950, 1971, 1981, US Amateur Championship 1916, 1924, 1930, 1966, 1989, Curtis Cup 1954

THE ORIGINAL MERION course consisted of nine holes designed in 1896 adjacent to the Merion cricket club. In 1900 it was extended to eighteen holes, but with the coming of the Haskell ball the need for a longer course dictated a move to farmland on the outskirts of Philadelphia. Ironically Merion is now one of the shortest of the American Championship courses, but it also judged by many to be the best.
● THE COURSE design has had a number of British influences, one being the National Links at Southampton designed by Charles MacDonald.
● MERION IS famous for its variety of holes, and also for its superb greens. The course has witnessed some incredible moments in golfing history which secure it as a national favourite. Bobby Jones completed his Grand Slam at the course in 1930, and 20 years later Ben Hogan completed his miraculous return from injury to win the US Open. In 1971 Lee Trevino beat his great rival Jack Nicklaus in a play-off, and in 1981 – the last time the US Open was held at Merion – David Graham became the first Australian to win the competition.

PHIL MICKELSON

Born: San Diego, CA, USA – 16/06/1970
First US Tour: 1992
Highest Ranking: 2 (1996)
US Tour Wins: 11
Major Wins: 0
Ryder Cup Appearances: 2
Tour Earnings: $5.1 million

PHIL MICKELSON could become the first left-hander to win a major championship since Bob Charles. Like Charles, Mickelson's reasons for playing left handed are unusual. Charles borrowed his parents left-handed clubs to practise, and similarly the naturally right-handed Mickelson mirrored the right-handed play of his father and thus played left-handed.
● THE ONLY left-handed player to have won the US Amateur Championship, Mickelson has been outstanding in his five years on the US Tour. He has averaged two wins a season, and in 1996 finished second in the US Money list after four victories – he was only overtaken by Tom Lehman in the last week of the season.

86

● MICKELSON has played in two Walker Cup teams and two Ryder Cup teams and has a brilliant record in both. In the Ryder Cup he lost only one out of his five matches.

● THE World Amateur Player of the Year in 1991, he turned pro a year later at the 1992 US Open, where he failed to meet the cut. The only setback in his career came away from the course, when Mickleson broke his ankle skiing in 1994.

CARY MIDDLECOFF

Born: Halls, TN, USA – 06/01/1921	
First US Tour: 1947	
Highest Ranking: 1 (1949, 1951)	
US Tour Wins: 40	
Major Wins: 3 (US Open 1949, 1956, US Masters 1955)	
Ryder Cup Appearances: 3	

NICKNAMED 'the Doc' on the US Tour, Cary Middlecoff was a qualified dentist who turned pro in the 1940s after a successful amateur spell. He was one of the dominant forces in 1950s golf, and his 40 wins before retiring in 1961 put him equal seventh with Walter Hagen on the all-time US PGA Tour winners list.

● A VERY SLOW and deliberate player, Middlecoff gained a reputation for slowing the game down, so much so that Dick Mayer took out a camping stool for their 1957 US Open play-off.

● SUCCESS came early to Middlecoff: he was second in the 1948 US Masters after turning pro the previous year, and he then won the US Open a year later, setting a course record in his second round at Medinah.

● A very nervous player, it was the putting 'yips' which eventually forced him to retire. Middlecoff was so lacking in confidence that he once placed a bet on himself losing the US Open while he waited in the clubhouse for players to try and catch him. They didn't.

Chipping in

'Nobody wins the Open. It wins you.'

Johnny Miller – great golfer, not so great trousers.

THE MIDDLE EAST

THE MIDDLE EAST has never been a rich source of golf courses, with the odd golf club literally an oasis in the desert. It was a case of plenty of bunkers and not enough fairways. This has changed in recent years, however, with the emergence of the Dubai Desert Classic, now a firm favourite on the European Tour. The Qatar Masters, staged at the Doha course, has joined the Dubai Classic on the European calendar. The Dubai Creek course is also set to stage events on the Asia PGA Tour in 1998.

JOHNNY MILLER

Born: San Francisco, CA, USA – 29/04/1947

First US Tour: 1969

Highest Ranking: 1 (1974)

US Tour Wins: 24

Major Wins: 2 (British Open 1976, US Open 1973)

Ryder Cup Appearances: 2

Tour Earnings: $2,757,432

IN 1974, JOHNNY MILLER was easily the best golfer in the world. He won eight events on the US Tour, headed the money list and was PGA Player of the Year.

● THE PREVIOUS year he had recorded an absolutely astonishing US Open victory. Miller seemed set to take the mantle of Nicklaus. But somehow it never materialised, and after his 1976 British Open win Miller never won another major.

● MILLER's final round in the 1973 US Open is often regarded as the best round of golf ever played. Miller took 63 to win the Championship at Oakmont, one of the hardest championship courses in America. Miller came into the final day six shots down on the leader and not amongst the top ten. He eventually won from John Schlee by a single stroke.

● HIS WIN IN 1976 was also impressive, as he held off Jack Nicklaus and a youthful Ballesteros and came home six shots clear of the field.

● AFTER MILLER's British Open win, he concentrated on his other careers of course architect and acerbic NBC commentator. He occasionally competes however, and won events in 1987 and 1994.

Chipping in

'The best thing that ever happened to me was coming second in the 1971 Masters. I couldn't have coped if I'd won.'

LARRY MIZE

Born: Augusta, GA, USA – 23/09/1958

First US Tour: 1982

Highest Ranking: 6 (1987)

US Tour Wins: 4

Major Wins: 1 (US Masters, 1987)

Ryder Cup Appearances: 1

Tour Earnings: $5 million

THE NAME Larry Mize is a familiar one, and yet Mize has only once finished in the top ten money earners after 15 years on tour. He has only four victories to his name, with the last of these coming in 1993.

● HIS FAME stems partly from his winning shot in the US Masters in 1987. In a play-off with Seve Ballesteros and Greg Norman, Ballesteros departed at the first hole. Then at the second hole, with Norman in a good position, Mize holed out from 42m (140 ft) and took the Championship. It seemed to be destiny for the locally-born man.

● MIZE ALSO won the Johnnie Walker World Championship in 1993, and played in the 1993 Ryder Cup. In 1997, however, Mize – also an accomplished pianist – barely managed to make the top 100 on the US Tour.

COLIN MONTGOMERIE

Born: Glasgow, Scotland – 23/06/1963

First European Tour: 1987

Highest Ranking: 1 (1993, 1994, 1995, 1996, 1997)

European Tour Wins: 14

European Tour Earnings: £5 million

First US Tour: 1992

US Tour Wins: 0

Highest Ranking: 37 (1997)

US Tour Earnings: $1,665,484

Major Wins: 0

Ryder Cup Appearances: 4

DESPITE NEVER having won a major championship, Montgomerie is probably the best British player of the 1990s, and certainly the most consistent. A great Ryder Cup competitor, Montgomerie has been leader of the European Tour Money List for five years running, breaking the record held by Peter Oosterhuis since the early 1970s.

● HE HAS indicated, however, that his goal now is to win a major, and that he has no intention of going for a sixth successive European Order title. He plans to compete in the three US majors and a reduced number of European events, starting with the Dubai Classic.

● MONTGOMERIE has already made something of an impression in America. In 1997 he finished in 37th place on the Money list, despite competing in only nine events, and he was the only player in the top 50 to have played in less than ten events.

● MONTGOMERIE's father was the secretary of Royal Troon, and after a successful amateur career (including winning the 1987 Scottish Amateur) Montgomerie turned pro in 1987. He was Rookie of the Year the following year, and in 1989 won his first event. His stroke average, ranking and money earning have all steadily improved year-on-year, and in the 1990s nobody has been able to touch him on the European circuit.

● HIS FORTUNES in the majors have been mixed. Never really a dangerous competitor in the British Open, Montgomerie has twice been second in the US Open, and was also runner up in the US PGA Championship, after a play-off with Steve Elkington in 1995.

● MONTGOMERIE made his Ryder Cup debut in 1991, and his brilliant halved match with Mark Calcavecchia was one of the highlights of the European campaign.

'Monty' – Europe's most consistent player.

GIL MORGAN

Born: Wewoka, OK, USA – 25/09/1946

First US Tour: 1973

Highest Ranking: 2 (1978)

US Tour Wins: 7

Tour Earnings: £5,253,117

First Senior Tour: 1996

Highest Ranking: 2 (1997)

Senior Tour Wins: 7

Major Wins: 0

Ryder Cup Appearances: 2

GIL MORGAN qualified as an optometrist before looking to golf as a career. Despite never having won a major, Morgan has made a great living from golf, earning over $5 million. He has been a winner in the 1970s, 1980s and 1990s, and seems set to have a lucrative career as a Senior well into the 21st century.

● IN HIS FIRST season on the Senior Tour, Morgan became the youngest ever winner – his win coming just eleven days after his 50th birthday. In his first full season, 1997, Morgan was second on the money list behind Hale Irwin, winning six events and earning over $2 million.

● MORGAN HAS never won a major event, and must rue his final holes at Pebble Beach in the 1992 US Open. Morgan was the first man to go 10 under in the event, and was at one point 12 shots below par. He faded badly, however, and finished back in 13th place.

TOM MORRIS JNR

Born: St Andrews, Scotland – 20/04/1851

Major Wins: 4 (British Open 1868, 1869, 1870, 1872)

'YOUNG' TOM MORRIS as he was also known, was the first golfer to achieve regular success in organised competitions.

● IN 1868, he succeeded his father as holder of the British Open title, when aged only 17. He retained the trophy for a following two years, and thus got to keep it. Morris won again in 1872, after a year's gap in the proceedings to find another trophy. Morris was the first winner of the new Claret Jug, and the only man to win four successive British Opens.

● UNFORTUNATELY, Young Tom did not have a long career – he died at the age of 24, just a few months after his wife.

TOM MORRIS SNR

Born: St Andrews, Scotland – 16/06/1821

Major Wins: 4 (British Open 1861, 1862, 1864, 1867)

THE FATHER of Young Tom, Morris Snr was in many ways the father of golf. He was the second winner of the British Open, popularised the 'gutty' ball, and was a great servant to his home town club over the years.

Young at heart, Gil Morgan continues to succeed on the Senior Tour.

● AS WELL AS his activities on the course, he was a partner with Allan Robertson in a business manufacturing feather balls. Seeing the benefits of the new gutta percha ball, he split from his partner and successfully produced and promoted the new ball.

● RUNNER-UP to Willie Park in the first British Open, Morris won a total of four Championships before his son took over the mantle. Morris continued his ball-manufacturing business and also became involved in course design. When he died in 1908 his funeral in St Andrews was attended by thousands, and his picture still hangs in the club to this day.

MUIRFIELD

Where: East Lothian, Scotland

Par: 71

Yardage: 6,941

Opened: 1891

Designer: Tom Morris Snr, Harry Colt

Major Events Staged: British Open 1892, 1896, 1901, 1906, 1912, 1929, 1935, 1948, 1959, 1966, 1972, 1980, 1987, 1992. British Amateur Championship 1897, 1903, 1909, 1920, 1926, 1932, 1954, 1974, 1990, Ryder Cup 1973

THE ORIGINAL course at Muirfield was designed by Tom Morris Snr and was not a great success. The course as it is today

was designed in the 1920s by Harry Colt.

● A VERY FLAT course, but with subtle dangers, Muirfield is much-loved by professionals. Its first hole is very testing, and the final two are very capable of robbing a player with a title virtually in hand.

Open Winners at Muirfield

1892	Harold Hilton	1948	Henry Cotton
1896	Harry Vardon	1959	Gary Player
1901	James Braid	1966	Jack Nicklaus
1906	James Braid	1972	Lee Trevino
1912	Ted Ray	1980	Tom Watson
1929	Walter Hagen	1987	Nick Faldo
1935	Alf Perry	1993	Greg Norman

MUIRFIELD VILLAGE

Where: Ohio, USA

Par: 72

Yardage: 7,104

Opened: 1974

Designer: Jack Nicklaus

Major Events Staged: Ryder Cup 1987

DESIGNED BY Jack Nicklaus in the 1970s, Muirfield Village is yet to stage a major, but was the venue for the Ryder Cup in 1987. Tony Jacklin took the European team to America, two years after their victory at The Belfry, to renew his duel with Jack Nicklaus. Jacklin's team won 15–13, the first ever European victory in the States.

Same name, vastly differing courses. Muirfield's 17th hole (above) and Muirfield Village's 12th.

KEL NAGLE

Born: Sydney, Australia – 21/12/1920
Career Spanned – 1940s–1970s
Major Wins: 1

KEL NAGLE was a late developer who won his first title at the age of 29, and didn't win a major until he was 40. A long and wild hitter in his youth, Nagle refined his technique and became a far better player for it, winning some 25 titles in the 1960s.
● AFTER WINNING the New Zealand Open and Australian Open, Nagle spread his wings further and won the centenary British Open in 1960 at St Andrews, holding off the favourite Arnold Palmer.
● HIS OTHER brush with major triumph was the 1965 US Open, when Nagle lost a play-off to Gary Player.

TOMMY NAKAJUIMA

TSUNEYUKI 'TOMMY' NAKAJUIMA is a star in Japan, where he has won over 50 events, including four Japanese Opens, three Japanese PGAs and three Matchplay Championships. Although he has occasionally been in contention for major tournaments in Europe and the US, it is for his disastrous attempts at the 1978 US Masters and British Open that he is best remembered.
● AT THE US Masters in 1978, he bizarrely scored a 13 at the 13th hole, Augusta's easiest. The same year, at the Road Hole at St Andrews, his problems at a bunker led to him carding a nine.

BYRON NELSON

Born: Fort Worth, TX, USA – 04/02/1912
First US Tour: 1932
Highest Ranking: 1 (1944, 1945)
US Tour Wins: 52
Major Wins: 5 (US Open 1939, US Masters 1937, 1942, US PGA 1940, 1945)
Ryder Cup Appearances: 2

BYRON NELSON is often overlooked in the ranks of the great golfers, but only Snead, Hogan, Palmer and Nicklaus have won more US Tournaments. From 1944 to 1946 there was not a golfer in the world that could match him: in 1945, Nelson played 113 tournaments without missing a cut. He won 19 of them, including a streak of 11 consecutive wins.
● IN 1946, after three incredible years, the quietly spoken Nelson retired at the age of 34. He played in the Ryder Cup a year later, and was a non-playing captain in the 1960s, but other than some television commentating he had little to do with the sport. In 1955, Nelson entered the French Open, almost for fun, and won it.
● IT COULD be said that Nelson's achievements were helped by the fact that many golfers were at war (illness prevented Nelson from taking part in the war effort), but his averages were remarkable and his consistency renowned.
● NELSON WON his first major in 1937, when his 66 in the opening round of the US Masters – then a course record – set him up for a two-stroke victory. He was to win the Masters again

five years later after a play-off with Hogan. In between he had secured the 1939 US Open, also in a play-off.
● AS THERE WAS no television during his peak playing years, Nelson was largely forgotten. But as mentor to Tom Watson in the 1970s, and now with a tournament, the Byron Nelson Classic, named after him, a whole new generation have been made aware of his remarkable career.

LARRY NELSON

Born: Fort Payne, AL, USA – 10/09/1947
First US Tour: 1973
Highest Ranking: 2 (1979)
US Tour Wins: 10
Major Wins: 3 (US Open 1983, US PGA 1981, 1987)
Ryder Cup Appearances: 3
Tour Earnings: $3,822,444

LARRY NELSON is something of an enigma. He didn't even play golf until he was 21, and even then he only took it up after being encouraged to do so while serving in Vietnam. And yet by the age of 26 Nelson was competing on the US Tour.
● ALTHOUGH HE has only won ten tournaments

Larry Nelson at the 1991 Johnie Walker World Championship.

Byron Nelson tees off in the 1994 US Masters at Augusta.

in some 25 years, three of those have been majors. Between 1981 and 1987 he only won five tournaments, but they included a US Open and two US PGA titles.

● WHEN WINNING the 1983 US Open, Nelson came from seven shots off the lead to win, with rounds of 65 and 67. His 132 for the last 36 holes remains a record.

● AS FOR HIS US PGA titles (both won on Sunday 9th August – six years apart), the first saw him hold off Fuzzy Zoeller with a strong final round of 71, while the second was won after a play-off with Lanny Wadkins.

● NOW ELIGIBLE for the Senior Tour, it is likely that Nelson will concentrate his efforts on the over-50s game, as his success on the PGA Tour appears to be on the wane.

LISELOTTE NEUMANN

Born: Finspang, Sweden – 20/05/1966

First LPGA Tour: 1988

Highest Ranking: 3 (1994)

Tour Wins: 8

Major Wins: 1 (US Open 1988)

Solheim Cup Appearances: 4

Tour Earnings: $3 million

LISELOTTE NEUMANN has won the Swedish Amateur Championship twice, and represented her country in many European events. She has also tasted victory in the German, European and French Opens.

● IN 1988 'Lotta', as she is known, joined the LPGA Tour, with her first win coming in the US Open that year. Not surprisingly she was named Rookie of the Year.

● SINCE THEN, Neumann has earned over $3 million. She won the British Women's Open and has also made her fourth Solheim Cup appearance. She is one of a number of Swedes who have helped to make the country one of the world's strongest golfing nations.

NEW ZEALAND

GOLF BEGAN in New Zealand at Dunedin in 1889, when Fogarty's pub was used as the nominal clubhouse. After the first club went bust, a more successful venture was set up in Christchurch, led by some Westward Ho! members. The course at Dunedin was later resurrected, and the first New Zealand Open was played there in 1907.

Major New Zealand Competitions

New Zealand Open

Famous New Zealand Players

Bob Charles
Michael Campbell
Frank Nobilo
Phil Tataurangi

Top Five Courses

Auckland
Dunedin
Paparamu
Wanganui
Wellington

Contact

New Zealand Golf Association,
PO Box 11842, Wellington Library,
65 Victoria Street, Wellington

'Lotta' – aka Liselotte Neumann – one of Sweden's many brilliant female golfers.

THE NEW ZEALAND OPEN

First Played: 1907

Most wins: 9 – Peter Thomson (1950, 1951, 1953, 1955, 1959, 1960, 1961, 1965, 1971)

Lowest 72-hole score: 262
(1986, Rodger Davis, Auckland)

New Zealand Open Last 25 Winners

Year	Winner	Score	Venue
1972	Bill Dunk	279	Paraparaumu
1973	Bob Charles	288	Palmerston North
1974	Bob Gilder	283	Christchurch
1975	Bill Dunk	272	Hamilton
1976	Simon Owen	284	Wellington
1977	Bob Byman	290	Auckland
1978	Bob Shearer	277	Wanganui
1979	Stewart Ginn	278	Dunedin
1980	Budd Allin	274	New Plymouth
1981	Bob Shearer	285	Wellington
1982	Terry Gale	284	Christchurch
1983	Ian Baker-Finch	280	Auckland
1984	Corey Pavin	269	Paraparaumu
1985	Corey Pavin	277	Russley
1986	Rodger Davis	262	Auckland
1987	Ronan Rafferty	279	Dunedin
1988	Ian Stanley	273	Paraparaumu
1989	Greg Turner	277	Wellington
1990	Not played		
1991	Rodger Davis	273	Paraparaumu
1992	Grant Waite	268	Paraparaumu
1993	Peter Fowler	274	Paraparaumu
1994	Craig Jones	277	Auckland
1995	Lucas Parsons	282	Wellington
1996	Michael Long	275	Paraparaumu
1997	Greg Turner	278	Auckland

Jack Nicklaus, the greatest golfer the world has ever seen – in familiar pose.

ALISON NICHOLAS

Born: Gibraltar – 06/03/1962
First LPGA Tour: 1990
Highest Ranking: 18 (1997)
Tour Wins: 3
Major Wins: 1 (US Women's Open 1997)
Solheim Cup Appearances: 4
Tour Earnings: £829,624

ALISON NICHOLAS didn't take up golf until the age of 17, perhaps because her home island of Gibraltar was not the ideal place to play. As an amateur in England, however, she won a number of regional titles, and in 1987 she won the British Women's Open aged 25. In 1990 she turned to the US circuit as well as continuing to play in Europe, and she has since won the Irish and Scottish Opens, as well as recording victories in the USA.

● IN 1997 Nicholas topped the European Order of Merit, and did well on the LPGA tour.

JACK NICKLAUS

Born: Columbus, OH, USA – 21/01/1940
First US Tour: 1962
Highest Ranking: 1 (1964, 1965, 1967, 1972, 1973, 1975, 1976)
US Tour Wins: 70
Tour Earnings: $5,679,136
First Senior Tour: 1990
Senior Tour Wins: 10
Senior Tour Earnings: $2,446,645
Major Wins: 18 (British Open 1966, 1970, 1978, US Open 1962, 1967, 1972, 1980, US Masters 1963, 1965, 1966, 1972, 1975, 1986, US PGA 1963, 1971, 1973, 1975, 1980)
Ryder Cup Appearances: 6

IT IS EASY to sum up Jack Nicklaus's career. He is simply the most successful golfer there has ever been.

● THE LIST of his achievements is seemingly endless, and deserves (and indeed on many occasions has warranted) a book in its own right. He has topped the US Money list more often than any other golfer, and his total of Tour victories is bettered only by Sam Snead.

● NOT ONLY has he won 18 majors, at least three in each of the four Championships, but he has also finished in the top three on another 28 occasions. From 1962 (his first season on Tour, in which he won the US Open) until 1978 he was never out of the top five players, and he won at least two tournaments every year.

● PERHAPS WHAT has marked out Nicklaus above any other player, however, is the span over which he has maintained consistency. During his years at the top, adversaries such as Arnold Palmer, Lee Trevino and Tom Watson have all come and gone.

● THERE WERE 24 years between his first major victory, the 1962 US Open, and

Frank Nobilo, New Zealand's All Black on the golf course.

his last, the 1986 US Masters. His record of 18 major wins is the highest total by some distance, with Walter Hagen trailing him a long way behind with only 11. Two majors have been secured in the same year on five occasions. And his total of 72 top ten finishes in major tournaments is almost double that of his nearest rival Sam Snead.

● ACCURACY and safe consistency were Nicklaus' strengths, and were attributes that saw him still achieving success into his 40s, despite a wealth of teaching books and course architecture taking up much of his time. Winning a record sixth US Masters at the age of 46 was perhaps the sweetest moment of all.

● PERHAPS HIS worst moment was losing the Ryder Cup to the Europeans in 1987, the first defeat on home soil. To add insult to injury, it was held at the Muirfield Village course he had designed in his own backyard. Luckily it was one of the few disappointments the Golden Bear ever suffered.

NICKNAMES

PLAYERS ON golfing tours are often given nicknames over the year. Graham Marsh was known as 'Swampy', for obvious reasons, and Cary Middlecoff as 'The Doc' because of his dental skills. Jack Nicklaus and Greg Norman are known as the Golden Bear and the Great White Shark respectively due to the colour of their hair. Other famous monikers include The Tex Mex (Trevino) and Zinger (Paul Azinger).

THE NINETEENTH HOLE

THE NINETEENTH hole, as even the most amateur of golfers knows, is the clubhouse. As soon as a round is finished, it's back to the bar for a long drink and some tall tales.

FRANK NOBILO

Born: Auckland, New Zealand – 14/05/1960
First US Tour: 1992
Highest Ranking: 23 (1997)
US Tour Wins: 1
Major Wins: 0
Tour Earnings: $1,268,518

FRANK NOBILO has mainly competed on the European Tour, where he has recorded five victories. Latterly he has chosen to compete in America, and he recorded his best year to date in 1997. As well as finishing 23rd in the US Tour list with close to a million dollars, Nobilo also recorded his first US win, the Greensboro Greater Classic.

● NOBILO's form in the US majors has always been consistent, his best finishes being fourth in the 1996 US Masters and eighth in the US PGA the same year. He caused a stir in the US Open two years earlier when he played the final round in his trademark all-black, despite temperatures in excess of 100 degrees.

GREG NORMAN

Born: Queensland, Australia – 10/02/1955
First US Tour: 1983
Highest Ranking: 1 (1986, 1990, 1995)
US Tour Wins: 18
Tour Earnings: $11,910,518
First European Tour: 1977
Highest Ranking: 1 (1982)
European Tour Wins: 17
Major Wins: 2 (British Open 1986, 1993)

GREG NORMAN must surely be the unluckiest golfer ever. But luck is relative: he is one of the three richest golfers in the world, has topped the European, US and World ranking lists, and has won the British Open twice. Many 'luckier' golfers would surely swap places with him.

● NORMAN HAS the unlucky tag, however, because he has been in contention for so many majors, but has either fallen away badly, been caught out by amazing play, or been on the wrong end of a once-in-a-lifetime shot. Nevertheless, Norman has

over $11 million in earnings and some 18 US Tour wins to add to the other 55 titles he has won in 13 countries.

● BOTH OF HIS major wins were impressive and the deserved result of superlative play. In the 1986 Open at Turnberry Norman equalled the Championship record with a 63 on the second day, and at Royal St Georges in 1993 he played four rounds below 70.

● THE LIST of majors he missed out on is, however, rather longer. In 1986 alone he led all four majors after three rounds, but only held on in the Open. And in the US he has finished second twice in all three of the important championships (the US Open in 1984 and 1995, US Masters in 1986 and 1987, and the US PGA in 1986 and 1993). In addition, Norman has lost play-offs in all four of the majors.

● DESPITE THIS tortuous record, Norman is the only player never to have been out of the Sony top ten rankings since they started in 1986.

Greg Norman – a powerful driver on and off the course.

ANDY NORTH

Born: Thorpe, WI, USA – 09/03/1950
First US Tour: 1973
Highest Ranking: 14 (1978)
US Tour Wins: 3
Major Wins: 2
Ryder Cup Appearances: 1
Tour Earnings: $1,364,013

ANDY NORTH has had a very strange career, but with the injuries that he has suffered it is surprising that he has had a career at all.

● NORTH WAS once a promising basketball player, but has over the years suffered bone defects in his legs, knees, elbows and neck which would have made it difficult to walk properly let alone play a sport professionally. Nevertheless, North has competed on the US PGA Tour, off and on, for over twenty years.

● NORTH HAS only recorded three wins on the US Tour, but two of those have come in the US Open – once in 1978, and then

again in 1985. Like the rest of his career, the wins were not distinguished: he just about bogeyed the last at Cherry Hills in 1978 to win by a stroke, and then in 1985 he won by a single stroke.

OAKMONT

Where: Pennsylvania, USA

Par: 71

Yardage: 6,921

Opened: 1904

Designer: Henry Fownes

Major Events Staged: US PGA 1922, 1951, 1978, US Open 1927, 1935, 1953, 1962, 1973, 1983, 1994, US Amateur Championship 1919, 1925, 1938, 1969, US Women's Open 1992

OAKMONT IS often regarded as the hardest course in the world, and certainly the hardest in America. And it was designed to be that way.

● HENRY FOWNES's original course was built in a year, and when completed had eight par fives and a par six as part of its 85 total for par. Trees had been felled to give it the open feel of a Scottish course. If people seemed to be mastering the course, Fownes simply moved a bunker to make it harder.

● SUCH TOUGH tests make it all the more strange that some of the best rounds of the US Open have been witnessed at Oakmont. In 1953, the US Open was staged on a relatively easy Oakmont setting with less hazards, and Ben Hogan stunned audiences with an opening 67. Hogan went on to win by six strokes.

● IN 1973, Johnny Miller recorded a final round 63, probably the best final round ever played. And in 1983 when Larry Nelson won the Open, his last two rounds had an aggregate of 132, the lowest recorded in the US Open.

The Oakmont 'Church Pews' have necessitated prayers from many players.

CHRISTY O'CONNOR JNR

Born: Galway, Ireland – 19/08/1948

First European Tour: 1970

Highest Ranking: 7 (1975)

European Tour Wins: 4

Major Wins: 0

Ryder Cup Appearances: 2

Tour Earnings: £1,066,214

THE YOUNGER Christy O'Connor has been a European player for almost 30 years, although his playing career has dwindled in the 1990s due to a foot injury. Undoubtedly the highlight of his career was his win over Fred Couples at the Belfry in 1989, which helped secure the European victory.

CHRISTY O'CONNOR SNR

Born: Galway, Ireland 21/12/1924

First European Tour: 1951

Highest Ranking: 1 (1961)

European Tour Wins: 24

Major Wins: 0

Ryder Cup Appearances: 10

CHRISTY O'CONNOR played in ten Ryder Cups in succession – a record – and fifteen times for Ireland in competition. Together with Harry Bradshaw he won the World Cup for Ireland in 1958. He is without doubt the finest golfer that Ireland has ever produced.

● OFTEN IN contention for the British Open, the closest O'Connor came was losing to Peter Thomson by a single stroke in 1965. He also had numerous top five finishes in the competition throughout the 1960s.

O

JOSE MARIA OLAZABAL

Born: Fuenterrabia, Spain – 05/02/1966

First European Tour: 1986

Highest Ranking: 2 (1986, 1989)

European Tour Wins: 17

Major Wins: 1 (US Masters 1994)

Ryder Cup Appearances: 5

Tour Earnings: £3,162,006

JOSE MARIA OLAZABAL exploded onto the golfing scene in 1986, winning two European tournaments in his first year and finishing second in the Order of Merit. Olazabal had already put together a very impressive amateur career, including beating Colin Montgomerie in the 1984 British Amateur Championship.

● OLAZABAL continued to win trophies and also formed a formidable partnership with friend and fellow countryman Seve Ballesteros in Ryder Cup competitions.

● IN 1994 he won the major he deserved, taking the Masters ahead of Tom Lehman. He finished fourth in the European Order of Merit, and seventh in the US Money list in the same year. Then, however, his world seemingly fell apart when a foot complaint cast doubt on his future career. Olazabal thankfully returned to competition in 1997, and finished in the top ten on the European Tour with a win to his credit.

OLYMPICS

GOLF ONLY featured twice in the Olympic Games. In the 1900 Paris Olympics Charles Sands won gold, then four years later in St Louis a Canadian, George Lyon, beat American Chandler Egan in the final. In 1908 George Lyon travelled to London to defend his title, only to discover that nobody else had entered.

MARK O'MEARA

Born: Goldsboro, NC, USA – 13/01/1957

First US Tour: 1981

Highest Ranking: 2 (1984)

US Tour Wins: 14

Major Wins: 1 (US Masters 1998)

Ryder Cup Appearances: 4

Tour Earnings: $8,506,775

UNTIL 1998 Mark O'Meara had never won a major championship, even though he had been successful in winning tournaments throughout the United States, Europe, Australia, Japan and South America. His favourite course seems to be Pebble Beach, as he has won there on five occasions.

● A CONSISTENT performer, O'Meara has remained a top 30 player for all but two years since 1984. His lean years came in 1993 and 1994, but since then he has won two tournaments in each of the last three years.

● IN THE 1998 Masters, with spectators concentrating on Fred Couples and Davis

Jose Maria Olazabal, now back on track after recovering from injury.

Love III, O'Meara snuck up on the rails and pipped them both at the final hole at Augusta.

● ADDING A SECOND major to his collection this year, O'Meara also took the 1998 British Open Championship at Royal Birkdale, beating fellow American Brian Watts in a tense play-off.

THOSE OLD CHAMPIONS

'You're never too old,' they say, and here are the players that have proved that adage:

— British Open —
Tom Morris Snr 1867
(46 years old)

— US Open —
Hale Irwin 1990
(45 years old)

— US Masters —
Jack Nicklaus 1986
(46 years old)

— US PGA —
Julius Boros 1968 (48 years old)

— European Tour win —
Neil Coles 1982 Sanyo Open
(48 years old)

— US Tour Win —
Sam Snead 1965
Gt Greensboro Open
(52 years old)

PETER OOSTERHUIS

Born: London, England – 03/05/1948
First European Tour: 1967
Highest Ranking: 1 (1971, 1972, 1973, 1974)
European Tour Wins: 20
Major Wins: 0
Ryder Cup Appearances: 6

PETER OOSTERHUIS never won a major tournament, despite topping the European Order of Merit for four successive years. In many ways his career was similar to Colin Montgomerie's, for after years dominating the European scene and as a pillar of the Ryder Cup team, Oosterhuis decided that his future lay in America and

that he wanted to win a major.

● UNFORTUNATELY it was not to be. After winning only one US Tour event, the 1981 Canadian Open, his career wound down and he faded from contention.

They say that all good things come to those who wait. Mark O'Meara had to wait for the 1998 US Masters.

The *Virgin* Book Of Golf Records　**99**

FRANCIS OUIMET

Born: Brookline, MA, USA – 08/05/1893
Career Spanned: 1910s to 1930s
Major Wins: 1 (US Open 1913)

FRANCIS OUIMET was the US Amateur who humbled the great Harry Vardon by winning the US Open in 1913. It did not convince him to turn professional, however, and he went on to win the US Amateur Championship in 1914 and again in 1931.

● A RESPECTED and well-loved man, Ouimet was involved in every Walker Cup as either player or non-playing captain from 1922 to 1949.

ALF PADGHAM

Born: Caterham, England – 1906
Career Spanned: 1920s to 1940s
Major Wins: 1 (British Open 1936)

ALF PADGHAM had a swing admired by all of his more successful contemporaries, including the great Harry Vardon. Like Vardon he had a good short game, but was let down by his putting, in which he experimented with new methods.

● MOST SUCCESSFUL in the 1930s, his one British Open win was almost denied to him. Arriving at Hoylake early in the morning he found the shop shut with his clubs inside. Padgham smashed the window with a brick, retrieved his clubs and went on to take the trophy.

Arnold Palmer waves farewell to St Andrews at the end of the 1995 British Open.

ARNOLD PALMER

Born: Latrobe, PA, USA – 10/09/1929
First US Tour: 1955
Highest Ranking: 1 (1958, 1960, 1962, 1963)
US Tour Wins: 60
First Senior Tour: 1980
Senior Tour Wins: 10
Senior Tour Earnings: $1,634,966
Major Wins: 7 (British Open 1961, 1962, US Open 1960, US Masters 1958, 1960, 1962, 1964)
Ryder Cup Appearances: 6

IF NICKLAUS WAS the dominant American professional of the 1960s, Palmer was the best loved. His style was anything but artistic and he would thrash his drives and race his putts to the flag, but his expressive personality and whirlwind play endeared him to crowds in the way that Ballesteros did in the 1970s and 1980s.

● ARNIE'S ARMY, as his followers were known, had the good fortune to witness Palmer play through four decades, and even in his later years his popularity has never waned, even if his nerve has. And they saw him win more titles than almost any other player of his generation, Nicklaus being the exception.

● PALMER TURNED PRO in 1954 after winning the US Amateur Championship, his first pro win – the Canadian Open – coming in 1955, his first year on tour. His first major was to come three years later in the US Masters.

● IT WAS BETWEEN 1960 and 1964 that Palmer achieved his greatest moments. In these four years he won six major championships, including two titles in both 1960 and 1962. In 1960 he had already won the US Masters when he came to the US Open at Cherry Hills in good form. He went into the final round seven strokes behind the leaders, but a barnstorming 65 saw him home two ahead of promising amateur Jack Nicklaus.

● IN 1961 he won his first British Open by a stroke, despite calling a penalty against himself as he prepared to take a bunker shot in round two – just another crowd-pleasing moment which added to the legend.

● DURING THIS brilliant period, Palmer became the last playing Ryder Cup captain in 1963, leading the USA to victory. His record of 22 Ryder Cup victories remains the best ever by a US player.

● IT IS A MYSTERY why Palmer did not add to his tally of major wins. After the 1964 Masters he recorded another 17 wins on the US Tour up until 1973, but never again raised a major trophy.

● IN 1980 Palmer gave credibility to the Senior Tour

at its inception and recorded ten victories up until 1988, before turning to course design.

PAR

PAR IS THE NUMBER of shots that a scratch golfer is expected to take to complete a hole. On any one course, there are normally two par fives, a few par threes and a majority of par fours.

● GOOD PLAYERS are expected to two-putt every green and take one, two or three shots to reach the green depending on whether it is a par three, four or five respectively.

Jesper Parnevik is the son of Sweden's most famous comedian. Unfortunately, in this photograph he looks like Norman Wisdom.

WILLIE PARK JNR

Born: Musselburgh, Scotland – 04/02/1864
Career Spanned: 1880s to 1900s
Major Wins: 2 (British Open 1887, 1889)

LIKE HIS FATHER before him, Willie Park Jnr was a winner of the British Open on more than one occasion. And like Tom Morris Jnr and Snr, the pair had a massive effect on the game in its early days. As well as their playing abilities, the Parks (especially the younger) helped with course design, club and ball making, and wrote extensively about the game.

● WILLIE PARK JNR wrote two large tomes about golf (The Game of Golf and The Art of Putting), and is also credited with course designs throughout the British Isles, Europe and America. Among his greatest achievements are those at Sunningdale, Carnoustie and Royal Antwerp. A great businessman, Park also owned shops in London and Scotland devoted to golf.

● IN ADDITION to these family achievements, uncle Mungo Park (brother of Willie Snr) was also Open champion, in 1874.

WILLIE PARK SNR

Born: Musselburgh, Scotland – 1833
Career Spanned: 1850s to 1870s
Major Wins: 4 (British Open 1860, 1863, 1866, 1875)

UNLIKE HIS entrepreneurial son, Park Snr was happy to let his playing do the talking. Along with his peer Tom Morris Snr, they dominated Open golf in its early stages, and Park won the trophy on four occasions, including the first time it was played in 1860.

● LEGEND HAS IT that Park was so good that he used to play people for money, offering to stand on one leg and use only one hand. An unlikely tale, and one made taller by the suggestion that he lost only once while indulging in the practice.

JESPER PARNEVIK

Born: Stockholm, Sweden – 07/03/1965
First US Tour: 1994
Highest Ranking: 12 (1997)
US Tour Wins: 1
Major Wins: 0
Ryder Cup Appearances: 1
Tour Earnings: $1,978,127

PARNEVIK FIRST played on the US Tour in 1994 after three wins on the European Tour. He continued to compete in Europe, becoming the first Swede to win on home soil when he took the 1995 Scandinavian Masters.

● A CONSISTENT competitor on the American circuit, Parnevik reaped over a million dollars in 1997, finishing 12th on the money list.

● PARNEVIK IS also the son of Sweden's most famous comedian, Bosse.

CRAIG PARRY

Born: Sunshine, Australia – 12/01/1966
First US Tour: 1992
Highest Ranking: 43 (1996)
US Tour Wins: 0
Major Wins: 0
Tour Earnings: $2,163,558

KNOWN AS POPEYE because of his huge forearms, Craig Parry has 14 international wins to his name, but is yet to add a US Tour win. After working his way up the field, he dropped off somewhat in 1997,

finishing 63rd, and his chances on the US Tour look to be fading.

● PARRY HAD wins in Australia and Canada before he tried his luck on the European Tour. He won four times, and finished third in the 1989 European Order of Merit before concentrating his efforts on the States.

● PARRY HAS come close to winning a major several times, finishing third behind Lee Janzen in the 1993 US Open, and leading the US Masters after three rounds in 1992, before fading to 13th.

Former Rookie Jerry Pate with his own Rookie son Wesley.

JERRY PATE

Born: Macon, GA, USA – 16/09/1953
First US Tour: 1976
Highest Ranking: 6 (1980, 1981)
US Tour Wins: 8
Major Wins: 1 (US Open 1976)
Ryder Cup Appearances: 1
Tour Earnings: $1,556,873

JERRY PATE had the best ever start as a rookie in 1976. He repeated Nicklaus's feat of winning the US Open in his first year on tour, and earned more than any other rookie had before in their first season.

● HE WAS ALSO the first player since Nicklaus to have won both US Amateur and US Open titles. He won the Open in thrilling circumstances, hitting a five iron from rough on the 18th hole to within 90cm (3ft) of the hole, and putting for a birdie when he needed a par to win the tournament.

● UNFORTUNATELY this early promise was never fulfilled, and although Pate went on to become the youngest player to win $1 million at the age of 27, and continued earning regularly until 1982, his career was cut short by injury.

COREY PAVIN

Born: Oxnard, CA, USA – 16/11/1959
First US Tour: 1983
Highest Ranking: 1 (1991)
US Tour Wins: 14
Major Wins: 1 (US Open 1995)
Ryder Cup Appearances: 3
Tour Earnings: $8 million

PAVIN'S CAREER seems to consist of a number of peaks and troughs. By 1985 he had worked his way to sixth on the US Tour before dropping to outside the top 50 in 1989. Two years later he fought his way to the very top after two wins, and again fell back down the rankings two years later.

● HIS GREATEST peak came in 1995 when, although only fourth on the Money list, he won the US Open and had a superlative Ryder Cup campaign, winning four out of five matches.

● HIS US Open win at Shinnecock Hills was well overdue and, like Jerry Pate in 1976, his final approach shot was perhaps the greatest he has ever played. A four-wood from over 220 yards ended five feet from the hole, and Pavin pipped Greg Norman to take the title.

● IN 1993, Pavin came close in the British Open eventually won by Norman, and won the World Matchplay Championship.

Corey Pavin has played flat out since joining the tour in 1983.

PEBBLE BEACH

Where: Monterey, CA, USA
Par: 72
Yardage: 6,799
Opened: 1919
Designer: Jack Neville
Major Events Staged: US Open 1972, 1982, 1992, US PGA 1977, US Amateur Championship 1929, 1947, 1961

PEBBLE BEACH is set in stunning surroundings and has witnessed some thrilling encounters over the years.
● THE COURSE was designed by Jack Neville, a local amateur champion, who had very little experience of course design, but the geography of the area meant that it was not a difficult task. As Neville later said, it was simply a case of deciding where to put the holes.
● TEN YEARS after Pebble Beach opened, it was the venue for the Amateur Championship, which saw Bobby Jones lose a shock first round encounter to unknown Johnny Goodman (who would later go on to win the US Open).
● THE US Open itself did not come to Pebble Beach until 1972, when it was won by Jack Nicklaus with a stunning shot at the 17th hole. Nicklaus had also won the last Amateur Championship to be held on the course in 1961. In 1982, Tom Watson pulled an amazing shot out of the bag when he holed out at 17 with a chip and birdied the final hole to beat Nicklaus into an uncharacteristic second place.
● THE US OPEN next returns to Pebble Beach in the year 2000, when Tom Kite will be looking to repeat his 1992 win.

CALVIN PEETE

Born: Detroit, MI, USA – 18/07/1943
First US Tour: 1975
Highest Ranking: 3 (1985)
US Tour Wins: 12
Major Wins: 0
Ryder Cup Appearances: 2

CALVIN PEETE did not swing a golf club until the age of 23, and even then he did so awkwardly due to a previously broken elbow. From this poor start, however, he went on to record the highest average in hitting fairways for ten seasons in a row. It was perhaps only his putting that prevented him winning a major.
● OFTEN AMONGST the money in the early 1980s, Peete competed twice in the Ryder Cup and recorded 12 US victories, before back injuries hampered his progress. He has since dabbled with the Senior Tour.
● PEETE is one of 19 children.

DOTTIE PEPPER

Born: Saratoga Springs, NY, USA – 17/08/1965
First LPGA Tour: 1987
Highest Ranking: 1 (1992)
Tour Wins: 14
Major Wins: 1 (Dinah Shore 1992)
Solheim Cup Appearances: 4
Tour Earnings: $3,977,769

DOTTIE PEPPER (née Mochrie) earned over $130,000 in her first year on Tour and has been a steady money earner ever since. She has been a top five player for the last seven years, and has won a tournament every year since 1992.
● IN 1992 she won her only major to date, the Dinah Shore, and also finished top of the money list. Since then Pepper has passed the $3 million mark in earnings and appeared in every Solheim Cup competition.
● PEPPER IS always accompanied on tour by her chow-chow dog, Furman.

PIN

THE PIN is another name for the flag, and is the origin of the term 'pin-high' which denotes a shot which is the correct length but just slightly off line. The pin gives a guide to where the hole is when playing a shot from a distance. It may be left in for chipping, but is best removed for putting, as a penalty is incurred if the pin is struck by a putt.

PINE VALLEY

Where: New Jersey, USA
Par: 70
Yardage: 6,765
Opened: 1919
Designer: George Crump
Major Events Staged: Walker Cup 1936, 1985

OPENED IN 1919, Pine Valley has never staged a major championship because its layout cannot cope with the crowds. It is still regarded as one of the best courses in the world, and one of the toughest. A wild

P

mixture of sand, swamp and exacting greens, every shot needs to be carefully assessed. Local members tend to bet that players attempting the course for the first time will not break 80, and although Arnold Palmer hit a 68 in his first round, many others have come a cropper.

● THE COURSE WAS designed by George Crump, who became obsessed with his project. He lived on a small property on the course while it was being built and invested $250,000 of his own money. Unfortunately he died with only 14 holes in place, and Hugh Wilson helped finish Crump's brainchild.

Pinero in Ryder Cup action.

PINEHURST COUNTRY CLUB

Where: North Carolina, USA

Par: 72

Yardage: 7,020

Opened: 1895

Designer: Donald Ross

Major Events Staged: US PGA 1936,
US Amateur Championship 1962,
Ryder Cup 1951

BOBBY JONES once referred to Pinehurst as the St Andrews of US golf. There are over 30 courses spread over some of the most beautiful American countryside, and as the name suggests it is surrounded by lush woodland.

● THE ORIGINAL course, on which the legendary Harry Vardon is supposed to

have played, was commissioned by a Boston businessman named James Tufts. This was replaced as the main Championship course in 1907 by Pinehurst No.2. It was here that Densmore Shute won the 1936 PGA Championship.

● FURTHER COURSES have been added over the years: a third in 1910, a fourth in 1919, a fifth in 1961, a sixth in 1979 and yet another in 1986. An eighth course is currently being laid out, and the US Open is set to make its debut at Pinehurst in 1999.

MANUEL PINERO

Born: Puebla de la Calzada, Spain –
01/09/1952

First European Tour: 1972

Highest Ranking: 4 (1976, 1977)

European Tour Wins: 9

Major Wins: 0

Ryder Cup Appearances: 2

MANUEL PINERO was a great competitor on the European Tour in the 1970s and 1980s. Often in the top five money earners, his play was outstanding in his two Ryder Cup appearances, winning both his singles matches easily.

● PINERO HAD a number of wins on tour, and appeared nine times for Spain in the World Cup, winning the team event with Ballesteros in 1976 and with Canizares in 1982, collecting the individual prize in the latter. A winner of the PGA Championship and European Open, Pinero's great strength was his putting.

GARY PLAYER

Born: Johannesburg, South Africa –
01/11/1935

First US Tour: 1957

Highest Ranking: 1 (1961)

US Tour Wins: 21

First Senior Tour: 1985

Senior Tour Wins: 17

Senior Tour Earnings: $4 million

Major Wins: 9 (British Open 1959,
1968, 1974, US Open 1965,
US Masters 1961, 1974, 1978,
US PGA 1962, 1972)

PRACTICE, a strict health regime and the will to win made the man in black one of the most successful golfers of the 1960s and 1970s, and stood him in good stead for a career that has now lasted some 40 years.

● AS A YOUNG golfer in South Africa, Player's swing was criticised and few saw him as the successor to Bobby Locke. He proved them all wrong, becoming, at the age of 42, only the fourth player to win all four majors.

● AFTER TURNING pro at a young age Player headed for the States, the first of many journeys that have made him the world's most travelled sportsman. In 1959 he travelled to Britain to rack up his first major, winning the Open at Muirfield. That was followed by the first of his three Masters wins in 1961, and the US PGA the following year.

● THE TITLES gradually mounted up, one of the most memorable being the Open he won at Carnoustie in 1968, when Player came out on top in a head-to-head battle with Jack Nicklaus. This was only bettered by the 1978 Augusta win when he came from seven behind leader Hubert Green to take the final.

PLAY-OFFS

IF PLAYERS are tied at the end of a gruelling tournament, then the dreaded play-off takes place. This can either be a sudden death scenario in which the winner of one hole takes all. Or it can take place over a full 18 holes again, as in the Open Championship.

● MOST OF THE great players have been involved in play-offs for major championships with varying degrees of success. Jack Nicklaus won three of the four that he competed in, while Faldo won two of his three. Both players were known for their steely determination and consistent play and were well suited to such pressures.

● OTHERS THAT have fared less well

include Hogan, Palmer and Watson, who all lost more play-offs than they won.

● PERHAPS THE MAN who dreads play-offs more than any other is Greg Norman – he has taken part in four, and has lost in each of them.

PLUS-FOURS

PLUS-FOURS are stereotypical golf clothing, but although some players such as Payne Stewart favour them, they are rarely worn today. Also known as knickerbockers, they are half way between trousers and shorts, and are tucked into the socks at the calf to create a baggy effect. They are called plus-fours because of the extra four inches added to shorts to create them.

POINT SCORING

THE STABLEFORD method of point scoring (named after Dr Frank Stableford) provides meaningful matches between players of varying abilities. Under the system developed in the 1930s, a scratch player receives a point for a bogey, two for a par, three for a birdie and so on.

● PLAYERS ALLOWED a stroke at the hole add this to their score. So a double bogey earns one point and so on. The stroke index of the hole determines where a player takes his strokes dependant on his handicap.

Payne Stewart models his latest in plus-fours.

Gary Player in the 1994 Senior British Open at Lytham St Annes, showing his unusual approach to golf – or is that gardening?

PORTUGAL

PORTUGAL HAS some fine courses, most of them strung out along the Algarve, but has never produced a golfer of any note. Perhaps the most famous course is the Penina, designed by Henry Cotton, which has often been the venue for the Portuguese Open.

Top Portuguese Courses

San Lorenzo, Algarve
Quinta do Lago, Algarve
Troia, Setubal
Vila Sol, Algarve
Penina, Algarve

PRACTICE

THERE ARE some players who practise religiously and are students of the game, others who simply turn up and play. For most average players, the only way to succeed is to get out on the putting green and the driving range with a bucket of balls, fresh from watching the latest teaching video, and slog away until it comes good. Books and magazines also provide plenty of opportunities to improve your game, but the only real way to the top is through practice.

NICK PRICE

Born: Durban, South Africa – 28/01/1957	
First US Tour: 1983	
Highest Ranking: 1 (1993, 1994)	
US Tour Wins: 15	
Major Wins: 3 (British Open 1994, US PGA 1992, 1994)	
Tour Earnings: $8,794,431	

IN 1997, Nick Price won over $1 million on the US Tour for the fourth time in his career, and returned to his winning ways for the first time since 1994. His three-year barren spell was made all the more surprising because the 1994 season had seen Price register six wins – the first time anybody had done so in one season since Tom Watson in 1980. It added to a total of eight wins over the previous three years, and confirmed Price as the best player in the world at the time.

● THAT SAME year, the South African won his first British Open at Turnberry, when Parnevik bogeyed the final hole. It added to Price's two US PGA titles, the first of which he had won two years earlier, at the age of 35.

● PRICE SHOULD have won the British Open long before, and indeed he had thrown away the title in the 1982 Open at Troon. Three shots lost to par over the final four holes meant he finished behind Tom Watson. He also finished second in 1988, but this time to brilliant play by Ballesteros at Royal Lytham.

PROFESSIONALS

GOLFERS HAVE BEEN paid for playing since the very early days of the game, and indeed the difference between professional and amateur status is greater than in many other sports. Players are ranked by the amount of money they earn in a year, and even relatively unsuccessful players can make a tidy sum on tour.

● THERE IS A VAST difference between the touring professionals of Europe, America and Asia, who earn huge amounts of money travelling the world competing in sponsored events, and club professionals, attached to a local course, who are paid for providing help and guidance to club members.

● THE PRO-CELEBRITY circuit is now an established set of events, in which famous sportsmen and comedians, among others, play together to raise money for charities. The larger Pro-Celebrity events generally take place prior to a Tour event, and leading Tour pros will team up with three celebrities to play in a foursome.

● PRO-AM TOURNAMENTS involve teams consisting of amateur and professional players, and are usually held at the same time as the on-going professional tournaments.

Nick Price looks to have picked up half of Miami Beach.

PROFESSIONAL GOLFERS' ASSOCIATION

THE BRITISH PGA was formed in 1901 by the 1894 Open Champion JH Taylor, with help from the celebrated amateur player and editor of Golf Illustrated, Harold Hilton, and other notable professionals of the time.

● THERE SEEMED a need to raise the profile of the professional game and to keep some players in check, and after an exchange of correspondence in Golf Illustrated, a meeting was held after the Open and a committee was formed for South East and London professionals.

● BY SEPTEMBER a full annual meeting was held and the Hon. James Balfour, soon to be Prime Minister, was elected President. Membership was extended to the rest of the country by the end of the year, and by 1903 the News of the World was offering a staggering £200 to the winner of a national matchplay championship organised by the PGA.

● BY THE EARLY 1920s the PGA had become a business, and was responsible for managing the Ryder Cup. In 1971 the PGA European Tour went its own way and took over many activities, but the PGA, now based at the Belfry, continues to preside over the affairs of club professionals.

PUTTERS

THE PUTTER is perhaps the most important club in the bag, and certainly the one that players experiment with most. The length of the shaft has been extended over the years – to the 'broom handle' favoured by such pros as Torrance and Wayne Riley – and the club face itself has been altered in terms of shape and weight in pursuit of that elusive 'feel'. Some players carry more than one putter in their bag, and will favour the one with which they are lucky.

QUALIFICATION

THERE ARE two routes to becoming a pro on the European and US Tours, these are to take part in the Challenge or Nike Tours, or to put yourself through the agony of Qualifying School.

● ONE OF the most nerve-racking processes known to a golfer, the prize of a Tour card can make it worthwhile. Having said that, those that have made the transition from Challenge Tour to Pro Tour generally seem to succeed more than those who have taken the school route.

Nigel Mansell: an amateur and a celebrity – he once considered joining the pro tour.

The *Virgin* Book Of Golf Records **107**

'Don't Look Back in Anger' – Ronan Rafferty in pensive mood.

RANKINGS

AS WELL AS the European and US Tour money lists, there is also a World Ranking system, which is approved by the R&A and other governing bodies. Sponsored by Sony and initially devised by Mark McCormack's International Management Group, the points system is based on the results of players taking part in various tournaments around the world. The rankings are updated weekly and players are awarded points on a three-year rolling basis.

● ONE PLAYER more than any other has dominated the chart: Greg Norman has never been out of the top ten since it was introduced in Masters week 1986.

TED RAY

Born: Jersey, Channel Islands – 28/03/1877
Career Spanned: 1900s to 1930s
Major Wins: 2 (British Open 1912,
**   US Open 1920)**

LIKE HIS FRIEND Harry Vardon, Ted Ray was a native of the Channel Islands, and like Vardon (and Tony Jacklin) he is one of only three Brits to have won Opens on both sides of the Atlantic.

● AN OUTSPOKEN, pipe-smoking, fun-loving giant of a man, Ray was not adverse to giving the ball a thwack, but was very delicate around the greens.

● HIS US OPEN win was rather lucky, after Vardon fell apart over the last nine holes, but there was no doubt about his talent. He was three-times runner-up in the News of the World Matchplay Championship, and

RACISM

RACISM HAS BEEN a problem since the early days of golf, especially in America, and changes in the golf world have reflected society's changing attitudes to the colour of people's skin.

● UNTIL 1961 a clause in the US PGA rules barred black players from joining. Theodore Havemeyer was one of the first to make a stand against the bigots when he was president of the US PGA. In only the second US Open, held on Long Island in 1896, he was faced with player revolt because of the inclusion of a local black player, John Shippen. Havemeyer bravely told the field that the Championship would go ahead with or without them.

● IN THE South, however, views were not so liberal, and it was not until 1975 that a black golfer took part in the US Masters at Augusta. The success of Tiger Woods and other black players is an encouraging sign that race is no longer an issue in professional golf.

RONAN RAFFERTY

Born: Newry, Northern Ireland –
**   13/01/1964**
First European Tour: 1982
Highest Ranking: 1 (1989)
European Tour Wins: 7
Major Wins: 0
Ryder Cup Appearances: 1
Tour Earnings: £2,152,899

IN 1981, at the age of 17, Ronan Rafferty was the youngest player ever to appear in the Walker Cup (at the time). He turned pro that year and by 1989 had topped the European Order of Merit. That same year he made his only Ryder Cup appearance, and beat the Open champion Calcavecchia in his singles match.

● PUTTING PROBLEMS have meant his career has dwindled, but he has achieved some success in Australia, Europe and South Africa.

R

was second on two other memorable occasions, firstly when trailing JH Taylor by eight shots when defending the Open in 1913, and also in the last Open played at Prestwick, in 1925.

DAI REES

Born: Barry, Wales – 31/03/1913
Career Spanned: 1930s to 1960s
Major Wins: 0

DAI REES, the man from Barry, is another candidate for the best British player never to have won a major. He came close, being three-times runner-up in the Open.
● HE IS BEST remembered as the only winning Ryder Cup Captain in a period spanning over 50 years. In 1957 he was playing captain at Lytham, defeating former US Open champion Ed Furgol easily in a singles encounter. Indeed, he was the last man to captain a victorious Great Britain side in the Ryder Cup, as the competition became a Europe/US battle in 1979.

JOSE RIVERO

Born: Madrid, Spain – 20/09/1955
First European Tour: 1983
Highest Ranking: 10 (1988)
European Tour Wins: 4
Ryder Cup Appearances: 2
Tour Earnings: £1,647,881

JOSE RIVERO is not the most ambitious golfer on the European circuit, but has nevertheless recorded four victories in

15 years on tour, including the French Open. He has won almost £2 million, and has appeared in two Ryder Cups.
● THE MAN from Madrid, who was a caddie and then club pro for some years before deciding to compete on Tour, has also been a World Cup winner for Spain.

THE ROAD HOLE

ALONG WITH the Postage Stamp, the Road Hole at St Andrews is one of the most famous holes at any golf club in the world. The 17th hole of the Old Course is a 421m (461 yd) par four, called the Road Hole because a road and a wall lie beyond the green ready to ruin a golfer's dreams.
● TO MAKE the green, one must hit a drive way out to the right and flirt with the out-of-bounds, before coming back to the tight green. Ironically, after the Road Hole, the 18th at St Andrews is one of the easiest final holes in Championship golf.

ALLAN ROBERTSON

Born: St Andrews,
        Scotland – 1815
Career Spanned: 1850s

WAS ALLAN ROBERTSON the father of professional golf? The St Andrews man was certainly the player of his

Jose Rivero displays one of his four trophy wins – the 1992 Catalan Open.

Dai Rees with the USA's Jackie Rees, in the 1957 Ryder Cup.

generation. The only reason he didn't win any major championships was that they hadn't been invented. In fact it was in tribute to Robertson that the Open was originally set up, the year after his death in 1859.
● ROBERTSON was also a golf ball maker, but fell out with his partner Tom Morris Snr in a dispute over the gutta percha ball. Robertson was not a fan and continued to make feathery balls. It was with a gutty, however, that he became the first man to break 80 on the St Andrews Old Course in 1858.

COSTANTINO ROCCA

Born: Bergamo, Italy – 4/12/56
First European Tour: 1983
Highest Ranking: 4 (1995, 1996)
European Tour Wins: 4
Major Wins: 0
Ryder Cup Appearances: 3
Tour Earnings: £2,307,374

COSTANTINO ROCCA is a passionate man, and one whose best and worst moments have all been in the public eye. Losing to Davis Love III on his Ryder Cup debut in 1993 was seen by many as the defeat that lost Europe the cup.

● HE RETURNED in 1995, however, and won three out the five points which secured Europe the cup. He was also one of the success stories of the 1997 victory in Valderrama, and with his consistent form on the European Tour has become an established member of the team.

● HIS OTHER memorable moment came in the 1995 Open at St Andrews. Needing a chip and a putt to take John Daly to a play-off, he choked on the chip and the chance looked to have gone. An amazing 18m (60 ft) putt, however, forced the play-off. Daly eventually won, but Rocca had cemented himself in the hearts of the St Andrews crowds.

CHI CHI RODRIGUEZ

Born: Puerto Rica – 23/10/1935
First US Tour: 1960
US Tour Wins: 8
Tour Earnings: $1 million
First Senior Tour: 1985
Senior Tour Wins: 22
Senior Tour Earnings: $5,696,544
Major Wins: 0
Ryder Cup Appearances: 1

RODRIGUEZ is possibly better suited to the laid back style of the Senior Tour than he ever was to the regular one. His talkative manner – even more so than Trevino – was loved by the crowds, but hated by the other players. After an

Constantino Rocca in subdued mood.

average career which saw him record eight wins and a Ryder Cup appearance, the Puerto Rican turned to the Seniors in 1986.

● HE HAS so far won 22 times and is the fifth highest earner on the Senior Tour, earning five times more in ten years than he did in twenty on the regular PGA Tour.

BILL ROGERS

Born: Waco, TX, USA – 10/09/1951
First US Tour: 1975
Highest Ranking: 5 (1981)
US Tour Wins: 5
Major Wins: 1 (British Open 1981)
Ryder Cup Appearances: 1

LOOKING BACK, Bill Rogers' career seems to consist of one tumultuous year and a rapid decline. In 1981, he was the Player of the Year, won the British Open after taking a five stroke lead into the final round, and made his only Ryder Cup appearance. Before that year and ever since, there is little to talk about!

EDUARDO ROMERO

Born: Cordoba, Argentina – 17/07/1954
First European Tour: 1985
Highest Ranking: 11 (1990)
European Tour Wins: 6
Major Wins: 0

EDUARDO ROMERO is without doubt the greatest Argentinian golfer of modern times. After huge success in South America, he joined the European Tour in 1985. Since then he has been reasonably successful, without ever having challenged in a major. 1997 was his best money-earning year to date.

ROOKIES

A ROOKIE is a player in their first full season on Tour, and the Rookie of the Year award is given to the debutante that makes the biggest impression – or wins the most money.

● IN 1962, Jack Nicklaus made a huge impression in his first year on tour and actually won the US Open before being named Rookie of the Year. Similarly, Jose-Maria Olazabal was named Rookie of the Year on the European Tour in 1986 after finishing his first full season at second in the Order of Merit.

THE ROYAL AND ANCIENT GOLF CLUB

ALTHOUGH the Royal and Ancient is the clubhouse for the St Andrews golf course, it is better known as the administrative home of golf outside of the USA.

● THE CLUB was formed by the '22 noblemen and gentlemen' who started the Society of St Andrews Golfers on 14 May 1754. They drafted 13 essential rules, which still form the basis for the rules of golf today.

● WITH THE QUALITY of the course and its booming membership, the club gradually gained prestige, and in 1873 the Open moved to St Andrews after previously being held at Prestwick. By the end of the 19th century it was suggested that the R&A should also take over the running of the competition, and so by degrees the club became the centre of the golfing world.

● IN 1919, the R&A became responsible not only for the running of championships, but also for maintaining rules. Over the years other responsibilities have been added and today the selection of Walker Cup teams also takes place within the stately clubhouse, built in 1857.

ROYAL BIRKDALE

Where: Southport, England
Par: 72
Yardage: 6,986
Opened: 1889
Designer: George Lowe
Major Events Staged: British Open 1954, 1961, 1965, 1971, 1976, 1983, 1991 Ryder Cup 1965, 1969.

THE ORIGINAL Birkdale course was designed in 1889 by George Lowe, but the course that we know today was built on its current site in 1897, where JH Taylor and Fred Hawtree made changes to accommodate the increasing skill of players.

● IN THE 1930s the course was complemented by a rather controversial clubhouse, and with the ideal amount of open spaces to cope with crowds, the club began to stage championships.

● AFTER HOSTING the Amateur Championship in 1946, the Open finally came to Royal Birkdale in 1954. And although the Open has been staged at Birkdale seven times now, it has never been won by a European.

● PETER THOMSON won the 1954 Open, and the Australian would win his fifth and final Open 11 years later on the same course. In between, Arnold Palmer won in 1961, beating the elements as much as the field.

● THE THREE BIG Americans who took over Nicklaus's crown all won at Birkdale – Trevino, Miller and Watson. Miller's final round was spectacular, carding a 66. Equally astounding was the outward 29 that Ian Baker-Finch played in winning the last Open held at Birkdale in 1991.

ROYAL LYTHAM AND ST ANNES

Where: St Annes, Lancashire, England
Par: 71
Yardage: 6,857
Opened: 1886
Designer: George Lowe
Major Events Staged: British Open 1926, 1952, 1958, 1963, 1969, 1974, 1979, 1988, 1996

ROYAL LYTHAM was the venue for Tony Jacklin's historic victory in the 1969 British Open. He was the first British player to win the tournament for 18 years.

● SEVE BALLESTEROS won his first Open at Lytham in 1979,

Eduardo Romero hangs on in there to score another win.

defeating Hale Irwin over the final few holes with some of the most wayward golf ever played by a champion. It was also the venue for his third and (to date) last victory in 1988, when he held off Nick Faldo and Nick Price with a 65 which Ballesteros described as the best round of his life.

● THE PRESENT COURSE was designed by the club's first professional, George Lowe, in 1897, although the club was formed in 1886. It is tucked away at the end of a residential road in the seaside resort of St Annes, near Blackpool.

● KEN COTTON and Harry Colt are among those who have helped maintain the course standards over the years, and great Open Champions such as Bobby Jones, Bobby Locke, Peter Thomson and Gary Player have also won there. Tom Lehman's win in 1996 was the first by a US professional.

THE ROYAL MELBOURNE

Where: Melbourne, Australia

Par: 71

Yardage: 6,946

Opened: 1931

Designers: Dr Alister MacKenzie and Alex Russell

Major Events Staged: Australian Open 1905, 1907, 1909, 1912, 1913, 1921, 1924, 1927, 1933, 1939, 1953, 1963, 1984, 1985, 1987, 1991, World Cup 1988

ALTHOUGH the original Melbourne golf club was founded as early as 1847, it is a composite course on the same site which is used for Australian Opens today. The East and West courses at Melbourne were both designed by Dr Alister MacKenzie, in between creating Cypress Point and Augusta National.

● WITH THE HELP of an Australian Open Champion, Alex Russell, MacKenzie created a golfing masterpiece, replete with a huge number of the sprawling bunkers for which MacKenzie became famous. The composite course marries six holes from the East course with twelve of those from the West.

● THE COURSE has become a favourite for Australian Opens and has also staged the Canada Cup in 1959 and the World Cup in 1988.

ROYAL NORTH DEVON

Where: Northam, Devon, England

Par: 71

Yardage: 6,662

Opened: 1864

Designer: Tom Morris Snr

Major Events Staged: British Amateur Championship 1912, 1925, 1931

ROYAL NORTH DEVON has the distinction of being the oldest golf club in England still occupying its original site. It has never staged an Open Championship but has been linked with some famous names over the years.

● THE GREAT Tom Morris Snr was the original designer, creating one course of 17 holes and another of 22. In later years the locally born JH Taylor, one of the Great Triumvirate, was made president.

● A TOUGH COURSE, originally built on barren moorland, it has the additional hazards of grazing sheep and cattle.

ROYAL ST GEORGES

Where: Sandwich, Kent, England

Par: 70

Yardage: 6,857

Opened: 1887

Designer: Dr Laidlaw Purves

Major Events Staged: British Open 1894, 1899, 1904, 1911, 1922, 1928, 1934, 1938, 1949, 1981, 1985, 1993, British Amateur Championship 1892, 1896, 1900, 1904, 1908, 1914, 1929, 1937, 1948, 1959, 1972, 1997

THE ORIGINAL course at Royal St Georges, usually known simply as Sandwich, was created by Dr Laidlaw Purves and a number of his associates who formed the Sandwich Golf Association in 1887.

● ST GEORGES is known for a number of firsts: in 1894 it was the first course outside Scotland to hold the Open, and that year's winner, JH Taylor, was the first English champion. The first American winner, Walter Hagen, also claimed his Open at St Georges in 1922, and the first televised hole-in-one occurred there, courtesy of Tony Jacklin in the 1967 Dunlop Masters.

● THE LAST TWO winners of the Open at Sandwich were Sandy Lyle in 1985, and Greg Norman in 1993, reflecting the fact that the course favours long-hitters. Bill Rogers was another example of this when he won the first Open staged at Sandwich for 32 years in 1981. The gap was due to the course not being able to cope with the logistics of the event, rather than any slight on the state of the course.

Westward Ho! – the oldest golf club in Britain, still occupying its original moorland site.

With the surrounding roads and amenities now brought up to date, the future looks bright for Sandwich.

RULES

TODAY THERE are a huge number of rules and regulations with subtle nuances and definitions – far too many to discuss here without sending most readers to sleep. Back in 1754 when the men of St Andrews got together, there were only 13 very basic rules, and they adhered to the principle of 'play it as it lies'.

● TODAY THE rules are enforced in the US by the United States Golf Association, and in the rest of the world by the R&A.

RUNNERS-UP

EVEN THE MOST successful golfers experience the agony of coming second occasionally. There are, however, some who seem destined to finish as runners-up, and Greg Norman is the unluckiest of the lot. The Great White Shark has eight times finished behind the leader, but only won a major twice. Other notable champions who have finished second more times than first include JH Taylor and Byron Nelson.

MOST TIMES AS RUNNER UP

Listed below are the players that have been regularly 'close but no cigar' in major championships – the number of times they have actually won is listed in brackets.

Jack Nicklaus	19	(18)
Arnold Palmer	10	(7)
Sam Snead	8	(7)
Greg Norman	8	(2)
JH Taylor	7	(5)
Tom Watson	7	(8)
Ben Hogan	6	(9)
Byron Nelson	6	(5)
Gary Player	6	(9)
Harry Vardon	6	(7)

RYDER CUP

First Played: 1927
Results: Played 32
United States 23 Wins
GB & I/Europe 7 Wins
2 Matches halved
Most Appearances: Nick Faldo (11)
Most Points Won: Nick Faldo (25)

THE RYDER CUP is the most famous team competition in golf, and has become hugely popular on both sides of the Atlantic as the balance of power has swung from the USA to Europe. In the last seven competitions, Europe has been victorious on four occasions – two on either side of the Atlantic. The USA have won twice and one match has been halved. The memorable scenes of celebration at The Belfry in 1985 were the start of a glorious period for Europe in a competition that has been dominated by the USA for most of its history.

● THE FIRST Ryder Cup took place in 1927, when Samuel Ryder donated a trophy for a golf match between the professionals of Great Britain and Ireland and the USA. After two victories in the first four competitions, the Great Britain team was to win only one tournament between 1935 and 1977. From 1979 onwards the competition was broadened, pitting the US team against players from all over Europe.

● PLAYERS are not usually paid for their efforts, but the prestige of the event means that competition is always fierce.

Ryder Cup results

1927	Worcester, USA	USA 9.5/2.5
1929	Moortown, Leeds	GB & I 7/5
1931	Scioto, Columbus	USA 9/3
1933	Southport	GB & I 6.5/5.5
1935	Ridgewood, NJ	USA 9/3
1937	Southport	USA 8/4
1947	Portland, OR	USA 11/1
1949	Ganton, Yorks	USA 7/5
1951	Pinehurst	USA 9.5/2.5
1953	Wentworth	USA 6.5/5.5
1955	Thunderbird, CA	USA 8/4
1957	Lindrick, Notts	GB & I 7.5/4.5
1959	Eldorado, CA	USA 8.5/3.5
1961	Lytham	USA 14.5/9.5
1963	Atlanta	USA 23/9
1965	Royal Birkdale	USA 19.5/12.5
1967	Houston, Texas	USA 23.5/8.5
1969	Royal Birkdale	Halved 16/16
1971	St Louis	USA 18.5/13.5
1973	Muirfield	USA 19/13
1975	Laurel Valley	USA 21/11
1977	Lytham	USA 12.5/7.5
1979	The Greenbrier	USA 17/11
1981	Walton Heath	USA 18.5/9.5
1983	PGA National, FL	USA 14.5/13.5
1985	The Belfry	Europe 16.5/11.5
1987	Muirfield Village	Europe 15/13
1989	The Belfry	Halved 14/14
1991	Kiawah Island	USA 14.5/13.5
1993	The Belfry	USA 15/13
1995	Rochester	Europe 14.5/13.5
1997	Valderrama, Spain	Europe 14.5/13.5

Victory for Europe at Valderrama, 1997.

SAND

SAND MIGHT be great for holidaymakers, but it isn't a welcome sight for golfers. Whether it is the fine white sand of Augusta or the coarse, damp, brown sand of a windy links course, a bunker is always to be avoided.

● FOR PROFESSIONALS in the modern game, a decent lie in a sand trap is sometimes preferred to a lie in the scruffy grass around the green. This was not always the case, but since the 1920s, when Gene Sarazen designed the first moulded sand wedges, players have had more control in bunkers and have been able to aim for the flag, rather than simply trying to get out of trouble.

● WHILE IN A sand trap, a golfer is forbidden from grounding the club as part of a practice swing, because it could affect the ball's lie. It incurs a penalty of two strokes in strokeplay and loss of the hole in matchplay.

Did You Know?

Perhaps the worst bunker experience ever was had by DJ Bayly MacArthur in a 1931 Australian tournament. After heavy rain, the contents of the bunker had turned to quicksand, and MacArthur was up to his armpits before his cries for help brought a rescue.

DOUG SANDERS

Born: Cedartown, GA, USA – 24/07/1933
First US Tour: 1957
US Tour Wins: 19
Major Wins: 0
Ryder Cup Appearances: 1

DOUG SANDERS was a useful golfer in the late 1950s and early 1960s. Of the 19 tournaments he secured between 1956 and 1972, five were won in 1961, the year in which he lost the US Open by one shot to Gene Littler.

● IT WAS HIS other brush with a major that brought him more attention, however. In 1970, when past his best, Sanders had qualified for the British Open, and was in sight of victory. With only the last two holes at St Andrews to play, he needed pars at both. He saved par at the difficult 17th, and was left with a downhill putt of 1.2m (4ft) to clinch the title. He missed, and Jack Nicklaus won the play-off by one shot the following day.

Chipping in

'A champion is not a champion because he wins, but how he conducts himself.'

Doug Sanders thinking up another pearl of golfing wisdom.

GENE SARAZEN

Born: Harrison, NY, USA – 27/02/1902
Career Spanned 1920s – 1930s
US Tour Wins: 38
Major Wins: 7 (British Open 1932, US Open 1922, 1932, US Masters 1935, US PGA 1922, 1923, 1933)
Ryder Cup Appearances: 6

GENE SARAZEN started his career at a very early age, and he continues to make news even as he approaches his 100th birthday.

● WINNING THE US Open and US PGA in 1922, aged 20, Sarazen became the first player ever to win two majors in the same year. By the age of 21 he had won three majors, something not even Tiger Woods has accomplished.

● THE ENSUING success of Bobby Jones meant that although Sarazen won pro tournaments regularly after 1923, the major successes that had come early to him dried up somewhat. Within five years of Jones' retirement in 1930, Sarazen had completed his Grand Slam with the 1932 British Open and 1935 Masters. He was the first player to win all four majors.

● IN THE 1935 Masters he holed a fairway wood for an albatross two at Augusta's 15th and beat Craig Wood in a play-off the next day. The wood shot is regarded by many as the greatest shot ever played.

● A MAN OF firsts, Sarazen invented the sand iron, remains the youngest ever winner of the US PGA, and won the US Open and the British Open in the space of 15 days in 1932.

● AS A 71-year-old, Sarazen returned to Troon and was caught on camera shooting a hole-in-one at the Postage Stamp. Some 25 years later, aged 96, he teed off at the 1998 US Masters in Augusta and looked in fine health – the small man as brash and ebullient as ever.

Chipping in

'Even when times were good, I realised that my earning power as a golf professional depended on too many ifs and putts.'

SAWGRASS

Where: Ponte Vedra Beach, FL, USA
Par: 7000 yards
Yardage: 72
Opened: 1982
Designer: Pete Dye
Major Events Staged: The Players Championship (formerly The Tournament Players Championship) has been held at Sawgrass since 1982

JUST WHEN PEOPLE thought Pete Dye had created his very worst courses, he designed the stadium-style Tournament Players Course at Sawgrass. With its high grassy banks, it was designed specifically with spectators in mind.

● THE PLAYERS weren't so keen. Jack Nicklaus said of the course: 'I've never been very good at stopping a 5-iron on the hood of a car.' Jerry Pate even threw Pete Dye in the lake when winning the first Players Championship there in 1982.

● GRADUALLY THE

Gene Sarazen, the elder statesman of American golf, in 1997.

course has been refined, however, and has helped the Players Championship, held two weeks before The Masters, become one of the most popular US tour events. It is sometimes described as the fifth major.

SCOTLAND

ALTHOUGH SOME historians have suggested that golf originates from the Romans or from Dutch sailors, most people believe that the game has its origins in Scotland – certainly the game in its modern form began there.

● THE HONOURABLE COMPANY of Edinburgh Golfers coined the first documented rules of the game, the first British Opens were held on Scottish courses and won by Scotsmen, and when America took up the game, the Scots still dominated tournaments.

● TODAY THERE are fewer great Scottish players than the past, but Colin Montgomerie, Sandy Lyle and Sam Torrance still fly the flag. Indeed Scotland won the Alfred Dunhill Cup in 1995, with Andrew Coltart joining Torrance and Montgomerie in the winning side.

● ST ANDREWS remains the home of world golf, and some of the best courses in the world are to be found on the linksland of Scotland.

Major competitions held in Scotland

The British Open
The Loch Lomond Invitational
The Alfred Dunhill Cup

Ten Famous Scottish Players

James Braid
Willie Anderson
Tommy Armour
Sandy Herd
Sandy Lyle
Colin Montgomerie
Tom Morris Jnr
Willie Park Snr
MacDonald Smith
Sam Torrance

Top Courses

Carnoustie
Gleneagles
Loch Lomond
Muirfield
Royal Dornoch
St Andrews
Troon
Turnberry

Did You Know?

Golf was banned in Scotland in the 15th century because the authorities thought that its popularity was undermining the country's defences.

The par-five 11th at Sawgrass Course, until recently one of the least popular courses on the US Tour.

PETER SENIOR

Born: Singapore – 31/07/1959

First European Tour: 1979

Highest Ranking: 7 (1987)

European Wins: 4

Major Wins: 0

PETER SENIOR has been most successful on home ground, winning both the Australian Open and the Australian PGA Championship, and topping the Australasia money list three times, in 1987, 1989 and 1993. He has a total of 20 wins worldwide, the most significant being the European Open, which he won at Sunningdale in 1990, forcing Ian Woosnam into second place.

● HE IS RENOWNED for his long 'broomstick' putter, which rests just below his chin. Recommended to him by Sam Torrance, the club has gone some way to curing his putting 'yips'.

THE SENIOR TOURS

THE US SENIOR TOUR was established in 1980 as an outlet for players like Palmer, Casper and January, over the age of 50, who still attracted attention from spectators but were no longer winning tournaments.

● THE TOUR has proved very lucrative, with good players such as Trevino quickly earning twice what they did in 20 years on the regular tour. Today players like Hale Irwin and Gil Morgan currently dominate the 30-odd competitions, which include four Senior majors.

● IN EUROPE a similar tour also takes place, but with much less prize money than in the US. Tommy Horton and Noel Ratcliffe were the top two players in 1997.

Senior Major Championships

The US Senior Open Championship
Senior PGA Championship
The Tradition
Ford Senior Players Championship

Leading Senior Tour Players

Jack Nicklaus
Lee Trevino
Hale Irwin
Ray Floyd
Tom Wargo
Dave Stockton
Bob Charles

Peter Senior pictured with his extra-long putter.

SHANK

SHANK is the hosel part of an iron just above the clubface. A shank is also a shot in which that part of the club connects with the ball, generally sending the ball right off its intended line.

PATTY SHEEHAN

Born: Middlebury, VT, USA – 27/10/1956

First LPGA Tour: 1980

Highest Ranking: 2 (1983, 1984, 1988, 1990, 1993)

Tour Wins: 35

Major Wins: 6 (US Women's Open 1992, 1994, LPGA 1983, 1984, 1993, Dinah Shore 1996)

Solheim Cup Appearances: 4

Tour Earnings: $5.2 million

AFTER A VERY successful amateur career during which she won National Championships and competed in the Curtis Cup, Patty Sheehan turned pro in 1980.

● HER CAREER since has been spectacular, and in less than 20 years she has won over 30 titles on the LPGA Tour, secured six major wins (with 13 years between the first and last) and contributed to three Solheim Cup wins.

● ALTHOUGH SHE has never topped the Money List, Sheehan has earned over $5 million, and in 1993 she secured her place in the Golf Hall of Fame.

● IN ADDITION to her six majors, she also won the British Open in 1992 at Woburn.

Chipping in

'It wasn't much fun being an amateur. I got tired of polishing the silverware.'

Patty Sheehan jumps in the lake after winning the Dinah Shore at Mission Hills, California 1998.

SHINNECOCK HILLS

Where: Southampton, Long Island, USA

Par: 70

Yardage: 6,697

Opened: 1891

Designer: Willie Dunn

Major Events Staged: US Open 1896, 1986, 1995, US Amateur Championship 1896, Walker Cup 1977

ALTHOUGH IT HAS had many overhauls since its creation in the late 19th century, the original Shinnecock Hills course was designed by the rather squat Willie Dunn, of Musselburgh fame. After creating a course in the resort of Biarritz, he was asked to design one at Long Island, and did so two miles from the coast with the help of a team of Indians from a nearby reservation.

● IN 1896 Shinnecock Hills staged the second US Open and US Amateur Championships, but would not hold another major championship for 90 years. When the US Open returned there in 1986, it seemed to many that American golf had come home.

● RAY FLOYD was a popular winner and the only man to break par with a one-under

279. In 1995 the tournament returned and Corey Pavin proved an equally appreciated champ, holding off Greg Norman with a par score of 280.

SHOCKS

THERE HAVE BEEN a few shocks over the years in golf, but in a sport which is based very much on consistency and application they are few and far between.

● WHEN JACK FLECK, the unknown pro from Iowa, beat Ben Hogan to win the 1955 US Open it was perhaps the biggest shock of all time. Bill Rogers' win in the 1981 British Open at Sandwich was also a surprise, as was John Daly's success in the 1991 PGA at Crooked Stick.

Did you know?

When John Daly won at Crooked Stick in his first US PGA, he was the ninth reserve in line for a place, and only qualified as a result of eight others dropping out ahead of him. Their diverse reasons included a pregnant wife, an unwell mother-in-law, injury, not wishing to travel, and, in Lee Trevino's case, the excessive length of the course.

● IN THE team game, perhaps the greatest shock was Europe's victory over the US in the Solheim Cup in 1992, winning by $11\frac{1}{2}$ to $6\frac{1}{2}$. This bombshell came after the US captain Mickey Wright had said that 'any of the US team could improve that of Europe by joining it'.

● IN GOLF, such shocks that do occur are usually more subtle. For example, when Mark O'Meara won the US Masters in 1998 at the last hole, he had hardly been mentioned as a contender throughout the four rounds.

CHARLIE SIFFORD

Born: Charlotte, NC, USA – 2/6/1923

Career Spanned: 1930s – 1960s

Major Wins: 0

CHARLIE SIFFORD became a golf pro after leaving the army, but despite winning US Tour events regularly he was never accepted by the racist establishment. He didn't qualify for the Masters and was turned down for jobs as the registered pro at clubs as his career wound down.

● IN LATER life, however, he was successful on the Senior tour. His efforts and eventual success have helped to further the acceptance of black players in America.

JAY SIGEL

Born: Narberth, PA, USA – 13/11/1943
Major Amateur Wins: 3 (British Amateur 1979, US Amateur 1982, 1983)
Major Wins: 0
First Senior Tour: 1993
Senior Tour Wins: 2
Senior Tour Earnings: $2.5 million

JAY SIGEL didn't turn professional until he was 50, and then only for the Senior Tour – he has never competed on the regular PGA Tour. Nevertheless, he has competed in the British and US Opens, and was of the most successful amateurs in the modern competition.

● A WINNER OF the Amateur Championships on both sides of the Atlantic, he has also made more Walker Cup appearances than anybody else, and accumulated more points.

● ALTHOUGH COMING late to the professional game, Sigel soon adapted and was Rookie of the Year on the Senior Tour – aged 51. He has since won two tournaments and accumulated over $2 million in his five years as an older professional.

SCOTT SIMPSON

Born: San Diego, CA, USA – 17/09/1955
First US Tour: 1978
Highest Ranking: 4 (1987)
US Tour Wins: 6
Major Wins: 1 (US Open 1987)
Ryder Cup Appearances: 1
Tour Earnings: $5 million

A FORMER WALKER CUP player, it took Simpson two attempts to qualify for the professional tour, but tasted victory in only his second full season, winning the 1980 Western Open.

● ALTHOUGH HIS career is now on the wane, Simpson won over $700,000 in 1995 alone, finishing in the top 20 for only the third time in his career.

● THE US OPEN seems to bring out the best in Simpson – as well as holding off Watson in the 1987 Open at the Olympic Club, he lost a play-off to Payne Stewart in the 1991 Open at Hazeltine, and had two more top ten finishes in the intervening years.

Scott Simpson at the 1995 US Open.

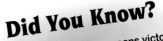

Vijay Singh takes a short break from practising.

VIJAY SINGH

Born: Lautoka, Fiji – 22/02/1963
First European Tour: 1988
European Tour Wins: 7
Highest Ranking: 6 (1994)
Tour Earnings: £1,553,558
First US Tour: 1992
Highest Ranking: 9 (1995)
US Tour Wins: 5
Major Wins: 0
Tour Earnings: $3,987,559

WELL KNOWN for his endless practice sessions, Fiji's only internationally-known golfer is probably the hardest working player in the world. Since he started on the European Tour in 1988, Vijay Singh's most lucrative victory has been the 1997 World Matchplay Championship, although he also triumphed in the South African Open ahead of Nick Price in 1997.

● HE NOW concentrates his efforts on the US Tour, where he recorded two more victories in 1997, as his earnings approached the $4 million mark.

Did You Know?

Vijay Singh's first name means victory in Hindi.

SKINS GAME

IN A SKINS GAME, four players compete against each other, with cash prizes available at every hole to the player that outscores the other three. As holes are halved the money is carried forward until somebody wins a hole outright, which can result in huge amounts of cash.

● THE SENIOR Skins Tournament is the most famous example of a tournament employing this method of scoring, with Ray Floyd having held the Skins title for three years from 1994 to 1996.

SLICE

THE OPPOSITE of a hook, a slice (for right-handers) is a shot where the ball spins clockwise and moves far to the right of its intended path. For left-handers it will spin in the opposite direction and veer off to the left.

● IT IS PERHAPS the most common of all poor shots and is a result of the clubface being open to the line of swing at impact.

JEFF SLUMAN

Born: Rochester, NY, USA – 11/09/1957
First US Tour: 1983
Highest Ranking: 14 (1992)
US Tour Wins: 2
Major Wins: 1 (US PGA 1988)
Ryder Cup Appearances: 0
Tour Earnings: $5,145,365

JEFF SLUMAN is best known for being the most anonymous man ever to win a major in golf.

● SLUMAN HAS never finished in the top ten of the money list, has no victories abroad and has only won twice on the US Tour in 14 years.

● SLUMAN IS probably not complaining about his lack of wins, however, as he has racked up over $4 million.

MACDONALD SMITH

Born: Carnoustie, Scotland – 1890
Career Spanned: 1900s to 1930s
Career Wins: 30
Major Wins: 0

MACDONALD SMITH is the greatest golfer there never was. He was three strokes off of the lead in an incredible eight US and British Opens without ever winning once. He lost the 1910 US Open in a play-off when a par at either of the last two holes would have secured victory.

● AS LATE AS 1925 he was still throwing chances away, losing the British Open at Prestwick when, needing only 79 to take the trophy, he recorded an 82.

● SMITH CAME from a remarkable family: all five of his brothers emigrated to America, and his brother Alex twice won the US Open.

Did You Know?

When Jeff Sluman won the 1988 PGA Championship, he was such an unknown that the newspaper USA Today commented 'An empty cab drew up at Oak Tree last week and Jeff Sluman got out.'

Jeff Sluman tries to identify himself by wearing an unusual hat.

SAM SNEAD

Born: Hot Springs, VA, USA – 27/05/1912

First US Tour: 1937

Highest Ranking: 1 (1938, 1949, 1950)

US Tour Wins: 81

Major Wins: 7 (British Open 1946,
US Masters 1949, 1952, 1954,
US PGA 1942, 1949, 1951)

Ryder Cup Appearances: 7

SAM SNEAD's career lasted for over 40 years, and he became the oldest man ever to win a tour event when he took the Greensboro Open in 1965 at the age of 52. It was mainly due to his great swing and good shape that kept Snead genuinely challenging for honours into his 60s – he was third behind Nicklaus and Trevino in the 1974 US PGA, aged 62.

● THIS EXTENDED career helped him to win 81 PGA Tour victories, more than any other golfer and a record which is never likely to be broken.

● IN THE 1940s and 1950s he won seven majors, but despite being second on four occasions he never managed to win the US Open. Although he lost a play-off to Lew Worsham in 1947, it was perhaps the 1939 Open which was his most tragic near-miss. Taking a triple bogey eight at the last hole, he missed a play-off by two strokes. Snead had thought he required a birdie, when a par would have secured the win.

● BORN INTO a poor family in Virginia, Snead was something of a novelty on tour at first, where players regarded him as a country boy. Encouraged by his manager Fred Corcoran, Snead was encouraged to play a few holes of the US Open in bare feet to reinforce the hillbilly caricature. As Snead was to show over the years, however, he was nobody's fool.

Sam Snead, still playing at the age of 84.

Chipping in

'Good golfing temperament falls between taking it with a grin or shrug, and throwing a fit.'

THE SOLHEIM CUP

First Played: 1990

Wins: America 3 Europe 1

THE FEMALE equivalent of the Ryder Cup was started in 1990 and is a three-day event with teams of 12, held every two years. The competition includes foursomes, best ball and singles and, apart from a shock in 1992, has been dominated by the US.

● THE COMPETITION is named after the engineer Karsten Solheim, the man behind the Ping company, in recognition of his contribution to the world of golf.

The Solheim Cup winners			
1990	Lake Nona, Orlando, FL	US	11½–4½
1992	Dalmahoy, Edinburgh	Eur	11½–6½
1994	The Greenbrier, WV	US	13–7
1996	Chepstow, Wales	US	17–11

ANNIKA SORENSTAM

Born: Stockholm, Sweden – 09/10/1970

First LPGA Tour: 1994

Highest Ranking: 1 (1995)

Tour Wins: 6

Major Wins: 2 (US Women's Open 1995, 1996)

Solheim Cup Appearances: 2

Tour Earnings: $2 million

ANNIKA SORENSTAM turned pro in 1992 after winning the All-American Collegiate title, and has been one of the success stories of the 1990s. In six short years she has since taken two US Women's Opens, topped the Tour List in both America and Europe, been voted Player of the Year, and even won the award for Swedish Athlete of the Year.

SOUTH AFRICA

SOUTH AFRICA has had golf clubs since the 1890s, when The Bedford Club at Cape Province and the Royal Cape club at Wynberg were formed. A century later the country is home to some of the world's best players in Bobby Locke, Gary Player and Ernie Els, and one of its richest competitions in the Million Dollar Challenge – originally known as the Sun City Classic.

● DUE TO APARTHEID, South Africa were barred from playing in the World Cup after the 1979 championships in Greece, but the political problems did not affect individual players travelling to and from South Africa for tournaments.

● THE APARTHEID YEARS also stunted the progress of many promising black players, but the country is now a true golfing force, with Ernie Els topping the World Rankings in the 1990s, and the South African team of Els and Westner beating the US in the 1996 World Cup in Cape Town.

S

Major South African Competitions

The South African Open
Alfred Dunhill South African PGA
Championship
The Million Dollar Challenge

Five Famous South African Players

Ernie Els
David Frost
Bobby Locke
Gary Player
Wayne Westner

Top South African Courses

Durban Country Club
Fancourt Golf and Country Club
Houghton, Johannesburg
Gary Player Country Club at Sun City
Royal Johannesburg

THE SOUTH AFRICAN OPEN

First Played: 1903

Most Wins: 13 – Gary Player (1956, 1960, 1965, 1966, 1967, 1968, 1969, 1972, 1975, 1976, 1977, 1979, 1981)

Lowest 72-hole Score: 267 – Tony Johnstone (Durban 1993)

OLDER THAN THE Australian or New Zealand Opens, the South African Open is one of the oldest competitions in the world, and has largely been dominated by native players, with Gary Player and Bobby Locke alone sharing 22 titles.

Did you know?

Gary Player and Dale Hayes both won the 1976 South African Open. It was held twice in the same year at different venues, because the date of the Championship was changed. The same thing happened in 1993, when Tony Johnstone and Clinton Whitelaw both won.

The South African Open Last 25 Winners

1972	Gary Player, Royal Johannesburg	274
1973	Bob Charles, Royal Durban	282
1974	Bobby Cole, Royal Johannesburg	272
1975	Gary Player, Mowbray	278
1976	Dale Hayes, Houghton	287
1976	Gary Player, Royal Durban	280
1977	Gary Player, Royal Johannesburg	273
1978	Hugh Baiocchi, Mowbray	285
1979	Gary Player, Houghton	279
1980	Bobby Cole, Durban	279
1981	Gary Player, Royal Johannesburg	272
1982	Not played	
1983	Charles Bolling, Mowbray	278
1984	Tony Johnstone, Houghton	274
1985	Gary Levenson, Royal Durban	280
1986	David Frost, Royal Johannesburg	275
1987	Mark McNulty, Mowbray	278
1988	Wayne Westner, Durban	275
1989	Fred Wadsworth, Glendower	278
1990	Trevor Dodds, Royal Cape	285
1991	Wayne Westner, Durban	272
1992	Ernie Els, Houghton	273
1993	Clinton Whitelaw, Glendower	279
1993	Tony Johnstone, Durban	267
1994	Not played	
1995	Retief Goosen, Randpark	275
1996	Ernie Els, Royal Cape	275
1997	Vijay Singh, Glendower	270

Annika Sorenstam in action at the Women's British Open at Woburn.

S

The Walrus eyeing up his chances.

SPAIN

GOLF DID NOT take off in Spain as early as it did in many nations, but in the 1970s and 1980s the Spanish were a world force, winning the World Cup four times (1976, 1977, 1982 and 1984). During this time Spain was also home to Europe's most famous player, Seve Ballesteros. With the resurgence of Olazabal and the form of newcomer Ignacio Garrido, it seems he may have some natural successors.

Major Spanish Competitions

The Peugeot Spanish Open
Volvo Masters

Five Famous Spanish Players

Seve Ballesteros
Jose Maria Canizares
Jose Maria Olazabal
Manuel Pinero
Jose Rivero

Top Five Spanish Courses

Club De Campo, Madrid
El Saler, Valencia
Montecastillo, Jerez
Sotogrande, Costa del Sol
Valderrama, Costa del Sol

SPECTATORS

THE MAJOR championships and Ryder Cup competitions would not be the same without the huge crowds which flock to the events. Indeed the majors are now only played at courses which can cope with the travel and accommodation requirements of

Did You Know?

In the 1968 World Series of Golf a drive by Gary Player bounced and then landed between a woman's chest and her folded arms. She stood there not knowing what to do. It was ruled that the ball should be placed at her feet. Player made par and went on to win the tournament.

the swarms of people who follow the tournaments.

● IN AMERICA, designers have taken to creating 'stadium' courses such as the Tournament Players course at Sawgrass, which incorporate large hills from which spectators can watch.

● DESPITE THEIR NUMBERS, spectators tend to observe the strict rules of etiquette, such as keeping still and quiet, when a player plays a shot. It all adds up to make the roar that much more dramatic when a vital putt drops.

SPORTING CLUB BERLIN

Where: Berlin, Germany
Par: 72
Yardage: 6,054
Opened: 1996
Designer: Nick Faldo
Major Events Staged: None

ONE OF THE newest courses in Europe has already become one of its most exciting. Yet to stage a championship of any note, the Germans already regard the Sporting Club as one of their premier courses – mainly because a lack of golfing tradition in the country has provided few rivals.

● THE FALDO STAMP is all over the course, not only in his signature which appears everywhere, but in the meticulous way that the course is designed and kept. The greens are beautifully placed, and the grass is beautifully cut.

● AN EXHIBITION match between Faldo, Parnevik and Langer is the biggest show the club has staged so far, but a big future lies ahead for the Sporting Club, and perhaps also for its famous designer.

CRAIG STADLER

Born: San Diego, CA, USA – 02/06/1953
First US Tour: 1976
Highest Ranking: 1 (1982)
US Tour Wins: 12
Major Wins: 1 (US Masters 1982)
Ryder Cup Appearances: 2
Tour Earnings: $6.8 million

THE WALRUS, as he is known, is one of the most loved characters on the US Tour – the players like him and the spectators adore him. Weighing in at over 14 stone, and with a distinctive moustache, he is one of the most recognisable figures on the Tour.

● HIS SECOND WIN, the World Series of Golf in 1992, means he is now exempt from qualification for the next ten years, by the end of which he will be only a year away from a place on the Senior Tour.

● STADLER's greatest win was the 1982 Masters, although he only just made it. Five strokes up with only nine holes to play, Stadler eventually took the title after a play-off.

● STADLER MUST have fond memories of a tree at Torrey Pines. He was disqualified

from an event there in 1987 when he knelt on a towel to play a shot from under the tree. When the tree required felling in 1995 due to disease, officials asked Stadler back to do the honours with a chainsaw.

Chipping in

'I wish they would talk more about my golf than my wardrobe. Print my score, not my measurements.'

STANCE

THE STANCE is the position of the golfers feet and body in relation to the ball as he addresses it, prior to striking. An open stance will often be used if a fade or a loft are required, while a closed stance (involving moving the back foot away from the line of the shot) will keep the ball low and help to draw it. Too closed a stance will result in a hook.

ST ANDREWS

Where: Fife, Scotland
Par: 72
Yardage: 7,090
Opened: Unknown
Designer: Unknown
Major Events Staged: British Open 1873, 1876, 1879, 1882, 1885, 1888, 1891, 1895, 1900, 1905, 1910, 1921, 1927, 1933, 1939, 1946, 1955, 1957, 1960, 1964, 1970, 1978, 1984, 1990, 1995, British Amateur Championship 1886, 1889, 1891, 1895, 1901, 1907, 1913, 1924, 1930, 1936, 1950, 1958, 1963, 1976, 1981

THE TRADITION of the Royal and Ancient Golf Club and its position as the administrative centre of world golf has given St Andrews a worldwide reputation. But golf has been played in the old town since the very beginnings of the sport.

The Swilken Bridge and Old Course Hotel at St Andrews.

S

There are no records of when the old course was opened, or who designed it, but the Royal and Ancient Golf Club was formed in 1754.
● THE NEW COURSE was designed in 1895, but it is the Old Course which has consistently been updated, and which will again hold the Open in 2000.
● A STRANGE COURSE in many ways, it is not actually that difficult when the wind stops blowing, and indeed the first ten holes are among the easiest in major golf, as is the 18th. The Road Hole 17th is a nightmare, however, and many great golfers have come to grief at the 421m (461yd) par four.
● NICK FALDO dominated the Open at St Andrews in 1990, when he achieved a then record aggregate score of 270, romping home by five shots from Mark McNulty and Payne Stewart.
● THE LAST Old Course winner at St Andrews was John Daly in 1995, when he defeated Constantino Rocca in a play off, after the Italian had drawn level on the 72nd hole with a dramatic 60-foot putt.

Did you know?

In the 1885 British Open, David Ayton took an 11 at St Andrews' 17th, the Road Hole, to lose the championship by two strokes.

JAN STEPHENSON

Born: Sydney, Australia – 22/12/1951
First LPGA Tour: 1974
Highest Ranking: 4 (1983, 1987)
Tour Wins: 16
Major Wins: 2 (US Women's Open 1983, US LPGA 1982)
Tour Earnings: $2,427,142

AFTER DOMINATING at both amateur and professional levels in her own country, Stephenson turned to the US LPGA in 1974 and was voted Rookie of the Year. Since then she has won two majors and 14 other tournaments, as well as numerous other competitions around the world.
● STEPHENSON has done some modelling work, but turned down an offer of $150,000 to pose for Playboy after winning the LPGA in 1982. She has also turned down offers from Penthouse, but did appear topless in a French magazine.
● RECENTLY Jan Stephenson has been working on the idea of setting up a Women's Senior Tour, and has also been negotiating to start a match between the female professionals of Australia and America. She is confident that, as non-playing captain of a team including Karrie Webb, she could lead the Australians to victory.

Chipping in

'Look like a woman, but play like a man.'

PAYNE STEWART

Born: Springfield, MO, USA – 30/01/1957
First US Tour: 1981
Highest Ranking: 2 (1989)
US Tour Wins: 9
Major Wins: 2 (US Open 1991, US PGA 1989)
Ryder Cup Appearances: 4
Tour Earnings: $8,465,062

STEWART COMES across as a colourful character on the course, due mainly to his garish outfits, which usually include plus fours and clothes in many different hues. Stewart was at one point sponsored to wear the colours of various American football teams – he still commits many outrageous crimes of fashion.
● ALTHOUGH NOT a prolific winner on the US Tour, Stewart is at his best in the majors and has managed to earn a huge amount of money. In 1993, for instance, he earned just short of $1 million without recording a single victory.
● PAYNE STEWART's greatest win came in the 1991 US Open at Hazeltine when he caught Scott Simpson to force a play-off, and again came from behind over the extra 18 holes before taking the title. He added this to the US PGA that he'd won two years earlier. Stewart has also been a runner up in the British Open on several occasions.
● AFTER HIS WIN in the 1987 Hertz Bay Hill Classic, Stewart donated $100,000 to a Florida Hospital in memory of his father who had died of cancer two years earlier.

Payne Stewart in flamboyant form, winning the US Open.

CURTIS STRANGE

Born: Norfolk, VA, USA – 30/01/1955
First US Tour: 1977
Highest Ranking: 1 (1985, 1987, 1988)
US Tour Wins: 17
Major Wins: 2 (US Open 1988, 1989)
Ryder Cup Appearances: 5
Tour Earnings: $7 million

THE 1990s have not been kind to Curtis Strange, and it looks like his best years are behind him. Having said that, the late 1980s couldn't have been much kinder. Strange three-times topped the money winners list from 1985 to 1988, and in 1988 was the first man to earn over $1 million in a single season.

● STRANGE ALSO won back-to-back US Opens in 1988 and 1989 – the first man to do so since Ben Hogan. In winning at Oak Hill in 1989, Strange wore the same red shirt on the last day that he'd worn on the final round at Brookline the previous season. Since 1990, however, Strange has not made the top 40 and has failed to win a single tournament.

Did you know?
Curtis Strange has an identical twin brother called Allen who was at one time a PGA Tour player.

STROKE PLAY

ALSO KNOWN as medal play, stroke play is the basis of most modern golfing tournaments, having succeeded match play as the preferred format. Players compete on a lowest aggregate total basis, rather than the number of holes won. Generally this aggregate will be over 72 holes.

● STROKE PLAY originated in 1764 in a tournament hosted by the Society of St Andrews Golfers. The British Open, US Masters and US Open have always been held on a stroke play basis, and only the US PGA has ever been based on match play. In 1958, however, this remaining major became a stroke play event.

STYMIE

THIS SITUATION occurs when one player's ball lies between another player's ball and the hole, making the player furthest away have to putt round it. In 1951 the R&A and USGA did away with the rule and players were allowed to mark their ball, thus making their opponents shot a playable one.

Curtis Strange without his lucky shirt.

LOUISE SUGGS

Born: Atlanta, GA, USA – 07/09/1923
First LPGA Tour: 1947
Highest Ranking: 1 (1953)
Tour Wins: 50
Major Wins: 3 (US Women's Open 1949, 1952, LPGA 1957)

ALONG WITH Patty Berg and Babe Zaharias, Louise Suggs was one of the female triumvirate which formed the basis of the LPGA in its formative years. A successful amateur, Suggs won the Western Open (then a female major) while still an Amateur, and also won the Women's US Open before turning professional.

● DURING THE 1950s and 1960s she was a highly successful player on the LPGA Tour, winning 50 tournaments, including the Western Open and the Titleholders four times each at a time when both were considered majors.

● SUGGS' greatest victory came in the 1949 US Open which she won by a record 14 strokes from her great rival Babe Zaharias.

FANNY SUNESSON

PERHAPS THE most famous caddie on any of the tours is Nick Faldo's bag carrier Fanny Sunesson. The lively Swede is a lover of dangerous sports and has also been known to wield a golf club pretty well herself. A lucky charm for Faldo, her effusive manner of celebration is well known.

SUNNINGDALE

Where: Surrey, England
Par: 72
Yardage: 6,601
Opened: 1901
Designer: Willie Park
Major Events Staged: Walker Cup 1987

THE SURREY sand belt, with its lush greenery, is home to some of the most beautiful golf courses in England, including Walton Heath, Wentworth and of course Sunningdale.
● SUNNINGDALE was built in 1900 by TA Roberts, who employed Willie Park Jnr to design the course. An Open Champion, Park was one of golf's greatest thinkers and he created a masterpiece.
● HARRY COLT updated the course as the gutty was introduced and he also designed

Fanny Sunesson in exuberant form – or just waiting to make a phone call?

a par 68 New Course which was opened in 1922. Between them, the 36 holes provide one of the greatest golfing experiences south of the Scottish border.

● THE GREATEST round ever recorded at the course was Bobby Jones' 'Perfect Round' in a 1926 Open qualifying event. Jones took 66 strokes: 33 shots and 33 putts. The whole round is remembered shot by shot in the clubhouse. He hit every green except the 13th, and had a three or a four for every hole. Jones went on to win the Open at Royal Lytham, dispelling rumours that he had peaked too soon.

HAL SUTTON

Born: Shreveport, CA, USA – 28/04/1958	
First US Tour: 1982	
Highest Ranking: 1 (1983)	
US Tour Wins: 8	
Major Wins: 1 (US PGA 1983)	
Ryder Cup Appearances: 2	
Tour Earnings: $5,134,238	

AFTER TWICE playing in the Walker Cup, Sutton turned pro in 1981 and was 11th in his first season. A year later he topped the money list, including a remarkable win in the 1983 US PGA. His PGA win saw him set a record for two rounds with 131, and he eventually held off Jack Nicklaus by a single stroke.

● IN THE SAME year Sutton also won the Tournament Players Championship. He has

Did you know?

The grass bunker alongside the 18th green at Sunningdale was originally created by a bomb dropped by a German aircraft fleeing a Spitfire in 1940.

never repeated the success of that year, however.

● IN 1985 and 1986 Sutton was in the top ten on the money list, winning two tournaments in each of the years. Sutton still managed to pick up plenty of cash, and another win finally came his way in 1995, as he triumphed in the BC Open. He recorded a 61 in the final round, the best final round by a winner since Johnny Miller in 1975.

SWEDEN

SWEDEN NOT ONLY boasts some beautiful golf courses, it is also the fastest growing force in world golf in the 1990s. As early as 1991 Sweden announced their intentions by beating South Africa in the final of the Alfred Dunhill Cup. In 1993 Joakim Haeggman became the first Swede to play in the Ryder Cup, and with Annika Sorenstam twice winning the US Women's Open it can only be a matter of time before a Swedish man wins a major tournament.

The magnificent par-four 17th at Sunningdale.

Five Famous Swedish Players

Anders Forsbrand
Per Ulrik Johansson
Liselotte Neumann
Jesper Parnevik
Annika Sorenstam

Top Swedish Courses

Barseback, Loddekopinge
Falsterbo, Nr Malmo
Halmstad, Halmstad
Ullna, Rosenkalla

SWING

THE SWING is the complete motion of lifting the club and striking the ball. Players are continually refining and practising their swing to make it smoother and more consistent. In extreme circumstances some players will even take their swing apart and start again in a bid to come up with a technique which will work better under pressure.

● HAROLD HUTCHISON was one of the first players to study the swing, while Bobby Jones made films and flick books in an attempt to monitor what he was doing and improve his technique.

● OVER THE YEARS, players have learnt how to use their whole body to put the maximum effort into striking a ball, and coaches such as David Leadbetter have come up with elaborate methods for monitoring and correcting swings.

TAM O'SHANTER

A TAM O'SHANTER is a woollen hat, which fits closely around the head but is large and full on top. It is named after the mythical hero Tam O'Shanter, who escapes the clutches of witches in a narrative poem by Robert Burns.

● THE TAM O'SHANTER has become a part of the golf tradition in Scotland, being worn by many of the early players. Although the hat has passed into the mists of sartorial history, its name lives on in the Tam O'Shanter Club in Chicago, and the Tam O'Shanter Open, played there since 1941.

JH TAYLOR

Born: North Devon, England – 19/03/1871
Career Spanned: 1880s – 1910s
Major Wins: 5 (British Open 1894, 1895, 1900, 1909, 1913)

JOHN HENRY TAYLOR, known as 'JH', was one of the triumvirate of players (along with Harry Vardon and James Braid) who dominated golf at the start of the century. The three British golfers had a monopoly on the British Open, and also helped progress the sport in many different ways – raising the profile of the game and moving from the gutty to the wound ball.

● OF THE THREE, Taylor was the most direct, the only one to captain a Ryder Cup team, and the first to win the British Open, but overall he was probably the least successful of the trio.

Chipping in

'A man who can approach does not require to putt.'

TEES

TEES ARE the wooden pegs used to lift the ball off the turf before driving, but can also refer to the area itself from which players take their drives – hence 'teeing ground' and 'tee times' for when the players start their rounds.

● THE FIRST tee pegs were introduced in 1922. Previously, players had used a small amount of sand to tee up their ball, kept in a tee-box next to the teeing ground. Dr William Lowell, a dentist, invented the first tee pegs and eventually persuaded Walter Hagen to use them.

Did you know?

The ropes around teeing grounds were installed to keep out small boys who were becoming a nuisance by grabbing tee pegs as souvenirs.

TELEVISION

THE FIRST EVER televised golf event was the 1947 US Open at St Louis, with coverage in the local area only. Six years later two million people watched the Tam O'Shanter Open, and gradually national coverage of golfing tournaments became commonplace.

● IN 1957 the first British Open to be shown live on British television was at St Andrews, and in the 1960s and 1970s, television and the sponsorship which came with it meant prize money rocketed.

● NOW EVENTS such as the Ryder Cup and the Masters are beamed around the world to millions. In America there is even a Golf Channel 24 hours a day for those that need a fix.

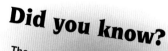

TERMINOLOGY

GOLF HAS a language all to itself, based partly on ancient words from the Scottish roots of the sport, and incorporating many phrases which developed from the wholesale adoption of golf in the USA.

Ace – American term for hole in one.

Air shot – A swing in which the player completely misses the ball.

Albatross – A score three less than the par of a hole.

Address – The position a player adopts before striking the ball.

Approach – A shot played at the green.

Apron – The area of close-cropped grass around the outside of the green.

Back nine – The second nine holes of an 18-hole course.

Birdie – A score one less than par for a hole.

Bisque – A handicap stroke given to a player for any particular hole that he wishes to nominate.

Bogey – A score of one over par.

Borrow – The amount of deviation from the direct line between hole and ball when putting, required to allow for the slope of the green.

Carry – The distance the ball travels in the air after being struck.

Cut – The point at which the field in a strokeplay competition is reduced to a pre-ordained number of players, e.g. after 18 or 36 holes depending on the number of rounds.

Dog-leg – A hole with a sharp turn, making an L-shape.

Dormie – When a player cannot be beaten in a matchplay event because the number of holes left is less than his score, the match is 'dormie'.

Eagle – A score two less than par for a hole.

Front nine – The first nine holes of an 18-hole course.

Honour – The privilege of being first off the tee.

Lay-up – To play a shot intentionally short usually to avoid a hazard.

Lie – How the ball sits on the fairway or rough.

Loft – The angle of the clubface.

Par – Standard score for a hole for a scratch player.

Pull – A shot which has a slight hook, making the ball move to the right.

Push – A shot with a small slice, making the ball move to the left.

Rough – Land left intentionally untended at the edges of the fairway to punish wayward strokes.

Scratch – The handicap of a player who can play the course to par.

Single – A match between just two players.

Stroke – The motion of striking the ball.

Top – To hit the ball above centre resulting in a shot which bobbles along the ground.

TEXAS SCRAMBLE

A FUN ALTERNATIVE for the weekend golfer, this is a strokeplay competition, usually between four players. Each takes it in turn to drive, and the best placed drive is the only one counted. The other three players move their balls to within a club's length of the best ball position and play their second shots, and so on until the hole is completed.

DAVE THOMAS

Born:	Newcastle, England – 16/08/1934
First European Tour:	1949
European Tour Wins:	16
Major Wins:	0
Ryder Cup Appearances:	4

D AVE THOMAS was a powerfully built player who turned pro at the age of 15. Over six feet tall, he was one of the longest, straightest drivers in the European game, and this more than anything brought him his 16 victories.
● THOMAS CAME closest to major victory in the 1958 and 1966 British Opens. In 1966 he had a par at Muirfield's 17th, while Nicklaus birdied to take the Championship by a shot. Even more agonisingly in 1958 at Lytham, Thomas missed the green with a simple iron at the 17th, after a massive drive. He had to settle for a play-off with Peter Thomson which he lost by four shots in tiring conditions.

● HAVING represented Wales 12 times in the World Cup, Thomas now lives in Spain and is a respected course architect.

PETER THOMSON

Born:	Melbourne, Australia – 23/08/1929
First US Tour:	1952
US Tour Wins:	2
Highest Ranking:	9 (1956)
Major Wins:	5 (British Open 1954, 1955, 1956, 1958, 1965)
First Senior Tour:	1979
Highest Ranking:	1 (1985)

P ETER THOMSON won tournaments wherever he played – except in America. He was three-times Australian Open Champion and nine-times New Zealand Open Champion, as well as winning tournaments in India, Italy and Spain.
● HIS RECORD in the British Open is one of the best of all time, and yet in America he could only manage two top ten finishes in 13 majors. He later returned to America to play in the Seniors, and topped the money list in 1985 with nine wins.
● IN THE US Open, he was the best player of the 1950s. Along with Bobby Locke he dominated the tournament, and in seven Championships from 1952 to 1958 he was

Peter Thompson, back on successful ground in Melbourne in 1998.

never out of the top two, winning three titles in a row from 1954 – the first and last man to do so this century.

TOP TENS

A S WELL AS the number of tournaments, a player's abilities, and in particular their consistency, is shown by the number of times they have finished in the top ten in a competition. Nobody has shown more consistency over the years than Jack Nicklaus, and even at the age of 58 he can still make the top ten, as he displayed in the 1998 US Masters.

Top Ten of Top Ten Finishes

Jack Nicklaus	73	Arnold Palmer	38
Sam Snead	46	Gene Sarazen	36
Gary Player	44	Walter Hagen	32
Tom Watson	42	Ray Floyd	28
Ben Hogan	39	Byron Nelson	28

Did you know?

Jack Nicklaus only finished outside the top ten in a major championship five times during the 1970s. In the British Open and US Masters he made the top ten in every single year of the decade.

SAM TORRANCE

Born: Largs, Scotland – 24/08/1953	
First European Tour: 1971	
Highest Ranking: 2 (1984, 1995)	
European Tour Wins: 20	
Major Wins: 0	
Ryder Cup Appearances: 8	
Tour Earnings: £3 million	

AMIABLE SCOT Sam Torrance has been a regular fixture on the European Tour since his sedate start in 1971. Success eluded him until 1976, when he finished third on the money list after a couple of good wins. Over 20 years later, he now has 20 Tour wins to his name, has twice finished runner-up in the European Rankings, but has never secured a major win.

● THE EARLY 1980s proved Torrance's most successful spell and it is for his Ryder

Torrance has now given up the nineteenth hole.

Cup exploits in 1985 that he is most fondly remembered. His emotional reaction to securing the Ryder Cup at the Belfry, with a 20-foot putt at the 18th, perfectly encapsulated the charged atmosphere of the historic European win.

● A CONSISTENT, long-hitting player, Torrance at one point struggled with his putting before switching to a long-putter which reached to just below his chin. A keen snooker player, Torrance reportedly practised with the pendulum putter on his table until he had regained his confidence.

● TORRANCE has lost two stone since giving up alcohol and the result has been a win at the 1998 French Open.

WALTER TRAVIS

Born: Maldon, Australia – 10/01/1867	
Career Spanned: 1900s to 1920s	
Significant Wins: 4 (British Amateur Championship 1904, US Amateur Championship 1900, 1901, 1903)	

TRAVIS WAS BORN in Australia, but moved to America at an early age. He did not take up golf, however, until his mid-thirties. But with relentless practice,

Travis became a formidable player, and was still winning tournaments in his 50s.

● HIS WIN in Britain at the age of 44 was not well received by the British public – as much as anything because Travis was such a reserved and quiet player. He won the tournament with a Schenectady putter (one in which the shaft enters the head at its centre) and the R&A banned the putter some years after. Travis was also the first foreigner to win the British Amateur.

TREES

THIS WOODY perennial is a hazard all golfers have encountered, and the need to punch a shot through can provide an exciting spectacle. The lack of any dropping privileges – except in the case of new saplings – can also lead to some strange scenes.

● IN THE 1990 Australian Open, Brett Ogle was a shot off the lead going into the penultimate hole. Attempting to play out of the trees after a wayward drive, his ball rebounded off a trunk and struck his knee. He decided to limp on after receiving medical attention but finished seven shots behind the winner after recording a nine – including a two-stroke penalty for being struck by his own ball.

Faldo uses his tree iron at the US Open.

British Open, US Open and US PGA Masters twice.

● BORN INTO POVERTY, Trevino spent four years in the Marines and was a tough, yet effervescent character. In the early 1960s he worked on municipal courses and did not attempt to qualify for the US Tour, instead taking part in arranged golf matches for money. After one such contest in which the short and scruffy amateur had beaten the already famous Ray Floyd, Floyd left in his expensive car saying that the US Tour was an easier way to make money.

● IN 1966, Trevino won the Texas State Open – a non Tour event – and entered the US Open, finishing 54th. He was back a year later and came 5th.

● IN 1968 Trevino exploded onto the world scene when he won the US Open at Oak Hill by four shots. He became the first man to break 70 in all four rounds of the competition, and he completely demoralised playing partner Bert Yancey on his final round. Many thought it a fluke, but they were soon proved wrong.

● IT WAS 1971 before Lee Trevino next won a major, winning the US Open again, this time at Merion. In the process he beat his great rival Nicklaus in a play-off. At the start of the play-off Trevino threw a pretend snake at Nicklaus which he had fished from his bag. Although later accused of gamesmanship, it was simply another crowd-pleasing antic.

● THE US OPEN victory saw Trevino mining a rich vein of form in which he won the US Open, Canadian Open and British Open in the space of five weeks. The 1971 Open win was secured at Birkdale by one shot from Taiwanese golfer Mr (Liang Huan) Lu, and by two from former champion Tony Jacklin.

● A YEAR LATER Trevino retained the British Open, this time at Muirfield, where he this time beat Jacklin and Nicklaus. Trevino was certainly leading a charmed life and none more so than when he chipped in at the 71st hole after missing the green with his fourth shot. After this tournament, however, his luck started to fade somewhat and Nicklaus regained world supremacy.

● AFTER WINNING his fifth major, the US PGA, in 1974, Trevino was seriously injured when struck by lightning in the Western Open at Ohio. He had surgery on his back and was out for a number of months. Trevino remained a consistent performer however, and was beaten by Tom Watson in the British Open at Muirfield in 1980.

● IN 1984, however, he won the US PGA for the second time at the age of 44. The victory at Shoal Creek was his last major title and was secured with all of the rounds being below 70.

● AT THE AGE of 50 Trevino looked to be tired of golf, but the Senior Tour

Lee Trevino, one of golf's greatest characters and players.

● IN A European Tour event Bernhard Langer was more lucky when he famously scaled a tree at Fulford and played his ball from an overhanging branch onto the green. He just failed to make par.

● AT PEBBLE BEACH in the 1992 US Open Nick Faldo similarly scaled a tree, but failed to find his ball. Upon returning to the course in 1995 he was upset to find that the tree had been destroyed in a storm. 'I loved that tree,' was his reported response.

LEE TREVINO

Born:	Dallas, TX, USA – 01/12/1939
First US PGA Tour:	1967
Highest Ranking:	1 (1970)
US Tour Wins:	27
Major Wins:	6 (US Open 1968, 1971, British Open 1971, 1972, US PGA 1974, 1984)
Ryder Cup Appearances:	6
Tour Earnings:	£3.4 million

THE PUDGY, wise-cracking Mexican-American is one of the legends of golf. With an unorthodox swing and a hooker's grip, but an amazing feel for the game, he dominated the game in the early 1970s along with Jack Nicklaus, winning the reawakened his interest, not least because he could renew his duels with Jack Nicklaus. Indeed Trevino has now earned far more on the Senior Tour than he ever did on the US Tour. In his first year alone he picked up more than a million dollars, winning seven events. And after five years he had accumulated $7.5 million, compared to the $3.4 million he earned in 20 years on the professional circuit.

● STILL A JOKER, Trevino is happy to share banter with the spectators and it takes a real chance of success to curb his jokes and focus him solely on winning. His pearly white teeth have become his trademark, and his acts of generosity, such as the donation of £2000 to a local orphanage after his British Open win at Birkdale in 1971, have endeared him to crowds the world over.

Chipping in

'You don't know the meaning of pressure until you play for five bucks with two bucks in your pocket.'

THE TRIUMVIRATE

NEVER HAS the definition of a triumvirate – joint rule by three people – been better exemplified than by the stranglehold that James Braid, JH Taylor and Harry Vardon held over the world of golf for 20 years spanning the turn of the 20th century.

The three were born only 14 months apart. The oldest, James Braid was the professional at Walton Heath where he remained until his death in 1950. He was noted for his resilient play, and his long-hitting and accurate putting won him four PGA Matchplay Championships. In later life he turned to course design and was responsible for the King's and Queen's courses at Gleneagles.

John Henry Taylor was a powerful man with a flat stance who punched the ball low to cope with Britain's vicious links weather. Born in Devon, Taylor was a founder-member of the British PGA in 1901, and a strong player who won all five of his British Open titles by at least four strokes.

His first Open victory came in 1894 at St George's in Kent – the first to be staged outside of Scotland – and it was a full 39 years later that he captained Great Britain to Ryder Cup victory.

Harry Vardon is the most commemorated of the trio, not just because he remains the only golfer ever to record six Open wins, but also because he gave his name to the Vardon grip.

Vardon was reportedly a latecomer to golf and had played only twenty rounds by the age of 20. His first triumph in 1896 was notable not only because he halted Taylor's progress towards a successive third Championship and began their long-running rivalry, but also because he came from 11 strokes behind after the first round.

If he had not suffered from the tuberculosis which was to cut short his career, we can only guess how many titles Vardon could have accumulated. As it was,

his last victory in 1914 robbed Taylor of the chance to match his record six titles. Vardon was also the only member of the Triumvirate to triumph in America, winning the US Open in 1900, again with Taylor as runner-up.

THE TRIUMVIRATE
ROLL OF HONOUR

— James Braid —
British Open Winner
1901, 1905, 1906, 1908, 1910

Runner-up
1897, 1902, 1904, 1909

— JH Taylor —
British Open Winner
1894, 1895, 1900, 1909, 1913

Runner-up
1896, 1904, 1905,1906, 1907, 1914

US Open Runner-up
1900

— Harry Vardon —
British Open Winner
1896, 1898, 1899, 1903, 1911, 1914

Runner-up
1900, 1901, 1902, 1912

US Open Winner
1900

US Open runner-up
1913, 1920

TROON

| Where: Ayrshire, Scotland |
| Par: 72 |
| Yardage: 7,097 |
| Opened: 1878 |
| Designer: Charles Hunter |
| Major Events Staged: British Open 1923, 1950, 1962, 1973, 1982, 1989, 1997 |

A CLOSE NEIGHBOUR of the Prestwick club, Old Troon is one of Scotland's greatest courses. Renamed Royal Troon in its centenary year of 1978, the course began as six holes laid out by Charles Hunter. In time architects including Willie Fernie, James Braid and Dr Alister Mackenzie created a course with dangerously narrow, undulating fairways, and one which boasts both the shortest and longest holes in British championship golf.

● ROYAL TROON also boasts one of the most famous holes in the Open, the Postage Stamp, so called because of the size of the green.

The jets from Prestwick airport are the most regular visitors to Troon. The 'postage stamp' looks just that from the sky.

● THE BEAUTIFUL seascape has made a perfect setting for the half-dozen Opens held at Troon over the years. The first in 1923 was won by Arthur Havers, with the great Bobby Locke and Arnold Palmer winning the next two in 1950 and 1962 respectively.

● THE LAST four winners have all been American: Tom Weiskopf in 1973, Tom Watson in 1982, Mark Calcavecchia in 1989 and Justin Leonard in 1997.

Did you know?

After years of failing to qualify for the Open at Troon, Gene Sarazen returned to the course at the age of 71. His round included a hole-in-one at the Postage Stamp.

TURNBERRY

Where: Ayrshire, Scotland

Par: 71

Yardage: 6,950

Opened: 1903

Designer: Willie Fernie

Major Events Staged: British Open 1977, 1986, 1994; British Amateur Championship 1961, 1984, 1996; Walker Cup 1963; British Women's Amateur Championship 1912, 1921, 1937

SET ON Scotland's beautiful and desolate west coast, Turnberry is famous for its stunning hotel and its two courses, the Ailsa – the original links designed by former Open Champion, Willie Fernie – and the Arran, opened in 1912 to cope with the venue's increasing popularity.

● AFTER A grand start, the course was variously used as a Royal Flying Corps training ground and an RAF Coastal Command Centre, and it was not until 1961 that a notable golfing event was staged, the British Amateur Championship. This was followed two years later by the Walker Cup.

● THE ALREADY testing weather conditions at Turnberry are further complicated because the first six holes are set perpendicular to the north-south lay of the last 12. Famous holes include the ninth, with its adjacent lighthouse, and the 16th, the Wee Burn, which offers a potentially watery grave.

● THE BRITISH OPEN was first staged at Turnberry in 1977, resulting in arguably the most exciting Championship ever. Four improbably sunny days culminated in a

Turnberry's Ailsa Course is beautiful and desolate, with the sea an ever-present threat to the unwary.

memorable final day duel between Tom Watson and Jack Nicklaus. Both men broke the existing 72-hole aggregate record for the Open as Watson's 268 beat Nicklaus by one stroke.

● WHEN THE OPEN returned in 1986, Greg Norman's main opponent was the weather. He overcame an unfavourably late tee-off time and the brunt of a gale to coast home by five shots.

● IN 1994 there was more excitement as Nick Price eagled with a 50-foot putt at the 17th on the final day, to turn around Swede Jesper Parnevik's one-shot lead. He held par to secure the tournament that had for so long evaded him.

MARK TWAIN

THE AMERICAN writer, famous for the Huckleberry Finn tales, is supposed to have made the most famous comment about golf ever, describing the sport as 'a good walk spoiled.'

BOB TWAY

Born: Edmond, OK, USA – 04/05/1959

First US Tour: 1985

Highest Ranking: 2 (1986)

US Tour Wins: 7

Major Wins: 1 (US PGA Championship 1986)

Ryder Cup Appearances: 0

Tour Earnings: $4,875,948

BOB TWAY is most famous for his chip at the 72nd hole of the US PGA at Inverness in 1986. Tway holed out from the bunker to steal another Championship from under Greg Norman's nose.

● THAT YEAR was by far Tway's best, with four wins. He was second in the money list – this time Norman pipped him to first place by only $516. He was still voted Player of the Year by the PGA.

● IN THE 1994 Memorial, Tway hit two hole-in-ones in the same tournament.

US AMATEUR CHAMPIONSHIP

First Played: 1895

Most Wins: 5 – Bobby Jones (1924, 1925, 1927, 1928, 1930)

THE US AMATEUR CHAMPIONSHIP predated the US Open by all of three days. Its first winner was Charles Macdonald, later a course architect, who took the title at Newport, Rhode Island. He beat Charles Sands by a brilliant 12 and 11 in the final. The event remained a matchplay tournament until 1965, when it reverted to strokeplay for eight years.

● THROUGHOUT the years there have been some notable winners, including Bobby Jones' record of five Championships. Other winners have included the Englishman Harold Hilton, the great Francis Ouimet and in later years Jack Nicklaus, Arnold Palmer, Lanny Wadkins, Hal Sutton

Bob Tway, and the greatest moment of his golfing career, the last hole of the 1986 US PGA.

and Mark O'Meara.

● THE MOST recent player to leave their mark on the tournament was of course Tiger Woods, whose win completed a record-breaking hat-trick of victories in 1996.

US Amateur - The Last 25 Winners

1972	Charlotte, NC	MM Giles	1985	Montclair, NJ	S Randolph
Championship returned to match play			1986	Shoal Creek, AL	S Alexander
1973	Inverness, OH	C Stadler	1987	Jupiter Hills, FL	W Mayfair
1974	Ridgewood, NJ	J Pate	1988	Hot Springs, VA	E Meeks
1975	Richmond, VA	F Ridley	1989	Merion, PA	C Patton
1976	Bel Air, CA	B Sander	1990	Cherry Hills, CO	P Mickelson
1977	Aronimink, PA	J Fought	1991	Honours Course, TN	M Voges
1978	Plainfield, NJ	J Cook	1992	Muirfield Village, OH	J Leonard
1979	Canterbury, OH	M O'Meara	1993	Houston, TX	J Harris
1980	Pinehurst, NC	H Sutton	1994	Sawgrass, FL	T Woods
1981	Olympic, CA	N Crosby	1995	Newport, RI	T Woods
1982	Brookline, MA	J Sigel	1996	Portland, OR	T Woods
1983	North Shore, IL	J Sigel	1997	Cog Hill, IL	M Kuchar
1984	Oak Tree, OK	S Verplank			

THE US GOLF ASSOCIATION

THE UNITED STATES Golf Association was formed in 1894 and within 12 months ha achieved its objective of staging a Mens and Women's Amateur event and the Open. The USGA presides over the rules of the amateur game in the United States as the R&A does in the rest of the world.

● IN 1953, eight years after its first Championship, the US Women's Open came under the USGA umbrella as well.

Contact

United States Golf Association, Far Hills, New Jersey 07931

THE US OPEN

First Played: 1895

Most Wins: 4 – Willie Anderson (1901, 1903, 1904, 1905),
Bobby Jones (1923, 1926, 1929, 1930),
Ben Hogan (1948, 1950, 1951, 1953),
Jack Nicklaus (1962, 1967, 1972, 1980)

Lowest 72-hole Score: 272 – Jack Nicklaus (1980 at Baltusrol),
Lee Janzen (1993 at Baltusrol)

THE US OPEN was less important than the US Amateur Championship in its first few years, and it was not actually won by a native-born American until 1911 when Johnny McDermott took the title. Initially a 36-hole tournament, it became a 72-hole event after three years.

The US Open winners

1895	H Rawlins	Newport, RI	173
1896	J Foulis	Shinnecock Hills, NY	152
1897	J Lloyd	Chicago, IL	162
1898	F Herd	Myopia, MA	328
1899	W Smith	Baltimore, MD	315
1900	H Vardon	Chicago, IL	313
1901	W Anderson	Myopia, MA	331
1902	L Auchterlonie	Garden City, MY	307
1903	W Anderson	Baltusrol, NJ	307
1904	W Anderson	Glenview, IL	303
1905	W Anderson	Myopia, MA	314
1906	A Smith	Onwentsia, IL	295
1907	A Ross	Philadelphia, PA	302
1908	F McLeod	Myopia, MA	322
1909	G Sargent	Englewood, NJ	290
1910	A Smith	Philadelphia, PA	298
1911	JJ McDermott	Chicago, IL	307
1912	JJ McDermott	Buffalo, NY	294
1913	F Ouimet	Brookline, MA	304
1914	W Hagen	Midlothian, IL	290
1915	JD Travers	Baltusrol, NJ	297
1916	C Evans Jnr	Minikahda, MN	286
1917 – 1918 No Championship			
1919	W Hagen	Brae Burn, MA	301

1920	T Ray	Inverness, OH	295
1921	J Barnes	Chevy Chase, MD	289
1922	G Sarazen	Skokie, Glencoe, IL	288
1923	R T Jones Jnr	Inwood, NY	296
1924	C Walker	Oakland Hills, MI	297
1925	W Macfarlane	Worcester, MA	291
1926	R T Jones Jnr	Scioto, OH	293
1927	T Armour	Oakmont, PA	301
1928	JJ Farrell	Olympia Fields, IL	294
1929	R T Jones Jnr	Winged Foot, NY	294
1930	R T Jones Jnr	Interlachan, MN	287
1931	B Burke	Inverness, OH	292
1932	G Sarazen	Fresh Meadow, NY	286
1933	J Goodman	N Shore, IL	287
1934	O Dutra	Merion, PA	293
1935	S Parks	Oakmont, PA	299
1936	T Manero	Baltusrol, NJ	282
1937	R Guldahl	Oakland Hills, MI	281
1938	R Guldahl	Cherry Hills, CO	284
1939	B Nelson	Philadelphia, PA	284
1940	W Lawson Little	Canterbury, OH	287
1941	C Wood	Fort Worth, TX	284
1942 – 1945 No Championship			
1946	L Mangrum	Canterbury, OH	284
1947	L Worsham	St Louis, Clayton, MO	282
1948	B Hogan	Riviera, CA	276
1949	C Middlecoff	Medinah, IL	286
1950	B Hogan	Merion, PA	287
1951	B Hogan	Oakland Hills, MI	287
1952	J Boros	Northwood, TX	281
1953	B Hogan	Oakmont, PA	283
1954	E Furgol	Baltusrol, NJ	284
1955	J Fleck	Olympic, CA	287
1956	C Middlecoff	Oak Hill, NY	281

Continued over page…

Did you know?

The first US Open took place in one day, over four rounds of the Newport nine-hole course, in 1895. Only 11 players took part, and so only one failed to make the top ten.

US Open winner Ernie Els, with his most prized possession. And his wife, of course.

The US Open winners continued

1957	R Mayer	Inverness, OH	282
1958	T Bolt	Southern Hills, OK	283
1959	W Casper	Winged Foot, NY	282
1960	A Palmer	Cherry Hills, CO	280
1961	G Littler	Oakland Hills, MI	281
1962	J Nicklaus	Oakmont, PA	283
1963	J Boros	Brookline, MA	293
1964	K Venturi	Congressional, MD	278
1965	G Player	Bellerive, MO	282
1966	W Casper	Olympic, CA	278
1967	J Nicklaus	Baltusrol, NJ	275
1968	L Trevino	Oak Hill, NY	275
1969	O Moody	Champions, Houston, TX	281
1970	A Jacklin	Hazeltine, MN	281
1971	L Trevino	Merion, PA	280
1972	J Nicklaus	Pebble Beach, CA	290
1973	J Miller	Oakmont, PA	279
1974	H Irwin	Winged Foot, NY	287
1975	L Graham	Medinah, IL	287
1976	J Pate	Duluth, GA	277
1977	H Green	Southern Hills, OK	278
1978	A North	Cherry Hills, CO	285
1979	H Irwin	Inverness, OH	284
1980	J Nicklaus	Baltusrol, NJ	272
1981	D Graham	Merion, PA	273
1982	T Watson	Pebble Beach, CA	282
1983	L Nelson	Oakmont, PA	280
1984	F Zoeller	Winged Foot, NY	276
1985	A North	Oakland Hills, MI	279
1986	R Floyd	Shinnecock Hills, NY	279
1987	S Simpson	Olympic, CA	277
1988	C Strange	Brookline, MA	278
1989	C Strange	Oak Hill, NY	278
1990	H Irwin	Medinah, IL	280
1991	P Stewart	Hazeltine, MN	282
1992	T Kite	Pebble Beach, CA	285
1993	L Janzen	Baltusrol, NJ	272
1994	E Els	Oakmont, PA	279
1995	C Pavin	Shinnecock Hills, NY	280
1996	S Jones	Oakland Hills, MI	278
1997	E Els	Congressional, MD	276

US PGA Championship winners

1916	Jim Barnes	Siwanoy, NY	1 hole
1917 – 1918 No Championship			
1919	Jim Barnes	Engineers, NY	6&5
1920	J Hutchison	Flossmoor, IL	1 hole
1921	W Hagen	Inwood, NY	3&2
1922	G Sarazen	Oakmont, PA	4&3
1923	G Sarazen	Pelham, NY	38 hole
1924	W Hagen	French Lick, IN	2 holes
1925	W Hagen	Olympic Fields, IL	6&5
1926	W Hagen	Salisbury, NY	5&3
1927	W Hagen	Cedar Crest, Dallas, TX	1 hole
1928	L Diegel	Five Farms, MD	6&5
1929	L Diegel	Hillcrest, CA	6&4
1930	T Armour	Fresh Meadow NY	1 hole
1931	T Creavy	Wannamoisett, RI	2&1
1932	O Dutra	Keller GC, St Paul, MN	4&3
1933	G Sarazen	Blue Mound, WI	5&4
1934	P Runyan	Park GC, Williamsville, NY	38 hole
1935	J Revolta	Twin Hills, OK	5&4
1936	D Shute	Pinehurst, NC	3&2
1937	D Shute	Pittsburgh Field Club, PA	37 hole
1938	P Runyan	Shawnee, PA	8&7
1939	H Picard	Pomonok, NY	37 hole
1940	B Nelson	Hershey, PA	1 hole
1941	V Ghezzi	Cherry Hills, CO	38 hole
1942	S Snead	Seaview GC, Atlantic City, NJ	2&1
1943 No Championship			
1944	R Hamilton	Manito, WA	1 hole
1945	B Nelson	Morraine, OH	4&3
1946	B Hogan	Portland, OR	6&4
1947	J Ferrier	Plum Hollow, MI	2&1
1948	B Hogan	Norwood Hills, MO	7&6
1949	S Snead	Hermitage, VA	3&2
1950	C Harper	Scioto, OH	4&3
1951	S Snead	Oakmont, PA	7&6
1952	J Turnesa	Big Spring, KY	1 hole
1953	W Burkemo	Birmingham, MI	2&1
1954	C Harbert	Keller, MI	4&3

1955	D Ford	Meadowbrook, MI	4&3
1956	J Burke	Blue Hill, MA	3&2
1957	L Herbert	Miami Val, OH	2&1
1958	D Finsterwald	Llanerch, PA	276
1959	B Rosburg	St Louis Park, MI	277
1960	J Herbert	Firestone, OH	281
1961	J Berber	Olympia Fields, IL	277
1962	G Player	Aronomink, PA	278
1963	J Nicklaus	Dallas, TX	279
1964	B Nichols	Columbus, OH	271
1965	D Marr	Laurel Valley, PA	280
1966	A Geiberger	Firestone, OH	280
1967	D January	Columbine, CO	281
1968	J Boros	Pecan Valley, TX	281
1969	R Floyd	NCR, Dayton, OH	276
1970	D Stockton	Southern Hills, OK	279
1971	J Nicklaus	PGA National, FL	281
1972	G Player	Oakland Hills, MI	281
1973	J Nicklaus	Canterbury, OH	277
1974	L Trevino	Tanglewood, NC	276
1975	J Nicklaus	Firestone, OH	276
1976	D Stockton	Congressional, MD	281
1977	L Wadkins	Pebble Beach, CA	282
1978	J Mahaffey	Oakmont, PA	276
1979	D Graham	Oakland Hills, MI	272
1980	J Nicklaus	Oak Hill, NY	274
1981	L Nelson	Atlanta, GA	273
1982	R Floyd	Southern Hills, OK	272
1983	H Sutton	Riviera, CA	274
1984	L Trevino	Shoal Creek, Al	273
1985	H Green	Cherry Hills, CO	278
1986	R Tway	Inverness, OH	276
1987	L Nelson	PGA National, FL	287
1988	J Sluman	Oak Tree, OK	272
1989	P Stewart	Kemper Lakes, IL	276
1990	W Grady	Shoal Creek, Al	282
1991	J Daly	Crooked Stick, IN	276
1992	N Price	Bellerive, MO	278
1993	P Azinger	Inverness, OH	272
1994	N Price	Southern Hills, OK	269
1995	S Elkington	Riviera, CA	267
1996	M Brooks	Valhalla, KY	277
1997	Davis Love III	Winged Foot, NY	269

THE US PGA CHAMPIONSHIP

First Played: 1916

Most Wins: 5 – Walter Hagen (1921, 1924, 1925, 1926, 1927), Jack Nicklaus (1963, 1971, 1973, 1975, 1980)

Lowest 72-hole Score: 267 – Steve Elkington and Colin Montgomerie (Riviera 1995)

THE US PGA Championship was started in 1916 by Rodman Wanamaker to provide the leading professional golfers in America with a dedicated tournament, and the prize remains the Wanamaker Trophy to this day.

● THE FIRST winner, Jim Barnes, was British born, but America soon took over in the form of Walter Hagen and Gene Sarazen. Hagen actually lost the trophy after one of his victories and a temporary trophy was used until it was found again.

● THE EVENT remained a match play tournament until 1958 when stroke play took over; Dow Finsterwald was the first victor under the new format.

Davis Love III with that loving feeling at Winged Foot in 1997.

THE US PGA TOUR

THE US Professional Golfers Association was formed in 1916 to protect the interests of pros and to provide a structure for organized competitions. Initially a haphazard organization, it has now become the biggest tour in the world, with millions of dollars of prize money available.

● IN 1934 the first money winners list was published – Paul Runyan came out top with $6,767. In 1937 Harry Cooper's earnings reached five figures, and in 1963 Arnold Palmer hit the six figure mark with $128,230. The first $1 million earner was Curtis Strange in 1988.

Leading US Tour Players

1934	Paul Runyan
1935	Johnny Revolta
1936	Horton Smith
1937	Harry Cooper
1938	Sam Snead
1939	Henry Picard
1940	Ben Hogan
1941	Ben Hogan
1942	Ben Hogan
1943	No Championship
1944	Byron Nelson
1945	Byron Nelson
1946	Ben Hogan
1947	Jimmy Demaret
1948	Ben Hogan
1949	Sam Snead
1950	Sam Snead
1951	Lloyd Mangrum
1952	Julius Boros
1953	Lew Worsham
1954	Bob Toski
1955	Julius Boros
1956	Ted Kroll
1957	Dick Mayer
1958	Arnold Palmer
1959	Art Wall
1960	Arnold Palmer
1961	Gary Player
1962	Arnold Palmer
1963	Arnold Palmer
1964	Jack Nicklaus
1965	Jack Nicklaus
1966	Billy Casper
1967	Jack Nicklaus
1968	Billy Casper
1969	Frank Beard
1970	Lee Trevino
1971	Jack Nicklaus
1972	Jack Nicklaus
1973	Jack Nicklaus
1974	Johnny Miller
1975	Jack Nicklaus
1976	Jack Nicklaus
1977	Tom Watson
1978	Tom Watson
1979	Tom Watson
1980	Tom Watson
1981	Tom Kite
1982	Craig Stadler
1983	Hal Sutton
1984	Tom Watson
1985	Curtis Strange
1986	Greg Norman
1987	Curtis Strange
1988	Curtis Strange
1989	Tom Kite
1990	Greg Norman
1991	Corey Pavin
1992	Fred Couples
1993	Nick Price
1994	Nick Price
1995	Greg Norman
1996	Tom Lehman
1997	Tiger Woods

Tom Lehman overtook Greg Norman on the US Tour, then a certain Mr Tiger Woods arrived on the scene.

THE US WOMEN'S OPEN

First Played: 1946

Most Wins: 4 – Betsy Rawls (1951, 1953, 1957, 1960), Mickey Wright (1958, 1959, 1961, 1964)

Lowest 72-hole Score: 272 – Annika Sorenstam (1996)

INITIALLY RUN by the LPGA and latterly by the USGA, the US Women's Open is the biggest event in women's golf today. Patty Berg was the first winner, in 1946, the only year that the Open was a matchplay event.

US Women's Open - Last 25 Winners

1972	Susie Berning
1973	Susie Berning
1974	Sandra Haynie
1975	Sandra Palmer
1976	JoAnne Carner
1977	Hollis Stacy
1978	Hollis Stacy
1979	Jerilyn Britz
1980	Amy Alcott
1981	Pat Bradley
1982	Janet Anderson
1983	Jan Stephenson
1984	Hollis Stacy
1985	Kathy Baker
1986	Jane Geddes
1987	Laura Davies
1988	Liselotte Neumann
1989	Betsy King
1990	Betsy King
1991	Meg Mallon
1992	Patty Sheehan
1993	Lauri Merton
1994	Patty Sheehan
1995	Annika Sorenstam
1996	Annika Sorenstam
1997	Alison Nicholas

VALDERRAMA

Where: Costa del Sol, Spain

Par: 71

Yardage: 6,734

Opened: 1975

Designer: Robert Trent Jones

Major Events Staged: Ryder Cup 1997

RECENTLY VOTED the best course in Europe by Golf World Magazine, Valderrama is known as the Augusta of Europe. The Ryder Cup was won by the European team in 1997 amid chaotic scenes at the beautiful club.

● THE COURSE as we know it today has gone through many stages of development. In 1975, Robert Trent Jones designed two reasonable courses at Sotogrande on Spain's Costa del Sol – Los Aves and Sotogrande Old. Los Aves was renamed Sotogrande New, but changed its name again to Valderrama after the millionaire Jaime Ortiz-Patino purchased the club in 1985.

● TRENT JONES was brought back to do

more work on the course, and gradually it was transformed into one of the best courses in Europe, if not the world. The Volvo Masters – the climax of the European season – was held at Valderrama every year from 1988-1996, and it was the venue for the Ryder Cup when it moved ouside Britain and America for the first time in 1997.

Alson Nicholas wins the 1997 Women's Open.

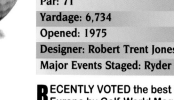

HARRY VARDON

Born: Grouville, Jersey – 1870

Career Spanned: 1880s to 1910s

Major Wins: 7 (British Open 1896, 1898, 1899, 1903, 1911, 1914, US Open 1900)

HARRY VARDON was the most successful and the most famous of the Great Triumvirate, winning the British Open more times than any other man before or since. He was

also the only one of the three to win the US Open – something Braid and Taylor never achieved.

● ALTHOUGH THE youngest of the three, Vardon was the first to die, when he lost a long battle with tuberculosis in 1937. He had escaped near-certain death in 1912, when injury forced him out of travelling to America for the US Open – on the Titanic.

● HARRY VARDON is remembered in two ways: the Vardon Trophy is awarded to the player who tops the European Order of Merit each year, while the Vardon grip was the forerunner of the modern day method of holding the club. Harry Vardon actually copied the style from Johnny Laidlaw, a former winner of the British Amateur Championship.

Chipping in

'At that time Vardon was the most atrocious putter I have ever seen. He didn't three-putt, he four-putted.'
Gene Sarazen talking about Vardon in the 1920s.

KEN VENTURI

Born: San Francisco, CA, USA – 15/05/1931	
First US Tour: 1957	
US Tour Wins: 14	
Major Wins: 1 (US Open 1964)	

KEN VENTURI came to the 1964 US Open during one of the worst slumps of his career. Playing badly in the practice rounds, he considering leaving the event, but after being persuaded to stay he played some of the best golf of his life and went on to his only major.

● SUFFERING in the extreme heat, Venturi had to be accompanied by a doctor on the final round. After this peak of success, ill health caused his career to tail off.

● AS AN AMATEUR, Venturi had almost won the Masters in 1956, but lost out over the final round. In 1960 as a professional he was even closer. Leading with two holes to play, Arnold Palmer birdied Augusta's 17th and 18th and stole the victory.

Chipping in

'Winning trophies is everything. You can spend the money, but you can never spend the memories.'

ROBERTO DE VICENZO

Born: Buenos Aires, Argentina – 14/04/1923	
Career Spanned 1940s to 1970s	
Major Wins: 1 (British Open 1967)	

ROBERTO DE VICENZO has had a remarkable career and is by far Argentina's greatest golfer. He has represented his country 15 times in the World Cup and has twice won the individual trophy.

● IN 1967, he won the Open Championship at Hoylake, holding off Gary Player and Jack Nicklaus with a steady nerve at the last few holes. At 44 he is the oldest man to have won the trophy this century.

● A YEAR LATER he could have added the Masters, but in one of the biggest errors of golfing history he signed a scorecard that his partner Bob Goalby had filled in incorrectly, and lost by one stroke.

● IN LATER LIFE de Vicenzo was awarded honorary membership of the R&A in 1976 and then won the US Senior Open in 1980, aged 57.

Did you know?

Roberto de Vicenzo has won over 200 tournaments worldwide, including 100 significant titles and 39 National Championships.

THE VOLVO MASTERS

THIS end-of-season tournament is one of the most prestigious competitions on the circuit, and reflects Volvo's commitment to the European golf scene.

● THE VOLVO MASTERS was held at Valderrama for nine years from until 1996, and provided a dramatic finish to the tour. The current champion Lee Westwood secured his second spot on the European List in 1997, while Colin Montgomerie confirmed his place at the top.

Roberto de Vicenzo, perhaps the unluckiest man golf has ever known.

LANNY WADKINS

Born: Richmond, VA, USA – 05/12/1949

First US Tour: 1971

Highest Ranking: 2

US Tour Wins: 21

Major Wins: 0

Ryder Cup Appearances: 7

Tour Earnings: $6.5 million

LANNY WADKINS has racked up more than 20 victories, has played on the Ryder Cup team eight times, and even captained it, but has never won a major.

● AN EXCITING player to watch, Wadkins always goes straight for the pin. Now his PGA career has wound down, fans are looking forward to next year when Wadkins will be eligible for the Senior Tour.

● IN 1995 Wadkins was the non-playing Ryder Cup captain when the USA lost the trophy to Europe at Oak Hill. Some of the blame for this defeat must fall to Wadkins, not least because one the players he personally picked for the team, Curtis Strange, lost all three of his matches.

Lanny Wadkins bends over backwards in his attempt to hole a putt.

Chipping in

'He's the most tenacious player I've ever seen. You out a pin in the middle of a lake, and Lanny will attack it.'
John Mahaffey, 1983 Golf Digest

WALES

WALES HAS steadily caught up with the rest of Britain in its enthusiasm for golf, but other than the trio of Huggett, Rees and Woosnam they have produced few golfers of note.

● DAI REES was the first Welsh golfer to compete on the world stage. A strong Ryder Cup player, he also topped the European Order of Merit twice in the 1950s. Brian Huggett then followed his example in 1968, before the Oswestry-born Ian Woosnam established himself as the greatest Welsh golfer of all time.

● WOOSNAM led Wales in their World Cup win in 1987, the year he also topped the European Order of Merit for the first time.

Famous Welsh Players

Brian Huggett
Dai Rees
Dave Thomas
Ian Woosnam

Top Welsh Courses

Royal Porthcawl
Royal St David's

THE WALKER CUP

First Played: 1922

Results: USA – 31, GB&I – 4, 1 match halved

THE WALKER CUP is an amateur competition between a US team and a team from Great Britain and Ireland. Started in 1922, it has been a bi-annual event since 1924, played on alternate sides of the Atlantic.

● TO DATE the US holds the upper hand by a considerable margin, although Great Britain has achieved notable success over the last ten years. Their start was less than impressive – in the first 30 years of the competition, the GB&I team won only twice.

Walker Cup Results

1922	National GL, NY	USA	8-4
1923	St Andrews	USA	$6^{1}/_2$-$5^{1}/_2$
1924	Garden City, NY	USA	9-3
1926	St Andrews	USA	$6^{1}/_2$-$5^{1}/_2$
1928	Chicago, IL	USA	11-1
1930	Royal St Georges	USA	10-2
1932	The Country Club, MA	USA	$9^{1}/_2$-$2^{1}/_2$
1934	St Andrews	USA	$9^{1}/_2$-$2^{1}/_2$
1936	Pine Valley, NJ	USA	$10^{1}/_2$-$1^{1}/_2$
1938	St Andrews	GB&I	$7^{1}/_2$-$4^{1}/_2$

1947	St Andrews	USA	8-4
1949	Winged Foot, NY	USA	10-2
1951	Royal Birkdale	USA	$7^{1}/_2$-$4^{1}/_2$
1953	Kittansett, MA	USA	9-3
1955	St Andrews	USA	10-2
1957	Minikahda, MI	USA	$8^{1}/_2$-$3^{1}/_2$
1959	Muirfield	USA	9-3
1961	Seattle, WA	USA	11-1
1963	Turnberry	USA	12-8
1965	Baltimore, MY	Match halved	11-11
1967	Royal St Georges	USA	13-7
1969	Milwaukee, WI	USA	10-8
1971	St Andrews	GB&I	13-11
1973	The Country Club, MA	USA	14-10
1975	St Andrews	USA	15.5-8.5
1977	Shinnecock Hills, NY	USA	16-8
1979	Muirfield	USA	$15^{1}/_2$-$8^{1}/_2$
1981	Cypress Point, CA	USA	15-9
1983	Royal Liverpool	USA	$13^{1}/_2$-$10^{1}/_2$
1985	Pine Valley, NJ	USA	13-11
1987	Sunningdale	USA	$16^{1}/_2$-$7^{1}/_2$
1989	Peachtree, GA	GB&I	$12^{1}/_2$-$11^{1}/_2$
1991	Portmarnock	USA	14-10
1993	Interlachen, MI	USA	19-5
1995	Royal Porthcawl	GB&I	14-10
1997	Quaker Ridge, NY	USA	18-6

Did you know?

When Britain did finally win back the Walker Cup in 1989, it went missing from a hotel where it was being displayed. It was later returned, having been taken as a prank.

TOM WATSON

Born: Kansas City, MO, USA – 04/09/1949

First US Tour: 1971

Highest Ranking: 1 (1977, 1978, 1979, 1980, 1984)

US Tour Wins: 33

Major Wins: 8 (British Open 1975, 1977, 1980, 1982, 1983, US Open 1982, US Masters 1977, 1981)

Ryder Cup Appearances: 4

Tour Earnings: $8 million

TOM WATSON is one of the most remarkable golfers of the modern age, and his duels with Jack Nicklaus at the end of the 1970s and beginning of the 1980s are legendary.

● HE NEVER achieved success on the scale of Nicklaus, but in winning five British Open Championships he did something the Golden Bear could never match. He was also the leading money winner in the US for four consecutive years, something else that Nicklaus never achieved.

● BEFORE WATSON achieved success he had to endure failure on a grand scale, throwing away the US Open title on the final day in both 1974 and 1975. A month after the second loss, however, he took his first major at Carnoustie when a long birdie at the last set a total that nobody could better. In a play-off he beat Jack Newton the following day.

● TWO YEARS LATER came the first of his

battles with Nicklaus. Watson was victorious at Turnberry by one stroke after a great head-to-head battle on the last round.

● THE SAME YEAR, Watson captured his first US major win when he took the Masters. He could have added the US PGA in 1978 but somehow threw away his five-shot lead over the last nine holes. The US PGA remains the only major that has proved elusive.

● IN 1983 Watson won his fifth British Open at Royal Birkdale, his last major success. Ten years later he captained the Ryder Cup team to a win at The Belfry. Having celebrated his first win for some time on the US Tour in 1996, it looks like Watson is in great shape as he heads for the Senior Tour in 1999.

Tom Watson – a career of great successes and grand failures.

Chipping in

'The person I fear most in the last two rounds is myself.'

Karrie Webb is leading Australia's challenge for world supremacy in the female game.

KARRIE WEBB

Born: Queensland, Australia – 21/12/1974
First LPGA Tour: 1996
Highest Ranking: 1 (1996)
Tour Wins: 4
Major Wins: 0
Tour Earnings: $1,002,000

KARRIE WEBB has made an unprecedented splash in the female golfing world. Having turned pro in 1994, Webb immediately joined the Women's European Tour, and having won the 1995 Women's European Open and topped the money list she headed for America.

● HER OPENING season in 1996 gave her three victories, and she finished second in the money list. Not surprisingly she was voted Rookie of the Year. Barely two years later, she is now rated the best female golfer in the world.

Tom Weiskopf and his majestic swing.

TOM WEISKOPF

Born: Massillon, OH, USA – 09/11/1942
First US Tour: 1965
Highest Ranking: 3 (1968, 1973, 1975)
US Tour Wins: 15
Major Wins: 1 (British Open 1973)
Ryder Cup Appearances: 2
Tour Earnings: $2.2 million
First Senior Tour: 1992
Senior Tour Wins: 4
Senior Tour Earnings: $1.7 million

A TALL PLAYER with a majestic swing but a suspect temper, Weiskopf was never a favourite with the press, who dubbed him the Towering Inferno. Were it not for putting problems he would surely have added to his one major, but certainly the 13 times he three-putted in the 1969 US Masters cost him the Championship. It was unlucky 13 again in 1980 at the 12th hole on the final round.

● WHEN IT DID come good for him at Troon in 1973, he led the Open from start to finish, the first man to do so since Henry Cotton in 1934.

● AS HIS CAREER has wound down, Weiskopf has dabbled with the Senior Tour and with commentary, but a career in course design may lie ahead, if the results of his work with Jay Morrish at Loch Lomond are anything to go by.

WENTWORTH

Where: Surrey, England

Par: 72

Yardage: 6,945

Opened: 1924

Designer: Harry Colt

Major Events Staged: Ryder Cup 1953,
World Cup 1956,
Women's British Open 1980

WENTWORTH was created in the 1920s by Harry Colt, while his friend Walter Tarrant built the clubhouse, complete with country club-style facilities. An adjacent building has been the administrative HQ of the European PGA Tour since 1981, and the course has hosted the World Matchplay Championship since 1964 and the Volvo PGA Championship since 1984.

● DESPITE BEING a relatively new course by British standards, Wentworth has its place in golfing history – the first professional match between America and Great Britain was played there in 1926 as a precursor to the Ryder Cup. Britain were

Did you know?

Wentworth is known as the Burma Road, because German prisoners of war worked on the restoration of the course after the Second World War.

easy winners. In 1953 the Ryder Cup was played at the course, but the US team gained their revenge with a narrow win.

● BEN HOGAN and Sam Snead also won the World Cup at Wentworth in 1956 – it was Hogan's only appearance in England.

● A TOUGH COURSE, with narrow fairways, it can test even the most even-tempered players. Sandy Lyle once snapped his club in a fit of anger during the World Matchplay Championships.

LEE WESTWOOD

Born: Worksop, England – 24/4/73

First European Tour: 1994

Highest Ranking: 3 (1997)

European Tour Wins: 2

Major Wins: 0

Ryder Cup Appearances: 1

Tour Earnings: £1,220,168

LEE WESTWOOD is rapidly becoming one of Britain's brightest hopes for the future. Westwood had a remarkable year in 1997. His first Ryder Cup appearance at Valderrama followed a win at Montecastillo in the Volvo Masters, which guaranteed him third place in the European Money List.

● HE ALSO SECURED a place in the top 150 in America despite appearing in only 5 US Tour events. He gained his first US Tour win in New Orleans in April 1997.

JOYCE WETHERED

Born: Surrey, England – 17/11/1901

Career Spanned: 1920s

Significant Wins: 9 (English Ladies Open 1920, 1921, 1922, 1923, 1924, British Ladies Open 1922, 1924, 1925, 1929)

LATER KNOWN as Lady Heathcote-Amory, Joyce Wethered died recently at the age of 96, leaving behind memories of perhaps the greatest female golfer Britain has produced.

● ENTERING HER first English Ladies Championship in 1920 simply to keep a friend company, she defeated Cecil Leitch in the final. She won the trophy for the following four years and then stopped competing. Her record in the British Ladies Championship was equally enigmatic. After winning it in 1922, 1924 and 1925, she decided not to enter from 1926 until 1928. She only entered in 1929 because it was being played at St Andrews, but came away victorious again.

● BOBBY JONES once described her as the greatest player, male or female, that he had ever seen.

Lee Westwood with his future opponents.

KATHY WHITWORTH

Born: Monahan, TA, USA – 27/09/1939

First LPGA Tour: 1959

Highest Ranking: 1 (1965, 1966, 1967, 1968, 1970, 1971, 1972, 1973)

Tour Wins: 88

Major Wins: 3 (US LPGA 1967, 1971, 1975)

KATHY WHITWORTH is very much the Sam Snead of women's golf, having won over 80 tournaments. She is the most prolific winner on the LPGA tour, but, like Snead, she has never won a National Championship. Her total of three majors is relatively low compared with the likes of Mickey Wright and Babe Zaharias.

● TURNING PRO in 1959, Whitworth immediately began winning tournaments, but it was 1965 before her phenomenal run began. From then until 1973 she only failed to top the money list on one occasion, and won two LPGA titles. Two years later she made it a hat-trick.

The denseley bunkered greens of 'man-sized' Winged Foot.

WINGED FOOT

Where: Mamaroneck, NY, USA

Par: 70

Yardage: 6,980

Opened: 1923

Designer: Albert Tillinghast

Major Events Staged: US Open 1929, 1959, 1974, 1984, Walker Cup 1949, US Women's Open 1957, 1972

THE WEST COURSE at Winged Foot is a long and treacherous one, which has only seen one winner score below par in the four US Opens it has staged. Its creator Albert Tillinghast was asked to create a 'man-sized' course by the gentlemen of the New York Athletic Club, and with its narrow fairways and densely-bunkered greens, he did just that.

● IN THE FIRST US Open held at Winged Foot, Bobby Jones made a legendary comeback against Al Espinosa, forcing a play-off with a 12-foot putt at the last hole. The play-off was less of a close affair, with Jones winning the 36-holes by some 23 strokes.

● BILLY CASPER won the Open there in 1959, Hale Irwin was victorious in 1974, but perhaps the most exciting was the 1984 US Open in which Fuzzy Zoeller was caught by Greg Norman, who holed a 30-foot putt for par to force a play-off. Zoeller exploited Norman's weakness in play-offs, however, romping home by eight shots in their extra 18 holes.

Did you know?

Playing at Winged Foot, Bing Crosby missed qualification for the 1940 American Amateur Championship by only five strokes.

PG WODEHOUSE

THE GREAT WRITER was a huge fan of the game and many of his novels included musings on the sport, while his characters, notably Bertie Wooster, occasionally played the odd round.

Chipping in

'If only I had taken up golf earlier and devoted my whole time to it instead of fooling about writing stories and things, I might have got my handicap down to under 18.'

THE WOMEN'S EUROPEAN TOUR

THE Women's European Tour has struggled to keep pace with its American equivalent, the LPGA, and sponsorship has been hard to come by in some years.

● IN RECENT years the profile of the tour has been raised considerably by Europe's Solheim Cup win in 1992, and by players such as Annika Sorenstam showing loyalty to the Tour.

Order of Merit Winners

1979	Catherine Panton
1980	Muriel Thomson
1981	Jenny Lee-Smith
1982	Jenny Lee-Smith
1983	Muriel Thomson
1984	Dale Reid
1985	Laura Davies
1986	Laura Davies
1987	Dale Reid
1988	Marie-Laure Taya
1989	Marie-Laure de Lorenzi
1990	Trish Johnson
1991	Corinne Dibnah
1992	Laura Davies
1993	Karen Lunn
1994	Liselotte Neuman
1995	Annika Sorenstam
1996	Laura Davies
1997	Alison Nicholas

WOODS

ALTHOUGH THEY are now almost all made from metal, some of the clubs in a golfer's armoury are still known as woods. Originally, the big-headed clubs were indeed made of wood, and the biggest of these was, and remains the driver. The two-wood was originally called a brassie, and the three and four-woods referred to as spoons.

TIGER WOODS

Born: Cypress, CA, USA – 30/12/1975

First US Tour: 1996

Highest Ranking: 1 (1997)

US Tour Wins: 6

Major Wins: 1 (US Masters 1997)

Ryder Cup Appearances: 1

Tour Earnings: $3.5 million

TIGER WOODS can only be described as a phenomenon. His youthful success has brought the game to a whole new generation of youngsters. With his good looks, slim figure, youth and Nike Sponsorship he has blown away in two short seasons the world's preconceptions about golf.

Annika Sorenstam, loyal to the European Tour.

Tiger Woods in the middle of a sandstorm. Like his bunker shot, Woods has exploded onto the scene.

● IN WINNING the Masters in 1997, Eldrick 'Tiger' Woods tore apart the record books by becoming the youngest Champion and recording the lowest aggregate total – 270. Only time will tell if Woods will live up to his potential, but if his amateur career is anything to go by he should have no trouble.

● BEFORE TURNING professional and becoming the first man to ever win more than $2 million in one season (his record breaking 1997 second full season on the US Tour) he had already put together a remarkable amateur career at an early age.

● BORN TO an Afro-American father and a Thai mother, Woods started playing golf at the age of five and proved a prodigious talent. At the age of 15 he won his first US Junior Amateur Title – he went on to win three in a row. He then stepped up to the full US Amateur Championship and again won three in a row – an unprecedented achievement.

● A SUBTLE PLAYER around the greens, Woods is also a massive driver, hitting the ball at least as far as John Daly. He has already made his mark on the Ryder Cup, as he did in the Walker Cup competition, and with huge sponsorship from Nike and Titleist, his financial future is secure. All that remains to be seen is whether he can win the 14 majors that his father Earl has predicted for him – one more than Bobby Jones.

IAN WOOSNAM

Born:	Oswestry, England – 02/03/1958
First European Tour:	1977
Highest Ranking:	1 (1987, 1990)
European Tour Wins:	28
Major Wins:	1 (US Masters 1991)
Ryder Cup Appearances:	8
Tour Earnings:	£4,173,192

THE LITTLE Welshman is a favourite on the European Tour, his explosive driving power belying his size. He has twice topped the European Tour list and in 1991 – his big year – he was also the World Player of the Year in the Sony Rankings.

● IN THAT YEAR Woosnam pipped Olazabal and Watson for the Masters, getting down in two from just off the 18th green for a par, and victory by a single stroke from Olazabal.

● WOOSNAM HAS also come close in the US Open, but has never really figured in the British Open. In 1987, however, he became the first British player to win the World Matchplay Championship at Wentworth. He did so by beating Faldo, Ballesteros and Lyle in the quarters, semis and final respectively.

● IN EIGHT consecutive Ryder Cup appearances since 1983, Woosnam has never won a singles match. That run continued in 1997 when he lost to Fred Couples.

Ian Woosnam, the mighty little man of Welsh golf.

THE WORLD CUP

First played: 1953

FIRST HELD in Canada in 1953, the World Cup was called the Canada Cup until 1967. It is held every year between teams of two players competing over four rounds. The individual with the lowest aggregate score also wins the International Trophy.

● JACK NICKLAUS has won the most individual titles (3) and been part of a winning team the most times (6) – he shares this second honour with Arnold Palmer.

● FRED COUPLES and Davis Love III have been the most successful partnership however, winning the title for four consecutive years in the 1990s.

A great couple: Fred Couples is the other half of Davis Love III in the most successful World Cup partnership.

The World Cup winners

Year	Venue	Winner
1953	Montreal	Argentina
1954	Montreal	Australia
1955	Washington DC	USA
1956	Wentworth	USA
1957	Tokyo	Japan
1958	Mexico City	Ireland
1959	Melbourne	Australia
1960	Dublin	USA
1961	Puerto Rico	USA
1962	Buenos Aires	USA
1963	Paris	USA
1964	Hawaii	USA
1965	Madrid	South Africa
1966	Tokyo	USA
1967	Mexico City	USA
1968	Rome	Canada
1969	Singapore	USA
1970	Buenes Aires	Australia
1971	Palm Beach, FL	USA
1972	Melbourne	China
1973	Marbella, Spain	USA
1974	Caracas	South Africa
1975	Bangkok	USA
1976	Palm Springs, CA	Spain
1977	Manila	Spain
1978	Hawaii	USA
1979	Athens	USA
1980	Bogota	Canada
1981	No Tournament held	
1982	Acapulco	Spain
1983	Jakarta	USA
1984	Rome	Spain
1985	La Quinta, CA	Canada
1986	No Tournament held	
1987	Hawaii	Wales
1988	Melbourne	USA
1989	Marbella, Spain	Australia
1990	Orlando, FL	Germany
1991	Rome	Sweden
1992	Madrid	USA
1993	Orlando, FL	USA
1994	Puerto Rico	USA
1995	Shenzheng, China	USA
1996	Cape Town	South Africa
1997	Kiawah Island, USA	Ireland

THE WORLD MATCHPLAY CHAMPIONSHIP

First played: 1964

Most Wins: 5 – Gary Player (1965, 1966, 1968, 1971, 1973),
Seve Ballesteros (1981, 1982, 1984, 1985, 1991)

THE WORLD Matchplay Championship is perhaps the most important tournament in Britain after the Open, and has seen some great moments over the years.

● GARY PLAYER, Seve Ballesteros, Sandy Lyle and Nick Faldo have been mainstays of the competition, with all four reaching the final at least five times. Lyle's sole victory came in 1988 against Faldo in one of the competitions most thrilling encounters.

● IN THE 1990s, Ernie Els has been the man to beat, taking a record three consecutive trophies.

The World Matchplay Championship results

Year	Winner		Year	Winner
1964	Arnold Palmer		1981	Seve Ballesteros
1965	Gary Player		1982	Seve Ballesteros
1966	Gary Player		1983	Greg Norman
1967	Arnold Palmer		1984	Seve Ballesteros
1968	Gary Player		1985	Seve Ballesteros
1969	Bob Charles		1986	Greg Norman
1970	Jack Nicklaus		1987	Ian Woosnam
1971	Gary Player		1988	Sandy Lyle
1972	Tom Weiskopf		1989	Nick Faldo
1973	Gary Player		1990	Ian Woosnam
1974	Hale Irwin		1991	Seve Ballesteros
1975	Hale Irwin		1992	Nick Faldo
1976	David Graham		1993	Corey Pavin
1977	Graham Marsh		1994	Ernie Els
1978	Isao Aoki		1995	Ernie Els
1979	Bill Rogers		1996	Ernie Els
1980	Greg Norman		1997	Vijay Singh

Sandy Lyle won the 1988 World Matchplay in the competition's greatest ever final.

THE WORLD OPEN

First played: 1994

Most Wins: 2 – Frank Nobilo (1995, 1996)

GENE SARAZEN's World Open Championship is played at the Legends Club in Atlanta, Georgia and boasts some $2 million in prize money.

The World Open results

1994	Ernie Els
1995	Frank Nobilo
1996	Frank Nobilo
1997	Mark Calcavecchia

Mark Calcavecchia competes in the Gene Sarazen World Open at Chateau Elan, Georgia, in 1997.

THE WORLD SERIES OF GOLF

First played: 1976

Most Wins: 2 – Craig Stadler (1982, 1992), JM Olazabal (1990, 1994), Greg Norman (1995, 1997)

STAGED EVERY YEAR but one on the South Course of the Firestone Country Clubin Ohio (it was held on the North Course in 1994), the World Series of Golf is one of the most important competitions on the US Tour, mainly because it offers the winner a ten-year qualifying exemption – something only the Players Championship and the three American majors offer.

● ONLY 50 players compete every year, and qualification is based on wins in other tournaments around the world. Although Jack Nicklaus, Tom Watson and Nick Price have all been winners, no one player has been dominant, with only Stadler, Norman and Olazabal taking the tournament more than once.

The World Series of Golf results

1976	Jack Nicklaus
1977	Lanny Wadkins
1978	Gil Morgan
1979	Lon Hinkle
1980	Tom Watson
1981	Bill Rogers
1982	Craig Stadler
1983	Nick Price
1984	Denis Watson
1985	Roger Maltbie
1986	Dan Pohl
1987	Curtis Strange
1988	Mike Reid
1989	David Frost
1990	JM Olazabal
1991	Tom Purtzer
1992	Craig Stadler
1993	Fulton Allem
1994	JM Olazabal
1995	Greg Norman
1996	Phil Mickelson
1997	Greg Norman

MICKEY WRIGHT

Born: San Diego, CA, USA – 14/02/1935

First LPGA Tour: 1955

Highest Ranking: 1 (1961, 1962, 1963, 1964)

Tour Wins: 82

Major Wins: 8 (US Women's Open 1958, 1959, 1961, 1964, LPGA 1958, 1960, 1961, 1963)

MICKEY WRIGHT is one of the greatest female golfers of all time. She has won the US Open four times, as has Betty Rawls, and has also won the LPGA title four times.

She has topped the Money List four times, and her total of 13 wins in 1963 remains a record for one season. Her overall total of 82 wins is second only to Kathy Whitworth (88), and a long way ahead of Patty Berg in third place with 57.

During the 1950s and 1960s she was perhaps the most consistent female golfer on tour, and her swing was certainly the sweetest.

YIPS

AN EXPRESSION first coined by Tommy Armour, the 'yips' are the shakes that can overcome a player when they are about to take a short putt.

● IN EXTREME CASES the yips can prevent a player from moving the club at all, or cause convulsive twitching. Players such as Bernhard Langer and even the great Ben Hogan have suffered from the yips (Also known as 'the twitch' or 'the jerks') at some time in their career.

YOUNG CHAMPIONS

IN GOLF's early days, Johnny McDermott and Tom Morris Jnr won their country's respective Opens while still in their teens. It is highly unlikely that these feats will ever be matched, but nevertheless some precocious talents have achieved great success at an early age in the modern era.
- TIGER WOODS is the latest, winning the US Masters at the age of 21, two years younger than Seve Ballesteros had been when he won the title.

THE YOUNGEST CHAMPIONS

— **European Tour** —
Dale Hayes
(1971 Spanish Open, aged 18 years 290 days)

— **US Tour** —
Johnny McDermott
(1911 US Open, aged 19 years 10 months)

— **British Open** —
Tom Morris Jnr
(1868, aged 17 years 5 months)

— **US Masters** —
Tiger Woods
(1997, aged 21 years)

— **US PGA** —
Gene Sarazen
(1922, aged 22 years 5 months)

Did you know?

Thuashni Selvaratnam won the 1989 Sri Lankan Ladies Amateur Championship aged 12 years and 324 days.

BABE ZAHARIAS

Born:	Port Arthur, TX, USA – 26/06/1915 (died 27/09/1956)
Career Spanned:	1930s to 1950s
First US Tour:	1948
Highest Rank:	1 (1948, 1949, 1950, 1951)
Major Wins:	3 (US Open 1948, 1950, 1954)

THE BABe, as she was known, was actually christened Mildred Didrickson. She married wrestler George Zaharias, and earned the nickname Babe, after the Baseball player Babe Ruth, when she hit five home runs in a game.
- PERHAPS NOT the greatest lady golfer of all time – though certainly she was at the turn of the 1950s – she was probably the

greatest female athlete ever.
- IN ADDITION to helping form the LPGA – which she topped for its first four years – she won the US Women's Open three times and the National Amateur titles both sides of the Atlantic.
- AS WELL AS GOLF and baseball, she also excelled in other sports. She was a great track athlete, and in 1932, before competing in that year's Olympics, she won five of the seven national events in which she took part. She went on to set a new world record in the 80 metres hurdles on the way to winning a gold medal, won another gold in the javelin, and tied in the high jump.

FUZZY ZOELLER

Born:	New Albany, IN, USA – 11/11/1951
First US Tour:	1975
Highest Ranking:	2 (1983)
US Tour Wins:	10
Major Wins:	2 (US Open 1984, US Masters 1979)
Ryder Cup Appearances:	3
Tour Earnings:	$5,400,000

FUZZY ZOELLER may not be the best golfer of the modern era, but he is certainly one of its favourite characters, and as the final entry in an A-Z, he sums up many of the things that are great about golf,

Fuzzy Zoeller, taking a light snack between holes.

notably the fun and companionship of the game.
- AS HE ENTERS his 40s, much of Zoeller's time is now devoted to course design, but he still manages to play competitively and sneaked into the top 150 money earners in 1997, although it was his lowest position since he first competed on the tour in 1975.
- IN TERMS of money, his best year came in 1994, when he earned the record for earnings without winning a single tournament – $1,016,804. He finished fifth overall, in a year when many thought his career was on the wane.
- IN HIS FIRST ever Masters, in 1979, he beat Tom Watson and Ed Sneed at the third hole of a sudden death play-off. Then after an exciting duel with Greg Norman in normal play, he beat the Australian by eight shots over an extra 18 holes at Winged Foot. Zoeller thought he had lost when Norman putted for par at the 18th, and waved a white handkerchief – he thought the putt had been for a birdie and outright victory.

Chipping in

'I have never led the tour in money winnings, but I have many times in alcohol consumption.'

THE 1998 PGA TOUR

Winners are shown for events played before this book went to press.

DATE	TOURNAMENT	COURSE	LOCATION
January 3-4	Andersen Consulting World Championship of Golf	Grayhawk Golf Club	Scottsdale, AZ
January 8-11	Mercedes Championships	La Costa Resort	Carlsbad, CA
January 14-18	Bob Hope Chrysler Classic	Indian Wells/Bermuda Dunes/LaQuinta	Indian Wells, CA
January 22-25	Phoenix Open	TPC of Scottsdale	Scottsdale, AZ
January 29-Feb 1	AT&T Pebble Beach National Pro-Am	Pebble Beach Golf Links/Spyglass Hill/Poppy Hills	Pebble Beach., CA
February 5-8	Buick Invitational	Torrey Pines Country Club, South Course/North Course	LaJolla, CA
February 12-15	United Airlines Hawaiian Open	Waialae Country Club	Honolulu, HI
February 19-22	Tucson Chrysler Classic	Omni Tucson National Golf Resort	Tucson, AZ
February 26-Mar 1	Nissan Open	Valencia Country Club	Valencia, CA
March 5-8	Doral-Ryder Open	Doral Resort and Country Club	Miami, FL
March 12-15	Honda Classic	TPC at Heron Bay	Coral Springs, FL
March 19-22	Bay Hill Invitational	Bay Hill Club and Lodge	Orlando, FL
March 26-29	The Players Championship	TPC at Sawgrass	Ponte Vedra Beach, FL
April 2-5	Freeport-McDermott Classic	English Turn Golf and Country Club	New Orleans, LA
April 9-12	Masters Tournament	Augusta National Golf Club	Augusta, GA
April 16-19	MCI Classic – The Heritage of Golf	Harbour Town Golf Links	Hilton Head Island, SC
April 23-26	Greater Greensboro Chrysler Classic	Forest Oaks Country Club	Greensboro, NC
April 30-May 3	Shell Houston Open	TPC at The Woodlands	The Woodlands, TX
May 7-10	BellSouth Classic	TPC at Sugarloaf	Duluth, GA
May 14-17	GTE Byron Nelson Classic	TPC at Las Colinas/ Cottonwood Valley CC	Irving, TX
May 21-24	MasterCard Colonial	Colonial Country Club	Fort Worth, TX
May 28-31	Memorial Tournament	Muirfield Village Golf Club	Dublin, OH
June 4-7	Kemper Open	TPC at Avenel	Potomac, MD
June 11-14	Buick Classic	Westchester Country Club	Rye, NY
June 18-21	US Open Championship	Olympic Club	San Francisco, CA
July 25-28	Motorola Western Open	Cog Hill Golf and Country Club	Lemont, IL
July 2-5	Canon Greater Hartford Open	TPC at River Highlands	Cromwell, CT
July 9-12	Quad City Classic	Oakwood Country Club	Coal Valley, IL
July 16-19	British Open	Royal Birkdale Golf Club	Southport, England
July 16-19	Deposit Guaranty Golf Classic	Annandale Golf Club	Madison, MS
July 23-26	CVS Charity Classic	Pleasant Valley Country Club	Sutton, MA
July 30-Aug 2	FedEx St Jude Classic	TPC at Southwind	Memphis, TN
August 6-9	Buick Open	Warwick Hills Golf and Country Club	Grand Blanc, MI
August 13-16	PGA Championship	Sahalee Country Club	Redmond, WA
August 20-23	Sprint International	Castle Pines Golf Club	Castle Rock, CO
August 27-30	NEC World Series of Golf	Firestone Country Club (South Course)	Akron, OH
August 27-30	Greater Vancouver Open presented by Air Canada	Northview Golf and Country Club	Surrey, BC, Canada
September 3-6	Greater Milwaukee Open presented by Miller Lite	Brown Deer Park Golf Course	Milwaukee, WI
September 10-13	Bell Canadian Open	Glen Abbey Golf Club	Oakville, Ontario, Canada
September 17-20	B.C. Open	En-Joie Golf Club	Endicott, NY
September 24-27	Westin Texas Open at LaCantera	LaCantera Golf Club	San Antonio, TX
October 1-4	Buick Challenge	Callaway Gardens Resort	Pine Mountain, GA
October 8-11	Michelob Championship	Kingsmill Golf Club	Williamsburg, VA
October 14-18	Las Vegas Invitational	TPC at Summerlin/Desert Inn Golf Club	Las Vegas, NV
October 22-25	National Car Rental Golf Classic at Walt Disney World Resort	Magnolia, Palm and Lake Buena Vista Golf Courses	Lake Buena Vista, FL
October 29-Nov 1	The Tour Championship	East Lake Golf Club	Atlanta, GA
November 5-8	Subaru Sarazen World Open	The Legends at Chateau Elan	Braselton, GA
November 12-15	Franklin Templeton Shark Shootout	Sherwood Country Club	Thousand Oaks, CA
November 19-22	World Cup of Golf		
November 28-29	Skins Game		
December 3-6	JCPenney Classic	Westin Innisbrook Resort	Palm Harbour, FL
December 11-13	The Presidents Cup	The Royal Melbourne Golf Club	Black Rock, Victoria, Australia
December 19-20	Wendy's Three-Tour Challenge	Lake Las Vegas Resort	Henderson, NV

WINNER

Colin Montgomerie
Phil Mickelson
Fred Couples
Jesper Parnevik

Scott Simpson
John Huston
David Duval
Billy Mayfair
Michael Bradley
Mark Calcavecchia
Ernie Els
Justin Leonard
Lee Westwood
Mark O'Meara
Davis Love III
Trevor Dodds
David Duval
Tiger Woods
John Cook
Tom Watson
Fred Couples
Stuart Appleby
J.P. Hayes
Lee Janzen
Joe Durant
Olin Brown
Steve Jones
Mark O'Meara

Mark O'Meara, triumphant at both the 1998 Masters and the British Open.

THE 1998 SENIOR PGA TOUR

Winners are shown for events played before this book went to press.

DATE	TOURNAMENT	COURSE	LOCATION
January 12-18	MasterCard Championship	Hualalai Golf Club	Kailua-Kona, HI
January 24-25	Senior Skins Game	Mauna Lani Resort	Kohala Coast, HI
January 26-Feb 1	Royal Caribbean Classic	Crandon Park Golf Club	Key Biscayne, FL
February 2-8	LG Championship	Bay Colony Golf	Naples, FL
February 9-15	GTE Classic	TPC of Tampa Bay	Lutz, FL
February 16-22	American Express Invitational	TPC at Prestancia	Sarasota, FL
March 9-10	Senior Slam	Cabo del Sol Golf Club	Los Cabos, Mexico
March 9-15	Toshiba Senior Classic	Newport Beach Country Club	Newport Beach, CA
March 16-22	Liberty Mutual Legends of Golf	Golf Club of Amelia Island at Summer Beach	Amelia Island, FL
March 23-29	Southwestern Bell Dominion	The Dominion Country Club	San Antonio, TX
March 30-Apr 5	The Tradition Presented by Countrywide	Desert Mountain (Cochise Course)	Scottsdale, AZ
April 13-19	PGA Seniors Championship	PGA National Golf Club	Palm Beach Gardens, FL
April 20-26	Las Vegas Senior Classic by TruGreen-ChemLawn	TPC at The Canyons	Las Vegas, NV
April 27-May 3	Bruno's Memorial Classic	Greystone Golf Club	Birmingham, AL
May 4-10	Home Depot Invitational	TPC at Piper Glen	Charlotte, NC
May 11-17	Saint Luke's Classic	Loch Lloyd Country Club	Belton, MO
May 18-24	Bell Atlantic Classic	Hartefeld National	Avondale, PA
May 25-31	Pittsburgh Senior Classic	Sewickley Heights Golf Club	Sewickley Heights, PA
June 1-7	Nationwide Championship	The Golf Club of Georgia	Alpharetta, GA
June 8-14	BellSouth Senior Classic at Opryland	Springhouse Golf Club	Nashville, TN
June 15-21	AT&T Canada Senior Open	Glencoe Golf and Country Club	Calgary, Alberta, Canada
June 22-28	Cadillac NFL Golf Classic	Upper Montclair Country Club	Clifton, NJ
June 29-Jul 5	State Farm Senior Classic	Hobbit's Glen Golf Club	Columbia, MD
July 6-12	Ford Senior Players Championship	TPC of Michigan	Dearborn, MI
July 13-19	Ameritech Senior Open	Kemper Lakes Golf Club	Long Grove, IL
July 20-26	US Senior Open	Riviera Country Club	Pacific Palisades, CA
July 27-Aug 2	Utah Showdown Presented by Smith's	Park Meadows Country Club	Park City, UT
August 3-9	Coldwell Banker Burnet Classic	Bunker Hills Golf Club	Coon Rapids, MN
August 10-16	First of America Classic	Egypt Valley Country Club	Grand Rapids, MI
August 17-23	Northville Long Island Classic	Meadow Brook Club	Jericho, NY
August 24-30	BankBoston Classic	Nashawtuc Country Club	Concord, MA
August 31-Sep 6	Emerald Coast Classic	The Moors Golf Club	Milton, FL
September 7-13	Comfort Classic	Brickyard Crossing	Indianapolis, IN
September 14-20	Kroger Senior Classic	The Golf Center at Kings Island	Mason, OH
September 21-27	Boone Valley Classic	Boone Valley Golf Club	Augusta, MO
September 28-Oct 4	Vantage Championship	Tanglewood Park	Clemmons, NC
October 5-11	The Transamerica	Silverado Resort	Napa, CA
October 12-18	Raley's Gold Rush Classic	Serrano Country Club	El Dorado Hills, CA
October 19-25	EMC2 Kaanapali Classic	Kaanapali Golf Course (North)	Lahaina, HI
October 26-Nov 1	Pacific Bell Senior Classic	The Wilshire Country Club	Los Angeles, CA
November 2-8	Energizer Senior Tour Championship	The Dunes Golf and Beach Club	Myrtle Beach, SC
December 19-20	Lexus Challenge	La Quinta Resort and Club (Citrus Course)	LaQuinta, CA
December 19-20	Wendy's Three-Tour Challenge	Lake Las Vegas Resort	Henderson, NV

WINNER

Gil Morgan

Ray Floyd

David Graham

Gil Morgan

Jim Albus

Larry Nelson

Gil Morgan

Hale Irwin

Charlie Coody, Dale Douglass

Lee Trevino

Gil Morgan

Hale Irwin

Hale Irwin

Hubert Green

Jim Dent

Larry Ziegler

Jay Sigel

Larry Nelson

John Jacobs

Isao Aoki

Brian Barnes

Bob Dickson

Bruce Summerhays

Jay Sigel, winner of the 1998 Bell Atlantic Classic.

THE 1998 EUROPEAN TOUR

Winners are shown for events played before this book went to press.

DATE	TOURNAMENT	COURSE	LOCATION	WINNER
January 22-25	Johnnie Walker Classic	Blue Canyon Country Club	Phuket, Thailand	Tiger Woods
January 29-Feb 1	Heineken Classic	The Vines	Perth, Australia	Thomas Bjorn
February 5-8	South African Open	Durban Country Club	Durban, South Africa	Ernie Els
February 12-15	Alfred Dunhill South African PGA	Houghton Golf Club	Johannesburg, South Africa	Nick Price
February 26-Mar 1	Dubai Desert Classic	Emirates Golf Club	Dubai	Jose Maria Olazabal
March 5-8	Qatar Masters	Doha Golf Club	Quatar	Andrew Coltart
March 12-15	Moroccan Open	Golf Royal d'Agadir	Agadir, Morocco	Stephen Leaney
March 19-22	Portuguese Open	Le Meridien Penina	Algarve, Portugal	Peter Mitchell
April 9-12	Masters Tournament	Augusta National	Augusta, GA, USA	Mark O'Meara
April 16-19	Cannes Open	Royal Mougins	Cannes, France	Thomas Levet
April 23-26	Peugeot Open de España	El Prat	Barcelona, Spain	Thomas Bjorn
April 30-May 3	Italian Open	Castleconturbia	Milan, Italy	Patrick Sjoland
May 7-10	Turespaña Masters	Santa Ponsa	Mallorca, Spain	Miguel Angel Jimenez
May 14-17	Benson and Hedges International Open	The Oxfordshire Golf Club	Thame, England	Darren Clarke
May 22-25	Volvo PGA Championship	Wentworth Club	Surrey, England	Colin Montgomerie
May 29-June 1	Deutsche Bank - SAP Open	TPC of Europe	Gut Kaden, Hamburg, Germany	Lee Westwood
June 4-7	National Car Rental English Open	Marriott Hanbury Manor	Ware, England	Lee Westwood
June 11-14	Compaq European Grand Prix	Slaley Hall	Northumberland, England	Tournament cancelled
June 18-21	Madeira Island Open	Santo da Serra	Madeira, Spain	Mats Lanner
June 18-21	US Open	Olympic Club	San Francisco, CA, USA	Lee Janzen
June 25-28	Peugeot Open de France	Golf National	Paris, France	Sam Torrance
July 2-5	Murphy's Irish Open	Druids Glen	Dublin, Ireland	David Carter
July 8-11	Standard Life Loch Lomond	Loch Lomond	Glasgow, Scotland	Lee Westwood
July 16-19	127th Open Golf Championship	Royal Birkdale	Southport, England	Mark O'Meara
July 23-26	TNT Dutch Open	Hilversumsche Golf Club	The Netherlands	
July 30-Aug 2	Volvo Scandinavian Masters	European Tour Club	Stockholm, Sweden	
August 6-9	German Open	Sporting Club	Bad Saarow, Berlin	
August 13-16	US PGA Championship	Sahalee	Seattle, WA, USA	
August 20-23	Smurfit European Open	The K Club	Dublin, Ireland	
August 27-30	BMW International Open	Golfclub München Nord-Eichenried	Munich, Germany	
September 3-6	Canon European Masters	Crans-sur-Sierre	Switzerland	
September 10-13	One 2 One British Masters	Marriott Forest of Arden	Coventry, England	
September 17-20	Trophée Lancôme	St. Nom la Bretèche	France	
September 24-27	Linde German Masters	Gut Lärchenhof	Cologne, Germany	
October 1-4	Belgacom Open	Royal Zoute	Knokke-le-Zoute, Belgium	
October 8-11	Alfred Dunhill Cup	St. Andrews	Scotland	
October 15-18	World Match Play Championship	Wentworth Club	Surrey, England	
October 29-Nov 1	Volvo Masters	Montecastillo	Jerez, Spain	
November 5-8	Subaru Sarazen World Open	Château Elan	Atlanta, GA, USA	
November 19-22	World Cup of Golf	Gulf Harbour	Auckland, New Zealand	

US Open 1998 winner, Lee Janzen.

THE 1998 NIKE TOUR

Winners are shown for events played before this book went to press.

DATE	TOURNAMENT	COURSE	LOCATION	WINNER
January 8-11	Lakeland Classic	Grasslands Golf Club	Lakeland, FL	Casey Martin
January 15-18	South Florida Classic	Palm-Aire Country Club	Pompano Beach, FL	Eric Johnson
March 5-8	Greater Austin Open	The Hills Country Club	Austin, TX	Michael Allen
March 19-22	Monterrey Open	Club Campestre	Monterrey, Mexico	Joe Ogilvie
March 26-29	Louisiana Open	Le Triomphe Country Club	Broussard, LA	John Wilson
April 9-12	Shreveport Open	Southern Trace Country Club	Shreveport, LA	Vance Veazey
April 16-19	Upstate Classic	Verdae Greens Golf Club	Greenville, SC	Tom Scherrer
April 23-26	Huntsville Open	Hampton Cove Golf Club	Huntsville, AL	Dennis Paulson
April 30-May 3	South Carolina Classic	Country Club of South Carolina	Florence, SC	Gene Sauer
May 7-10	Carolina Classic	Raleigh Country Club	Raleigh, NC	Brian Bateman
May 14-17	Dominion Open	Dominion Club	Glen Allen, VA	Bob Burns
May 28-31	Knoxville Open	Three Ridges Golf Club	Knoxville, TN	Robin Freeman
June 4-7	Miami Valley Open	Heatherwoode Golf Club	Springboro, OH	Craig Bowden
June 11-14	Cleveland Open	Quail Hollow Resort	Concord, OH	Doug Dunakey
June 18-21	Lehigh Valley Open	Center Valley Club	Center Valley, PA	Eric Booker
June 25-28	Greensboro Open	Sedgefield Country Club	Greensboro, NC	Joe Ogilvie
July2-5	Hershey Open	Country Club of Hershey (East)	Hershey, PA	Michael Clark
July 16-19	St. Louis Golf Classic	Missouri Bluffs Golf Club	St. Charles, MO	
July 23-26	Wichita Open	Willowbend Golf Club	Wichita, KS	
July 30-Aug 2	Dakota Dunes Open	Dakota Dunes Country Club	Dakota Dunes, SD	
August 6-9	Omaha Classic	Champions Club	Omaha, NE	
August 13-16	Ozarks Open	Highland Springs Country Club	Springfield, MO	
August 20-23	Fort Smith Classic	Hardscrabble Country Club	Fort Smith, AR	
August 27-30	Permian Basin Open	Mission Dorado Country Club	Odessa, TX	
September 10-13	Tri-Cities Open	Meadow Springs Country Club	Richland, WA	
September 17-20	Boise Open	Hillcrest Country Club	Boise, ID	
September 24-27	Oregon Classic	Shadow Hills Country Club	Eugene, OR	
October 1-4	San Jose Open	Almaden Country Club	San Jose, CA	
October 8-11	Inland Empire Open	Moreno Valley Ranch Golf Club	Moreno Valley, CA	
October 22-25	Tour Championship	Robert Trent Jones	Trail Semmes, AL	

David Duval, who qualified in 1994 from the Nike Tour, has gone on to huge success.

AUTHOR ACKNOWLEDGMENTS

Many thanks to Martin Roderick, Ed Lavender, Ian Cullen, Gary Tipp, Rick Seiles and Kit Bellamy for golfing knowledge and advice, to Tim Smith for pointing me in the right direction, to Jon Palmer for the odd tip, to my mum and dad for my first set of clubs at the age of 12, to James Bennett at Virgin Publishing for not losing his temper with me and most of all to Sanchia for her incredible patience, understanding and love throughout.

PUBLISHER ACKNOWLEDGMENTS

The publishers would like to thank the following for their help and enthusiasm:
Roger Kean, Oliver Frey and everyone at Prima Creative Services
David Hamilton for fact-checking and advice
Rick Mayston at Allsport for picture research
Diana Vowles and Conor Kilgallon for initial editorial work

PICTURE ACKNOWLEDGMENTS

All photographs in this book were supplied by Allsport/Hutlon Getty
Simon Bruty, David Cannon, Russell Cheyne, Mike Cooper, JD Cuban, Stephen Dunn, Stu Forster, Michael Hobbs, Hulton Deutsch, Phil Inglish, Rusty Jarrett, Craig Jones, David Leah, Andy Lyons, Clive Mason, Tim Matthews, Stephen Munday, Gary Newkirk, Doug Pensiger, Andrew Redington, Richard Saker, Paul Severn, Jamie Squire, Rick Stewart, Matthew Stockman, Anton Want, Aubrey Washington